Contents

KT-364-809

Topic 1A — Biological Molecules

Carbohydrates 2
Lipids 6
Proteins 8
Enzyme Action 10
Factors Affecting Enzyme Activity 12
Enzyme-Controlled Reactions.......................14

Topic 1B — More Biological Molecules

DNA and RNA 16
DNA Replication 18
Water 20
ATP 22
Inorganic Ions..23

Topic 2A — Cell Structure and Division

Eukaryotic Cells and Organelles 24
Prokaryotic Cells and Viruses.......................28
Analysis of Cell Components 30
Cell Division — Mitosis...............................32
Cell Division — Investigating Mitosis.............34

Topic 2B — Cell Membranes

Cell Membrane Structure.............................36
Exchange Across Cell Membranes
    — Diffusion 38
Exchange Across Cell Membranes
    — Osmosis 40
Exchange Across Cell Membranes
    — Active Transport.................................42

Topic 2C — Cells and the Immune System

The Immune System 44
Immunity and Vaccines 46
Antibodies in Medicine 48
Interpreting Vaccine and Antibody Data...........50
HIV and Viruses..52

Topic 3A — Exchange and Transport Systems

Size and Surface Area 54
Gas Exchange...56
Gas Exchange in Humans 58
The Effects of Lung Disease..........................60
Interpreting Lung Disease Data......................62
Dissecting Gas Exchange Systems...................64

Topic 3B — More Exchange and Transport Systems

Digestion and Absorption 66
Haemoglobin 68
The Circulatory System 70
The Heart 72
Cardiovascular Disease 75
Transport in Plants — Xylem.........................78
Transport in Plants — Phloem.......................80

Topic 4A — DNA, RNA and Protein Synthesis

DNA, Genes and Chromosomes......................82
RNA and Protein Synthesis 84
The Genetic Code and Nucleic Acids 86

Topic 4B — Diversity, Classification and Variation

Meiosis and Genetic Variation 88
Mutations 91
Genetic Diversity and Natural Selection 92
Investigating Selection 94
Classification of Organisms 96
DNA Technology, Classification and Diversity .98
Investigating Variation................................100
Biodiversity 102

Practical Skills

Planning an Experiment...............................104
Processing and Presenting Data.....................106
Drawing Conclusions and Evaluating.............108
Answers..110
Index..116

TOPIC 1A — BIOLOGICAL MOLECULES

Carbohydrates

Even though there is, and has been, a huge variety of different organisms on Earth, they all share some biochemistry — for example, they all contain a few carbon-based compounds that interact in similar ways.

Most Carbohydrates are Polymers

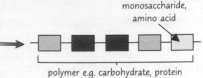

1) Most **carbohydrates** (as well as proteins and nucleic acids) are **polymers**.
2) Polymers are **large, complex molecules** composed of **long chains** of **monomers** joined together.
3) **Monomers** are **small, basic molecular units**.
4) Examples of monomers include **monosaccharides**, **amino acids** and **nucleotides**.

Carbohydrates are Made from Monosaccharides

1) All carbohydrates contain the elements **C**, **H** and **O**.
2) The **monomers** that they're made from are **monosaccharides**, e.g. **glucose**, **fructose** and **galactose**.

1) Glucose is a **hexose** sugar — a monosaccharide with **six carbon atoms** in each molecule.

2) There are **two types** of glucose, alpha (α) and beta (β) — they're **isomers** (molecules with the same molecular formula as each other, but with the atoms connected in a different way).

3) You need to know the structures of **both types** of glucose for your exam — it's pretty easy because there's only one difference between the two:

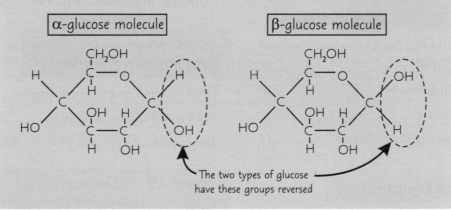

The two types of glucose have these groups reversed

Condensation Reactions Join Monosaccharides Together

1) A **condensation reaction** is when two molecules join together with the formation of a new **chemical bond**, and a **water** molecule is released when the bond is formed.
2) Monosaccharides are **joined together** by **condensation reactions**.
3) A **glycosidic bond** forms between the two monosaccharides as a molecule of water is released.
4) A **disaccharide** is formed when **two monosaccharides** join together.

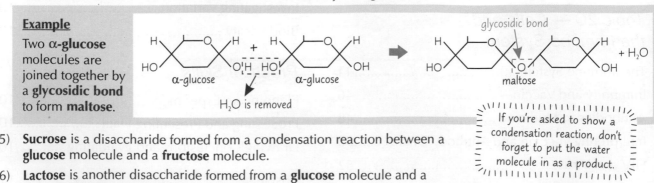

Example

Two α-**glucose** molecules are joined together by a **glycosidic bond** to form **maltose**.

If you're asked to show a condensation reaction, don't forget to put the water molecule in as a product.

5) **Sucrose** is a disaccharide formed from a condensation reaction between a **glucose** molecule and a **fructose** molecule.
6) **Lactose** is another disaccharide formed from a **glucose** molecule and a **galactose** molecule.

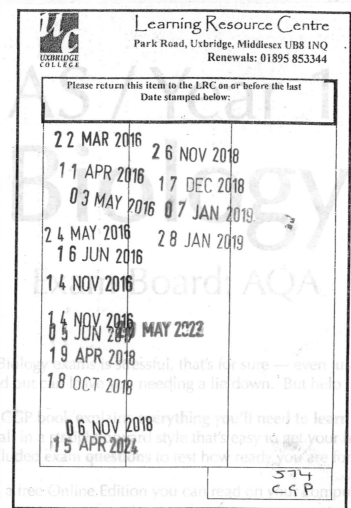
Revising for Biology exams is stressful, that's for sure — even just getting your
notes sorted out can leave you needing a lie-down. But help is at hand...

This brilliant CGP book explains everything you'll need to learn (and nothing
you won't), all in a plain and simple style that's easy to get your head around.
We've also included exam questions to test how ready you are for the real thing.

There's even a free Online Edition you can read on your computer or tablet!

How to get your free Online Edition

Go to **cgpbooks.co.uk/extras** and enter this code...

4365 2191 4628 7936

This code only works for one person. If somebody else has used
this book before you, they might have already claimed the Online Edition.

A-Level revision? It has to be CGP!

Published by CGP

From original material by Richard Parsons.

Editors:
Charlotte Burrows, Christopher Lindle, Christopher McGarry, Claire Plowman, Rachael Rogers, Hayley Thompson.

Contributors:
Gloria Barnett, Paddy Gannon, Liz Masters, Adrian Schmit.

ISBN: 978 1 78294 283 2

With thanks to Lauren Burns, Glenn Rogers and Karen Wells for the proofreading.
With thanks to Laura Jakubowski for the copyright research.

Cover image © duncan1890/iStockphoto.com

MMR graph on page 50 adapted from H. Honda, Y. Shimizu, M. Rutter. No effect of MMR withdrawal on the incidence of autism: a total population study. Journal of Child Psychology and Psychiatry 2005; 46(6):572-579.

Data used to construct Herceptin® graph on page 50 from M.J. Piccart-Gebhart, et al. Trastuzumab after Adjuvant Chemotherapy in HER2-positive Breast Cancer. NEJM 2005; 353: 1659-72.

Data used to construct the Hib graph on page 51 from the Health Protection Agency. Reproduced under the terms of the Open Government Licence https://www.nationalarchives.gov.uk/doc/open-government-licence/version/3/

Data used to construct the smoking graph on page 62 from Cancer Research UK, http://www.cancerresearchuk.org/cancc info/cancerstats/causes/tobacco-statistics/#Smoking, January 2015

Data used to construct the lung cancer graph on page 62 from Cancer Research UK, http://www.cancerresearchuk.org/cancer-info/cancerstats/types/lung/mortality/uk-lung-cancer-mortality-statistics, January 2015

Data used to construct asthma and sulfur dioxide graphs on page 63. Source: National Statistics. Crown copyright material is reproduced under the terms of the open government licence http://www.nationalarchives.gov.uk/doc/open-government licence/version/3/

Exam Question graph on page 63, The Relationship Between Smoke And Sulphur Dioxide Pollution And Deaths During The Great London Smog, December 1952, Source: Wilkins, 1954

Data used to construct the graph on page 77 from P.M. Ridker, et al. Comparison of C-reactive protein and low density lipoprotein cholesterol levels in the prediction of first cardiovascular events. NEJM 2002; 347: 1557-65.

With thanks to Science Photo Library for permission to reproduce the images on pages 34 and 64.

Every effort has been made to locate copyright holders and obtain permission to reproduce sources. For those sources wher it has been difficult to trace the originator of the work, we would be grateful for information. If any copyright holder woul like us to make an amendment to the acknowledgements, please notify us and we will gladly update the book at the next reprint. Thank you.

Clipart from Corel®
Printed by Elanders Ltd, Newcastle upon Tyne.

Carbohydrates

Hydrolysis Reactions Break Polymers Apart

1) **Polymers** can be broken down into **monomers** by **hydrolysis reactions**.

2) A **hydrolysis reaction breaks** the **chemical bond** between monomers using a **water molecule**. It's basically the **opposite** of a condensation reaction.

3) For example, **carbohydrates** can be broken down into their constituent **monosaccharides** by **hydrolysis** reactions.

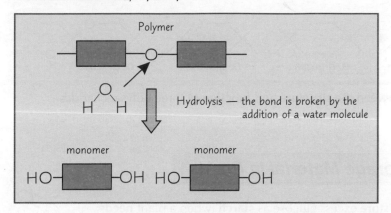

Even hydrolysis couldn't break this bond.

Use the Benedict's Test for Sugars

Sugar is a general term for **monosaccharides** and **disaccharides**. All sugars can be classified as **reducing** or **non-reducing**. The **Benedict's test** tests for sugars — it **differs** depending on the **type** of sugar you are testing for.

REDUCING SUGARS

1) Reducing sugars include **all monosaccharides** (e.g. glucose) and **some disaccharides** (e.g. maltose and lactose).

2) You add **Benedict's reagent** (which is **blue**) to a sample and **heat it** in a water bath that's been brought to the **boil**.

3) If the test's **positive** it will form a **coloured precipitate** (solid particles suspended in the solution).

The colour of the precipitate changes from:

blue ➡ **green** ➡ **yellow** ➡ **orange** ➡ **brick red**

Always use an excess of Benedict's solution — this makes sure that all the sugar reacts.

4) The higher the concentration of reducing sugar, the further the colour change goes — you can use this to **compare** the amount of reducing sugar in different solutions. A more accurate way of doing this is to **filter** the solution and **weigh the precipitate**.

NON-REDUCING SUGARS

1) If the result of the reducing sugars test is **negative**, there could still be a non-reducing sugar present. To test for **non-reducing sugars**, like sucrose, first you have to break them down into monosaccharides.

2) You do this by getting a new sample of the test solution, adding **dilute hydrochloric acid** and carefully heating it in a water bath that's been brought to the **boil**. You then **neutralise** it with **sodium hydrogencarbonate**. Then just carry out the **Benedict's test** as you would for a reducing sugar.

3) If the test's **positive** it will form a **coloured precipitate** (as for the reducing sugars test). If the test's **negative** the solution will **stay blue**, which means it **doesn't contain any sugar** (either reducing or non-reducing).

Carbohydrates

So, you've already looked at monosaccharides and disaccharides... now it's time to give polysaccharides some love.

Polysaccharides are Loads of Sugars Joined Together

A **polysaccharide** is formed when **more than two monosaccharides** are joined together by **condensation reactions**.

Example Lots of α–glucose molecules are joined together by **glycosidic bonds** to form **amylose**.

glycosidic bonds

α-glucose   α-glucose   α-glucose   α-glucose   α-glucose

You need to know about the relationship between the **structure** and **function** of three polysaccharides — starch, glycogen and cellulose.

Starch is the Main Energy Storage Material in Plants

1) Cells get **energy** from **glucose**. Plants **store** excess glucose as **starch** (when a plant **needs more glucose** for energy, it **breaks down** starch to release the glucose).

2) Starch is a mixture of **two** polysaccharides of **alpha-glucose** — **amylose** and **amylopectin**:
   - **Amylose** — a long, **unbranched chain** of α–glucose. The angles of the glycosidic bonds give it a **coiled structure**, almost like a cylinder. This makes it **compact**, so it's really **good for storage** because you can **fit more in** to a small space.
   - **Amylopectin** — a long, **branched chain** of α–glucose. Its **side branches** allow the **enzymes** that break down the molecule to get at the **glycosidic bonds easily**. This means that the glucose can be **released quickly**.

3) Starch is **insoluble** in water and doesn't affect **water potential** (see page 40), so it **doesn't** cause water to enter cells by **osmosis**, which would make them swell. This makes it good for **storage**.

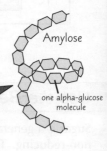
Amylose
one alpha-glucose molecule

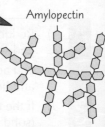
Amylopectin

Use the Iodine Test for Starch

If you do any **experiment** on the **digestion** of **starch** and want to find out if any is **left**, you'll need the **iodine test**.

Just add **iodine dissolved in potassium iodide solution** to the test sample. If there is **starch present**, the sample changes from **browny-orange** to a dark, **blue-black colour**.

Make sure you always talk about iodine in potassium iodide solution, not just iodine.

Glycogen is the Main Energy Storage Material in Animals

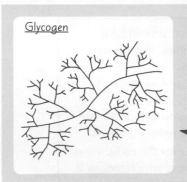
Glycogen

1) Animal cells get **energy** from **glucose** too. But animals **store** excess glucose as **glycogen** — another polysaccharide of **alpha-glucose**.

2) Its structure is very similar to amylopectin, except that it has **loads** more **side branches** coming off it. Loads of branches means that stored glucose can be **released quickly**, which is **important for energy release** in animals.

3) It's also a very **compact** molecule, so it's good for storage.

After throwing and fetching the ball no less than 312 times, Chappy and Stuart were finally out of glycogen.

Carbohydrates

Cellulose is the Major Component of Cell Walls in Plants

1) Cellulose is made of **long, unbranched** chains of **beta–glucose**.
2) When **beta–glucose** molecules **bond**, they form straight cellulose chains.
3) The cellulose chains are linked together by **hydrogen bonds** to form strong fibres called **microfibrils**. The strong fibres mean cellulose provides **structural support** for cells (e.g. in plant cell walls).

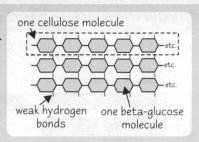

one cellulose molecule

etc.
etc.
etc.

weak hydrogen bonds   one beta-glucose molecule

Practice Questions

Q1 What is a polymer?

Q2 Draw the structure of α-glucose.

Q3 What type of bond holds monosaccharide molecules together in a polysaccharide?

Q4 Name the two polysaccharides present in starch.

Q5 Describe the iodine test for starch.

Exam Questions

Q1 Maltose is a sugar. Describe how a molecule of maltose is formed. [3 marks]

Q2 Sugars can be classed as reducing or non-reducing. Describe the test used to identify a non-reducing sugar. Include the different results you would expect to see if the test was positive or negative. [5 marks]

Q3 Read the following passage:

Chitin is a structural polysaccharide, similar to cellulose in plants, that is found in the exoskeletons of insects and crustaceans, as well as in the cell walls of fungi. It is made up of chains of the monosaccharide N-acetylglucosamine, which is derived from glucose. The polysaccharide chains are long, unbranched and linked together by weak hydrogen bonds.

Chitin can be broken down by enzymes called chitinases, which catalyse hydrolysis reactions. Some organisms are able to make their own chitinases. Amongst these are yeasts, such as *Saccharomyces cerevisiae*. In yeast reproduction, a newly formed yeast cell 'buds off' from the cell wall of its parent cell to become a new independent organism. This requires the separation of the cell wall of the new cell from the cell wall of the parent cell. *Saccharomyces cerevisiae* uses a chitinase for this purpose.

Use information from the passage and your own knowledge to answer the following questions:

a) Explain why chitin can be described as a polysaccharide (line 1). [1 mark]

b) Chitin is similar to cellulose in plants (line 1).
Describe the ways in which cellulose and chitin are similar. [3 marks]

c) Chitin can be broken down by enzymes called chitinases, which catalyse hydrolysis reactions (line 5).
Explain how these hydrolysis reactions break down chitin. [2 marks]

d) Some organisms are able to make their own chitinases (line 5 and 6).
Explain how it would be beneficial for plants to make and secrete chitinases as a defence system. [4 marks]

Starch — I thought that was just for shirt collars...

Every cell in an organism is adapted to perform a function — you can always trace some of its features back to its function. Different cells even use the exact same molecules to do completely different things. Take glucose, for example — all plant cells use it to make cellulose, but they can also make starch from it if they need to store energy. Smashing.

Lipids

Lipids are really nice. Without them, we'd have no cell membranes. You owe it to them to make sure you can remember all of the stuff about them on these pages. It'll help you and your membranes get a good grade.

Triglycerides are a Kind of Lipid

Triglycerides have one molecule of **glycerol** with **three fatty acids** attached to it.

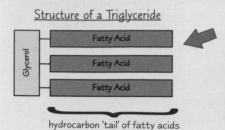
Structure of a Triglyceride

Fatty acid molecules have long 'tails' made of **hydrocarbons**. The tails are 'hydrophobic' (they repel water molecules). These tails make lipids **insoluble in water**. All fatty acids have the same basic structure, but the **hydrocarbon tail varies**.

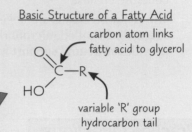
Basic Structure of a Fatty Acid
carbon atom links fatty acid to glycerol
variable 'R' group hydrocarbon tail

Triglycerides are Formed by Condensation Reactions

glycerol   triglyceride

H_2O is released   fatty acid

condensation reaction

Two more fatty acids are attached in the same way here and here.

The diagram shows a **fatty acid** joining to a **glycerol molecule**. When the **ester bond** is formed a molecule of **water** is **released**. — it's a **condensation reaction**. This process happens twice more to form a **triglyceride**.

Fatty Acids can be Saturated or Unsaturated

There are **two** kinds of fatty acids — **saturated** and **unsaturated**. The difference is in their **hydrocarbon tails (R group)**.

Saturated fatty acids **don't** have any **double bonds** between their **carbon atoms**. The fatty acid is 'saturated' with hydrogen.

saturated hydrocarbon tail

Unsaturated fatty acids have **at least one** double bond between **carbon atoms**, which cause the chain to kink.

unsaturated hydrocarbon tail

Phospholipids are Similar to Triglycerides

1) The lipids found in cell membranes **aren't** triglycerides — they're **phospholipids**

2) Phospholipids are pretty **similar** to triglycerides except one of the fatty acid molecules is replaced by a **phosphate group**.

3) The phosphate group is **hydrophilic** (attracts water). The fatty acid tails are **hydrophobic** (repel water). This is important in the cell membrane (see next page to find out why).

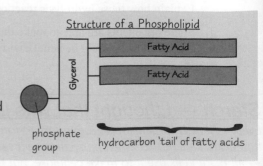
Structure of a Phospholipid
Fatty Acid
Fatty Acid
Glycerol
phosphate group
hydrocarbon 'tail' of fatty acids

Lipids

The **Structures** of Lipids Relate to Their **Functions**

You need to know how the **structures** of **triglycerides** and **phospholipids** are related to their **functions**:

Triglycerides

Triglycerides are mainly used as **energy storage molecules**. They're good for this because:

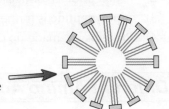

1) The **long hydrocarbon tails** of the fatty acids contain lots of **chemical energy** — a load of energy is **released** when they're **broken down**. Because of these tails, lipids contain about **twice** as much energy per gram as carbohydrates.

2) They're **insoluble**, so they don't affect the **water potential** (see p. 40) of the cell and cause water to enter the cells by **osmosis** (which would make them swell). The triglycerides clump together as **insoluble droplets** in cells because the fatty acid tails are **hydrophobic** (water-repelling) — the tails **face inwards**, shielding themselves from water with their glycerol heads.

Phospholipids

Phospholipids make up the **bilayer of cell membranes** (see p. 36).
Cell membranes **control** what **enters and leaves a cell**.

1) Their heads are **hydrophilic** and their tails are **hydrophobic**, so they form a **double** layer with their heads facing **out** towards the water on either side.

2) The **centre** of the bilayer is **hydrophobic**, so water-soluble substances **can't** easily pass through it — the membrane acts as a **barrier** to those substances.

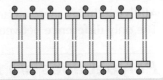

Use the **Emulsion Test** for **Lipids**

If you wanted to find out if there was any **fat** in a particular **food** you could do the **emulsion test**:

1) **Shake** the test substance with **ethanol** for about a minute so that it dissolves, then **pour** the solution into **water**.

2) Any lipid will show up as a **milky emulsion**.

3) The more lipid there is, the more noticeable the milky colour will be.

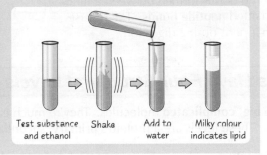

Test substance and ethanol — Shake — Add to water — Milky colour indicates lipid

Practice Questions

Q1 What type of bond is made from a condensation reaction between glycerol and a fatty acid molecule?

Q2 Describe how you would test for lipids in a solution.

Exam Questions

Q1 Triglycerides have a hydrophobic tail. Explain how this feature of a lipid is important for its function. [2 marks]

Q2 Cell membranes contain phospholipids.

a) Describe the structure of a phospholipid. [3 marks]

b) Explain the difference between a saturated fatty acid and an unsaturated fatty acid. [2 marks]

The test for lipids — stick them in a can of paint...

Not really. Otherwise you might upset your Biology teacher a bit. Instead, why not sit and contemplate all those phospholipids jumping around in your plasma membranes... their water-loving, phosphate heads poking out of the cell and into the cytoplasm, and their water-hating, hydrocarbon tails forming an impenetrable layer in between...

Proteins

There are loads of different proteins with loads of different functions. But what are proteins? What do they look like? Well, for your enjoyment, here are the answers to all those questions and many, many more...

Proteins *are Made from* Long Chains *of Amino Acids*

1) The **monomers** of proteins are **amino acids**.
2) A **dipeptide** is formed when **two** amino acids join together.
3) A **polypeptide** is formed when **more than two** amino acids join together.
4) **Proteins** are made up of **one or more polypeptides**.

Grant's cries of "die peptide, die" could be heard for miles around. He'd never forgiven it for sleeping with his wife.

Different Amino Acids *Have* Different Variable Groups

Amino acids have the same general structure — a **carboxyl group** (-COOH), an **amine** or **amino group** (-NH$_2$) and a **carbon-containing R group** (also known as a **variable** side group).

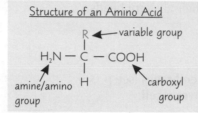

Structure of an Amino Acid

$$H_2N - C - COOH$$

R ← variable group

amine/amino group

carboxyl group

E.g. Structure of Alanine

$$H_2N - C - COOH$$

CH$_3$

All living things share a bank of only **20 amino acids**. The only **difference** between them is what makes up their carbon-containing **R group**.

Glycine is the only amino acid that doesn't have carbon in its side group. Its R group consists of just one hydrogen atom.

Polypeptides *are Formed by* Condensation Reactions

Amino acids are linked together by **condensation** reactions to form polypeptides. A molecule of **water** is **released** during the reaction. The bonds formed between amino acids are called **peptide bonds**. The reverse reaction happens during digestion.

amino acid 1   amino acid 2   dipeptide

condensation
hydrolysis

a molecule of water is formed during condensation.

peptide bond

Proteins *Have* Four Structural Levels

Proteins are **big**, **complicated** molecules. They're much easier to explain if you describe their structure in four 'levels'. These levels are a protein's **primary**, **secondary**, **tertiary** and **quaternary** structures.

<u>Primary Structure</u> — this is the **sequence** of **amino acids** in the **polypeptide chain**.

<u>Secondary Structure</u> — the polypeptide chain doesn't remain flat and straight. **Hydrogen bonds** form between the amino acids in the chain. This makes it automatically **coil** into an **alpha (α) helix** or **fold** into a **beta (β) pleated sheet** — this is the secondary structure.

<u>Tertiary Structure</u> — the coiled or folded chain of amino acids is often **coiled** and **folded further**. More **bonds** form between different parts of the polypeptide chain, including **hydrogen bonds** and **ionic bonds** (attractions between **negative** and **positive** charges on different parts of the molecule). **Disulfide bridges** also form whenever two molecules of the amino acid **cysteine** come **close together** — the **sulfur** atom in one cysteine **bonds** to the sulfur atom in the other. For proteins made from a **single** polypeptide chain, the tertiary structure forms their **final 3D structure**.

<u>Quaternary Structure</u> — some proteins are made of **several different polypeptide chains** held together by **bonds**. The **quaternary structure** is the way these polypeptide chains are assembled together. For proteins made from more than one polypeptide chain (e.g. haemoglobin, insulin, collagen), the quaternary structure is the protein's **final 3D structure**.

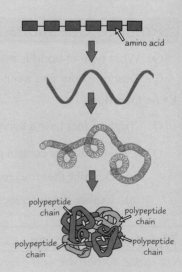

amino acid

polypeptide chain

polypeptide chain

polypeptide chain

polypeptide chain

Proteins

Proteins have a *Variety* of *Functions*

There are **loads** of different **proteins** found in **living organisms**. They've all got **different structures** and **shapes**, which makes them **specialised** to carry out particular **jobs**. For example:

1) <u>Enzymes</u> — they're usually roughly **spherical** in shape due to the **tight folding** of the polypeptide chains. They're **soluble** and often have roles in **metabolism**, e.g. some enzymes break down large food molecules (**digestive enzymes**, see pages 66-67) and other enzymes help to **synthesise** (make) large molecules.

2) <u>Antibodies</u> — are involved in the **immune response**. They're made up of **two light** (short) polypeptide chains and **two heavy** (long) polypeptide chains bonded together. Antibodies have **variable regions** (see p. 44) — the **amino acid sequences** in these regions **vary** greatly.

3) <u>Transport proteins</u> — e.g. channel proteins are present in **cell membranes** (p. 38). Channel proteins contain **hydrophobic** (water hating) and **hydrophilic** (water loving) amino acids, which cause the protein to **fold up** and form a **channel**. These proteins **transport molecules** and **ions across** membranes.

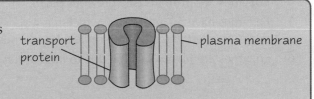
transport protein — plasma membrane

4) <u>Structural proteins</u> — are physically **strong**. They consist of **long polypeptide chains** lying **parallel** to each other with **cross-links** between them. Structural proteins include **keratin** (found in hair and nails) and **collagen** (found in connective tissue).

Use the *Biuret Test* for *Proteins*

If you needed to find out if a substance, e.g. a **food sample**, contained **protein** you'd use the **biuret test**.

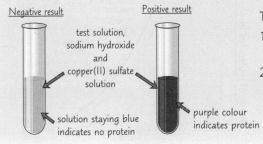
Negative result — test solution, sodium hydroxide and copper(II) sulfate solution — solution staying blue indicates no protein
Positive result — purple colour indicates protein

There are **two stages** to this test.
1) The test solution needs to be **alkaline**, so first you add a few drops of **sodium hydroxide solution**.
2) Then you add some **copper(II) sulfate solution**.
   - If protein **is** present the solution turns **purple**.
   - If there's **no protein**, the solution will **stay blue**. The colours are pale, so you need to look carefully.

Practice Questions

Q1 What groups do all amino acid molecules have in common?

Q2 Give three functions of proteins.

Q3 Describe how you would test for the presence of protein in a sample.

Exam Questions

Q1 Leucyl-alanine is a dipeptide. Describe how a dipeptide is formed. [3 marks]

Q2 Myoglobin is a protein formed from a single polypeptide chain.
Describe the tertiary structure of a protein like myoglobin. [2 marks]

Condensation — I can see the reaction happening on my car windows...

Protein structure is hard to imagine. I think of a Slinky® — the wire's the primary structure, it coils up to form the secondary structure and if you coil the Slinky around your arm, that's the tertiary structure. When a few Slinkies get tangled up, that's like the quaternary structure. I need to get out more. I wish I had more than a Slinky for company.

TOPIC 1A — BIOLOGICAL MOLECULES

Enzyme Action

Enzymes crop up loads in biology — they're really useful 'cos they make reactions work quickly. So, whether you feel the need for some speed or not, read on — because you really need to know this basic stuff about enzymes.

Enzymes are Biological Catalysts

Enzymes **speed up chemical reactions** by acting as **biological catalysts**.

A catalyst is a substance that speeds up a chemical reaction without being used up in the reaction itself.

1) Enzymes catalyse **metabolic reactions** — both at a **cellular level** (e.g. **respiration**) and for the **organism** as a **whole** (e.g. **digestion** in mammals).

2) Enzymes can affect **structures** in an organism (e.g. enzymes are involved in the production of **collagen**, an important protein in the **connective tissues** of animals) as well as **functions** (like **respiration**).

3) Enzyme action can be **intracellular** — **within** cells, or **extracellular** — **outside** cells.

4) Enzymes are **proteins** (see previous page).

5) Enzymes have an **active site**, which has a **specific shape**. The active site is the part of the enzyme where the **substrate** molecules (the substance that the enzyme interacts with) **bind to**.

6) Enzymes are **highly specific** due to their tertiary structure (see next page).

Enzymes Lower the Activation Energy of a Reaction

In a chemical reaction, a certain amount of **energy** needs to be supplied to the chemicals before the reaction will **start**. This is called the **activation energy** — it's often provided as **heat**. Enzymes **lower** the amount of activation energy that's needed, often making reactions happen at a **lower temperature** than they could without an enzyme. This **speeds up** the **rate of reaction**.

When a substrate fits into the enzyme's active site it forms an **enzyme-substrate complex** — it's this that lowers the activation energy. Here are two reasons why:

1) If two substrate molecules need to be **joined**, being attached to the enzyme holds them **close together**, **reducing** any **repulsion** between the molecules so they can bond more easily.

2) If the enzyme is catalysing a **breakdown reaction**, fitting into the active site puts a **strain** on bonds in the substrate, so the substrate molecule **breaks up** more easily.

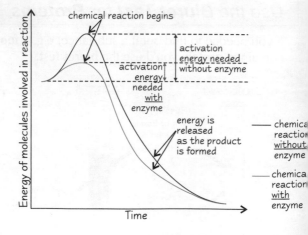

The 'Lock and Key' Model is a Good Start...

Enzymes are a bit picky — they only work with substrates that fit their active site. Early scientists studying the action of enzymes came up with the 'lock and key' model. This is where the **substrate fits** into the **enzyme** in the same way that a **key fits** into a **lock**.

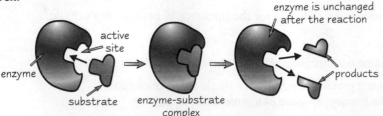

Scientists soon realised that the lock and key model didn't give the full story. The enzyme and substrate do have to fit together in the first place, but new evidence showed that the **enzyme-substrate complex changed shape** slightly to complete the fit. This **locks** the substrate even more tightly to the enzyme. Scientists modified the old lock and key model and came up with the 'induced fit' model.

Enzyme Action

...but the 'Induced Fit' Model is a Better Theory

The **'induced fit'** model helps to explain why enzymes are so **specific** and only bond to one particular substrate. The substrate doesn't only have to be the right shape to fit the active site, it has to make the active site **change shape** in the right way as well. This is a prime example of how a widely accepted theory can **change** when **new evidence** comes along. The 'induced fit' model is still widely accepted — for now, anyway.

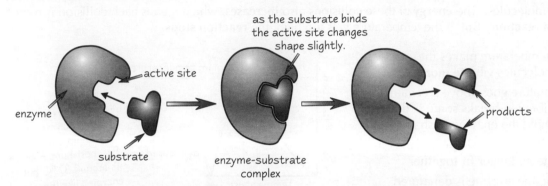

The 'Luminous Tights' model was popular in the 1980s but has since been found to be grossly inappropriate.

Enzyme Properties Relate to Their Tertiary Structure

1) Enzymes are **very specific** — they usually only catalyse **one** reaction, e.g. maltase only breaks down maltose, sucrase only breaks down sucrose.

2) This is because **only one complementary substrate will fit** into the active site.

3) The active site's **shape** is determined by the enzyme's **tertiary structure** (which is determined by the enzyme's **primary structure**).

4) Each **different enzyme** has a **different tertiary structure** and so a **different shaped active site**. If the substrate shape doesn't match the active site, an enzyme-substrate complex **won't** be formed and the reaction won't be catalysed.

5) If the tertiary structure of the enzyme is **altered** in any way, the **shape** of the active site will **change**. This means the **substrate won't fit** into the active site, an enzyme-substrate complex **won't** be formed and the enzyme will no longer be able to carry out its function.

6) The tertiary structure of an enzyme may be **altered** by changes in **pH** or **temperature** (see next page).

7) The **primary structure** (amino acid sequence) of a protein is determined by a **gene**. If a mutation occurs in that gene (see p. 91), it could change the tertiary structure of the enzyme **produced**.

Practice Questions

Q1 What is an enzyme?

Q2 What is the name given to the amount of energy needed to start a reaction?

Q3 What is an enzyme-substrate complex?

Q4 Why can an enzyme only bind to one substance?

Exam Questions

Q1 Describe the 'induced fit' model of enzyme action. [4 marks]

Q2 Explain how a change in the amino acid sequence of an enzyme may prevent it from functioning properly. [2 marks]

But why is the enzyme-substrate complex?

So enzymes lower the activation energy of a reaction. I like to think of it as an assault course (bear with me). Suppose the assault course starts with a massive wall — enzymes are like the person who gives you a leg up over the wall (see?). Without it you'd need lots of energy to get over the wall yourself and complete the rest of the course. Unlikely.

Factors Affecting Enzyme Activity

Now you know what enzymes are and how they work, let's take a look at what makes them tick. Humans need things like money and the newest mobile phone, but enzymes are quite content with the right temperature and pH.

Temperature *has a* Big Influence *on Enzyme Activity*

Like any chemical reaction, the **rate** of an enzyme-controlled reaction **increases** when the **temperature's increased**. More heat means **more kinetic energy**, so molecules **move faster**. This makes the enzymes **more likely** to **collide** with the substrate molecules. The **energy** of these collisions also **increases**, which means each collision is more likely to **result** in a **reaction**. But, if the temperature gets too high, the **reaction stops**.

1) The rise in temperature makes the enzyme's molecules **vibrate more**.

2) If the temperature goes above a certain level, this vibration **breaks** some of the **bonds** that hold the enzyme in shape.

3) The **active site changes shape** and the enzyme and substrate **no longer fit together**.

4) At this point, the enzyme is **denatured** — it no longer functions as a catalyst.

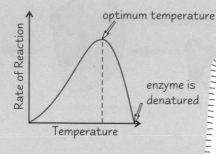

Every enzyme has an optimum temperature. For most human enzymes it's around 37 °C but some enzymes, like those used in biological washing powders, can work well at 60 °C.

pH *Also Affects Enzyme* Activity

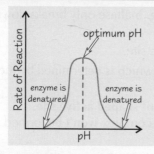

All enzymes have an **optimum pH value**. Most human enzymes work best at pH 7 (neutral), but there are exceptions. **Pepsin**, for example, works best at acidic pH 2, which is useful because it's found in the stomach. Above and below the optimum pH, the H^+ and OH^- ions found in acids and alkalis can mess up the **ionic bonds** and **hydrogen bonds** that hold the enzyme's tertiary structure in place. This makes the active site change shape, so the enzyme is **denatured**.

Enzyme Concentration *Affects the Rate of Reaction*

1) The **more enzyme molecules** there are in a solution, the more likely a substrate molecule is to **collide** with one and form an **enzyme-substrate complex**. So increasing the concentration of the enzyme **increases** the **rate of reaction**.

2) But, if the amount of **substrate** is **limited**, there comes a point when there's more than enough enzyme molecules to deal with all the available substrate, so adding more enzyme has **no further effect**.

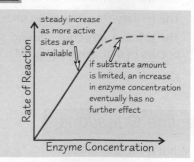

Substrate Concentration *Affects the Rate of Reaction* Up to a Point

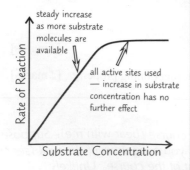

1) The **higher** the substrate concentration, the **faster** the reaction — more substrate molecules means a **collision** between substrate and enzyme is **more likely** and so more active sites will be used. This is only true up until a **'saturation'** point though. After that, there are so many substrate molecules that the enzymes have about as much as they can cope with (all the **active sites are full**), and adding more **makes no difference**.

2) Substrate concentration **decreases** with **time** during a reaction (unless more substrate is added to the reaction mixture), so if no other variables are changed, the **rate of reaction will decrease over time** too. This makes the **initial** rate of reaction (the reaction rate at the **start**) the **highest** rate of reaction.

Factors Affecting Enzyme Activity

Enzyme Activity can be Inhibited

Enzyme activity can be prevented by **enzyme inhibitors** — molecules that **bind to the enzyme** that they inhibit. Inhibition can be **competitive** or **non-competitive**.

COMPETITIVE INHIBITION

1) **Competitive inhibitor** molecules have a **similar shape** to that of the **substrate** molecules.
2) They **compete** with the substrate molecules to **bind** to the **active site**, but **no reaction** takes place.
3) Instead they **block** the active site, so **no substrate** molecules can **fit** in it.

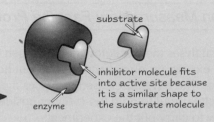

substrate

inhibitor molecule fits into active site because it is a similar shape to the substrate molecule

enzyme

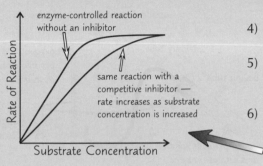

4) How much the enzyme is inhibited depends on the **relative concentrations** of the inhibitor and the substrate.
5) If there's a **high concentration** of the **inhibitor**, it'll take up **nearly all** the **active sites** and hardly any of the substrate will get to the enzyme.
6) But if there's a **higher concentration** of **substrate**, then the substrate's chances of getting to an active site before the inhibitor **increase**. So **increasing** the concentration of **substrate** will **increase** the **rate of reaction** (up to a point).

NON-COMPETITIVE INHIBITION

1) **Non-competitive inhibitor** molecules bind to the enzyme **away from its active site**.
2) This causes the active site to **change shape** so the substrate molecules can **no longer bind** to it.
3) They don't 'compete' with the substrate molecules to bind to the active site because they are a different shape.
4) **Increasing** the concentration of **substrate won't** make any difference to the reaction rate — enzyme activity will still be inhibited.

inhibitor molecule fits onto enzyme away from active site

substrate molecule can no longer fit into active site

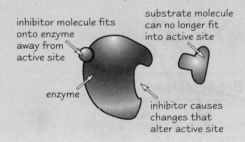

enzyme

inhibitor causes changes that alter active site

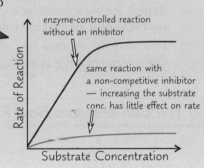

Practice Questions

Q1 Draw a graph to show the effect of temperature on enzyme activity.

Q2 Draw a graph to show the effect of pH on enzyme activity.

Q3 Explain the effect of increasing substrate concentration on the rate of an enzyme-catalysed reaction.

Exam Question

Q1 Inhibitors prevent enzymes from working properly. They can be competitive or non-competitive.
   a) Explain how a competitive inhibitor works. [3 marks]
   b) Explain how a non-competitive inhibitor works. [2 marks]

Activity — mine is usually inhibited by pizza and a movie...

Human enzymes work well under normal body conditions — a neutral pH and body temp of 37 °C. Many poisons are enzyme inhibitors, e.g. cyanide. Even though there are thousands of enzymes in our bodies, inhibiting just one of them can cause severe problems. Some drugs are enzyme inhibitors though, e.g. penicillin, so they're not all bad.

Enzyme-Controlled Reactions

Science isn't all about words and theory, it's also about getting your pipette dirty and making bad smells (in the name of discovery of course). These pages show you how to measure the rate of an enzyme-controlled reaction.

You can **Measure** the **Rate** of an **Enzyme-Controlled** Reaction

Here are two ways of measuring the **rate** of an enzyme-controlled reaction:

1) You Can Measure **How Fast** the **Product** of the Reaction is **Made**

Catalase catalyses the **breakdown** of **hydrogen peroxide** into **water** and **oxygen**. It's easy to measure the volume of oxygen produced and to work out **how fast** it's given off. The diagram below shows the **apparatus** you'll need. The oxygen released **displaces** the water from the measuring cylinder. (A **stand** and **clamp** would also be pretty useful to hold the cylinder upside down, as would a **stopwatch** and a **water bath**.) Here's how to carry out the experiment:

1) Set up boiling tubes containing the **same volume** and **concentration** of **hydrogen peroxide**. To keep the pH constant, add **equal volumes** of a suitable **buffer solution** to each tube. (A buffer solution is able to resist changes in pH when small amounts of acid or alkali are added.)

2) Set up the rest of the **apparatus** as shown in the diagram.

3) Put each boiling tube in a **water bath** set to a different temperature (e.g. 10 °C, 20 °C, 30 °C and 40 °C) along with another tube containing **catalase** (wait 5 minutes before moving onto the next step so the enzyme gets up to temperature).

4) Use a pipette to add the **same volume** and **concentration** of **catalase** to each boiling tube. Then **quickly attach** the **bung** and **delivery tube**.

5) **Record** how much oxygen is produced in the **first minute** (60 s) of the reaction. Use a **stopwatch** to measure the time.

6) **Repeat** the experiment at each temperature three times, and use the results to find an **average volume of oxygen produced**.

7) **Calculate** the **average rate of reaction** at each temperature by dividing the volume of oxygen produced by the time taken (i.e. 60 s). The units will be cm^{3}s^{-1}.

upside down measuring cylinder

volume of oxygen produced per minute is measured

delivery tube

boiling tube

bung

trough of water

hydrogen peroxide solution and catalase enzyme

A negative control reaction, i.e. a boiling tube not containing catalase, should also be carried out at each temperature.

2) You Can Measure **How Fast** the **Substrate** is **Broken Down**

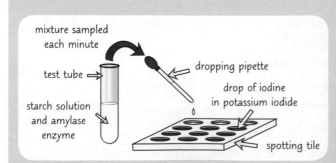

mixture sampled each minute

test tube

dropping pipette

drop of iodine in potassium iodide

starch solution and amylase enzyme

spotting tile

The enzyme **amylase** catalyses the breakdown of **starch** to **maltose**. The diagram shows how the experiment can be **set up**. You'll need the **apparatus** shown in the diagram as well as a **stopwatch**. A drop of **iodine in potassium iodide** is put into each well on a **spotting tile**. A known concentration of **amylase** and **starch** are then mixed together in a test tube. A **dropping pipette** is used to put a drop of this mixture into one of the wells containing the iodine solution on the spotting tile at **regular intervals** and the resulting colour is observed. The iodine solution goes **dark blue-black** when starch is **present** but remains its normal **browny-orange** colour when there's **no starch** around. You can see how fast **amylase** is working by **recording** how long it takes for the iodine solution to **no longer** turn blue-black when starch/amylase mixture is added. **Repeat** the experiment using **different concentrations** of **amylase**. Make sure that you also **repeat** the experiment three times at **each** amylase concentration.

The **experiments above** show you how you can investigate the effects of **temperature** and **enzyme concentration** on the rate of enzyme-controlled reactions. You can also **alter** these experiments to investigate the effect of a **different variable**, such as **pH** (by adding a **buffer solution** with a **different pH** to each test tube) or **substrate concentration** (you could use **serial dilutions** to make substrate solutions with **different** concentrations). The key to experiments like this is to remember to **only** change **one variable** — **everything else** should stay the **same**.

Enzyme-Controlled Reactions

You Need to be Able to *Interpret Graphs* of *Enzyme-Controlled* Reactions

The results of enzyme-controlled reactions are usually shown in **line graphs**. You might be asked to **interpret** the **graph** of an **enzyme-controlled** reaction in the exam. The graph below shows the **release of a product over time**:

① First look at the **start** of the graph and **compare** the rates of reaction here. E.g. the rate of reaction is **fastest** at **65 °C**. Use what you **know** about **factors affecting enzyme activity** to explain why (see p. 12). You might have to work out the **initial rate of reaction** (see below).

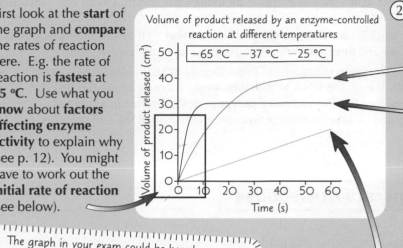

Volume of product released by an enzyme-controlled reaction at different temperatures
— 65 °C   — 37 °C   — 25 °C

The graph in your exam could be based on any variable — e.g. pH, temperature, enzyme concentration or substrate concentration. You'll have to use your knowledge of enzymes to explain what's going on.

② Now look at what **else** the graphs are **showing** you and make **comparisons** between the different temperatures.

At **37 °C** the graph has **plateaued** (flattened out) because all the **substrate** has been **used up**. At **65 °C** the graph has **plateaued earlier** than at 37 °C, because the high temperature caused the enzyme to **denature**, so the reaction **stopped sooner**. Not as much product was made because **not all** the substrate was **converted to product** before the enzyme was denatured, so there is still **substrate left**.

At **25 °C** the **rate of reaction** is remaining **constant** and the **volume of product** is **continuing to increase** because **not all** of the substrate has been used up.

You Can Use a *Tangent* to *Calculate* the *Initial Rate of Reaction*

The **initial** rate of reaction is the rate of reaction right at the **start** of the reaction, close to **time equals zero** (t = 0) on the graph. To work out the initial rate of reaction carry out the following steps:

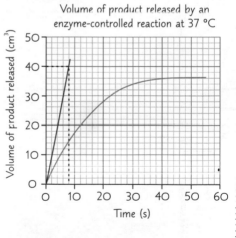

Volume of product released by an enzyme-controlled reaction at 37 °C

1) **Draw a tangent** to the curve at **t = 0**, using a ruler. Do this by positioning the ruler so it's an **equal distance** from the curve at **both sides** of where it's touching it. Here you'll have to **estimate** where the curve would **continue** if it carried on **below zero**. Then draw a **line** along the ruler. (For more on drawing tangents see p. 107.)

2) Then calculate the **gradient** of the **tangent** — this is the **initial rate of reaction**. Gradient = change in y axis ÷ change in x axis
In this graph it's: 40 cm³ ÷ 8 s = **5 cm³ s⁻¹**

If you're comparing the initial rate of reaction for two different reactions, you can work out the ratio of the rates to give you a quick and easy comparison.

Practice Question

Q1 You are testing the effects of pH on the action of an enzyme. What other variables must you keep constant?

Exam Question

Q1 A student carries out an enzyme-controlled reaction at 37 °C and 65 °C. Her results are shown in the graph above. Draw a tangent to find the initial rate of reaction at 65 °C. Show your working. [1 mark]

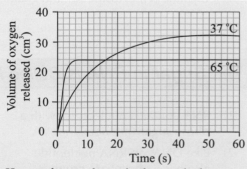

My rate of reaction depends on what time of day it is...

In your exam, you could get asked about methods used to measure the rate of an enzyme-controlled reaction or to calculate the rate from a graph. It's worth your time to memorise the examples and learn the maths on these pages.

DNA and RNA

These two pages are all about nucleic acids — DNA and RNA. These molecules are needed to build proteins, which are required for the cells in living organisms to function. They're right handy little things.

DNA and RNA Carry Important Information

DNA and RNA are both types of **nucleic acid**. They're found in **all living cells** and they both carry **information**.

1) **DNA** (deoxyribonucleic acid) is used to store **genetic information** — that's **all the instructions** an organism needs to **grow and develop** from a fertilised egg to a fully grown adult.

2) **RNA** (ribonucleic acid) is similar in structure to DNA. One of its main functions is to **transfer** genetic information from the **DNA** to the **ribosomes**. Ribosomes are the body's 'protein factories' — they read the RNA to make **polypeptides** (proteins) in a process called **translation** (see p. 85). Ribosomes themselves are made from **RNA** and **proteins**.

DNA and RNA are Polymers of Nucleotides

1) A **nucleotide** is a type of biological molecule. It's made from:

- a **pentose sugar** (that's a sugar with **5** carbon atoms),
- a **nitrogen-containing** organic **base**,
- a **phosphate** group.

'Organic' means that it contains carbon.

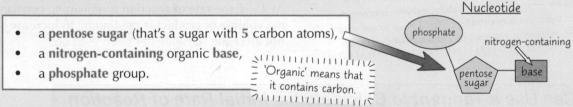

Nucleotide

phosphate / pentose sugar / base / nitrogen-containing

2) Nucleotides are really **important**. For a start, they're the **monomers** (see p. 2) that make up **DNA** and **RNA**.

The Sugar in DNA is Called Deoxyribose

1) The **pentose sugar** in a **DNA** nucleotide is called **deoxyribose**.

2) Each DNA nucleotide has the **same sugar** and a **phosphate group**. The **base** on each nucleotide can **vary** though.

3) There are **four** possible bases — adenine (**A**), thymine (**T**), cytosine (**C**) and guanine (**G**).

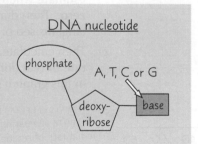

DNA nucleotide

phosphate / deoxy-ribose / base / A, T, C or G

The Sugar in RNA is Called Ribose

1) **RNA** contains nucleotides with a **ribose sugar** (not deoxyribose).

2) Like DNA, an RNA nucleotide also has a **phosphate group** and one of **four** different **bases**.

3) In RNA though, **uracil** (**U**) replaces **thymine** as a base.

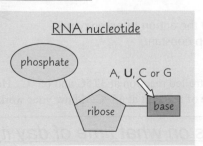

RNA nucleotide

phosphate / ribose / base / A, **U**, C or G

Mary didn't care if it was ribose or deoxyribose, she just wanted her cuppa.

DNA and RNA

Nucleotides Join Together to Form Polynucleotides

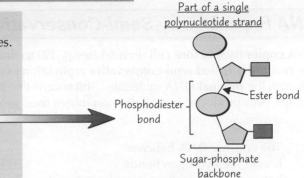

Part of a single polynucleotide strand

1) A **polynucleotide** is a **polymer** of **nucleotides**. Both DNA and RNA nucleotides form polynucleotides.

2) The nucleotides join up via a **condensation reaction** (see p. 2) between the **phosphate** group of one nucleotide and the **sugar** of another.

3) This forms a **phosphodiester bond** (consisting of the phosphate group and two ester bonds).

4) The chain of sugars and phosphates is known as the **sugar-phosphate backbone**.

Ester bond
Phosphodiester bond
Sugar-phosphate backbone

DNA is Made of Two Polynucleotide Chains in a Double-Helix Structure

1) **Two DNA** polynucleotide strands join together by **hydrogen bonding** between the bases.

2) Each base can only join with one particular partner — this is called **complementary base pairing** (or specific base pairing).

3) **Adenine** always pairs with **thymine** (**A - T**) and **cytosine** always pairs with **guanine** (**C - G**). This means that there are always **equal amounts** of adenine and thymine in a DNA molecule and **equal amounts** of cytosine and guanine.

4) **Two** hydrogen bonds form between **A and T**, and **three** hydrogen bonds form between **C and G**.

5) Two **antiparallel** (running in opposite directions) polynucleotide strands **twist** to form the **DNA double-helix**.

6) DNA was first observed in the 1800s, but lots of scientists at the time **doubted** that it could carry the **genetic code** because it has a **relatively simple chemical composition**. Some argued that genetic information must be carried by **proteins** — which are much more **chemically varied**.

7) By 1953, experiments had shown that DNA was the carrier of the genetic code. This was also the year in which the **double-helix structure**, which helps DNA to carry out its function, was determined by **Watson** and **Crick**.

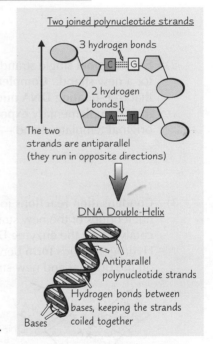

Two joined polynucleotide strands

3 hydrogen bonds
C··G
2 hydrogen bonds
A··T

The two strands are antiparallel (they run in opposite directions)

DNA Double-Helix

Antiparallel polynucleotide strands
Hydrogen bonds between bases, keeping the strands coiled together
Bases

RNA is a Relatively Short Polynucleotide Chain

RNA is made from a **single** polynucleotide chain (not a double one). It's much **shorter** than most DNA polynucleotides.

Practice Questions

Q1 Name the bases in RNA.

Exam Questions

Q1 The bar chart shows the percentage of the bases in a DNA sample that are adenine and cytosine. On the chart, sketch bars to show the percentages of thymine and guanine in the sample. [2 marks]

Q2 a) Describe how nucleotides are joined together in DNA. [3 marks]

b) Describe how two single polynucleotide strands are joined to make a double helix. [3 marks]

Give me a D, give me an N, give me an A! What do you get? — confused...

You need to learn the structure of DNA — the polynucleotide strands, the hydrogen bonds, and don't forget complementary base pairing. Make sure you know the differences between RNA and DNA too — interesting stuff.

DNA Replication

DNA has the amazing ability to replicate (copy) itself. These pages cover the facts behind the replication mechanism, as well as some of the history behind its discovery. This stuff is really clever. Honest.

DNA Replicates by Semi-Conservative Replication

DNA **copies** itself **before** cell division (see p. 32) so that each **new** cell has the **full** amount of **DNA**. The method is called **semi-conservative replication** because **half** of the strands in **each new DNA molecule** are from the **original** DNA molecule. This means that there's **genetic continuity** between generations of cells (i.e. the cells produced by cell division inherit their genes from their parent cells).

1) The enzyme **DNA helicase breaks** the **hydrogen bonds** between bases on the two **polynucleotide** DNA strands. This makes the helix **unwind** to form two single strands.

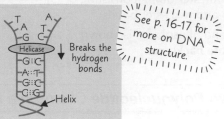

See p. 16-17 for more on DNA structure.

Gerald doesn't need helicase to unwind. He just needs a beach full of seals.

2) Each **original** single strand acts as a **template** for a new strand. **Complementary base pairing** means that **free-floating DNA nucleotides** are attracted to their complementary **exposed bases** on each original template strand — A with T and C with G.

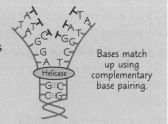

Bases match up using complementary base pairing.

3) **Condensation reactions** join the nucleotides of the new strands together — catalysed by the enzyme **DNA polymerase**. Hydrogen bonds **form** between the bases on the original and new strands.

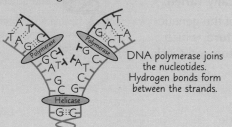

DNA polymerase joins the nucleotides. Hydrogen bonds form between the strands.

4) Each new DNA molecule contains **one strand** from the **original** DNA molecule and one **new strand**.

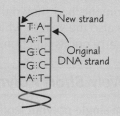

New strand

Original DNA strand

DNA Polymerase Moves in Opposite Ways Along Antiparallel DNA Strands

Each end of a DNA strand is slightly **different** in its structure.
One end is called the **3'** (pronounced 'three prime') end and one end is called the **5'** (five prime) end.
In a DNA helix, the strands run in **opposite** directions — they're **antiparallel**.

The **active site** of **DNA polymerase** is only **complementary** to the **3' end** of the newly forming DNA strand — so the enzyme can **only** add **nucleotides** to the new strand at the **3' end**.

This means that the **new strand** is made in a **5' to 3'** direction and that DNA polymerase moves down the **template strand** in a **3' to 5'** direction. Because the strands in the double-helix are **antiparallel**, the DNA polymerase working on **one** of the template strands **moves** in the **opposite direction** to the DNA polymerase working on the **other** template strand.

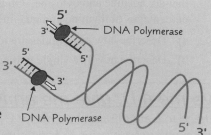

DNA Polymerase

DNA Polymerase

DNA Replication

Meselson and Stahl Provided Evidence for Semi-Conservative Replication

1) You might remember from page 17 that **Watson** and **Crick** determined the structure of DNA. They also came up with the theory of **semi-conservative DNA replication**.

2) It wasn't until **Meselson** and **Stahl's** experiment a few years **later** that this theory was **validated**. Before that, people were unsure whether DNA replication was **semi-conservative** or **conservative**. If the method was **conservative**, the original DNA strands would **stay together** and the new DNA molecules would contain **two new strands**.

3) Meselson and Stahl showed that DNA is replicated using the **semi-conservative method**. Their experiment used two **isotopes** of **nitrogen** (DNA contains nitrogen) — **heavy** nitrogen (^{15}N) and **light** nitrogen (^{14}N). Here's how it worked:

Isotopes are different forms of the same element.

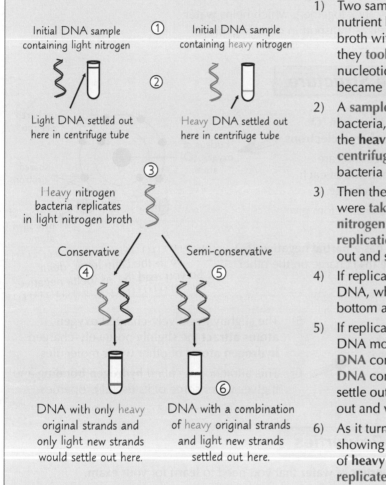

Initial DNA sample containing light nitrogen ①   Initial DNA sample containing heavy nitrogen

②

Light DNA settled out here in centrifuge tube   Heavy DNA settled out here in centrifuge tube

③

Heavy nitrogen bacteria replicates in light nitrogen broth

Conservative   Semi-conservative

④   ⑤

⑥

DNA with only heavy original strands and only light new strands would settle out here.   DNA with a combination of heavy original strands and light new strands settled out here.

1) Two samples of bacteria were grown — one in a nutrient broth containing **light** nitrogen, and one in a broth with **heavy** nitrogen. As the **bacteria reproduced**, they **took up nitrogen** from the broth to help make nucleotides for new DNA. So the nitrogen gradually became part of the bacteria's DNA.

2) A **sample of DNA** was taken from each batch of bacteria, and spun in a **centrifuge**. The DNA from the **heavy** nitrogen bacteria settled **lower** down the **centrifuge tube** than the DNA from the **light** nitrogen bacteria — because it's **heavier**.

3) Then the bacteria grown in the **heavy** nitrogen broth were **taken out** and put in a broth containing only **light** nitrogen. The bacteria were left for **one round of DNA replication**, and then **another DNA sample** was taken out and spun in the centrifuge.

4) If replication was **conservative**, the original **heavy** DNA, which would still be together, would settle at the bottom and the new **light** DNA would settle at the top.

5) If replication was **semi-conservative**, the new bacterial DNA molecules would contain **one strand** of the **old** DNA containing **heavy** nitrogen and **one strand** of **new** DNA containing **light** nitrogen. So the DNA would settle out **between** where the **light** nitrogen DNA settled out and where the **heavy** nitrogen DNA settled out.

6) As it turned out, the DNA settled out in the **middle**, showing that the DNA molecules contained a **mixture** of **heavy** and **light** nitrogen. The bacterial DNA had **replicated semi-conservatively** in the **light** nitrogen.

Once Meselson and Stahl had confirmed that **DNA replication** in **bacteria** was **semi-conservative**, other scientists carried out experiments to show that it was the **universal method** for DNA replication in **all living things**.

Practice Questions

Q1 What is the role of DNA helicase in DNA replication?

Q2 What's the key difference between the conservative and semi-conservative theories of DNA replication?

Exam Question

Q1 Describe the process of semi-conservative DNA replication. [5 marks]

DNA DNA Replication Replication is is Semi-Conservative Semi-Conservative

Make sure you can recall the mechanism of DNA replication — you might be asked for it in your exam. You might also be asked to evaluate the work of the scientists who validated Watson and Crick's theory of semi-conservative replication.

Water

Your body needs lots of molecules to stay alive, and these pages cover one of the most important — water.

Water is Vital to Living Organisms

Water makes up about 80% of a cell's contents. It has loads of important **functions**, inside and outside of cells:

1) Water is a **metabolite** in loads of important **metabolic reactions**, including **condensation** and **hydrolysis reactions** (see below).

2) Water is a **solvent**, which means some substances **dissolve** in it. Most metabolic reactions take place **in solution** (e.g. in the **cytoplasm** of eukaryotic and prokaryotic cells) so water's pretty essential.

3) Water helps with **temperature control** because it has a **high latent heat of vaporisation** (see below) and a **high specific heat capacity** (see next page).

4) Water molecules are very **cohesive** (they stick together), which helps **water transport** in **plants** (see next page) as well as transport in other organisms.

A metabolic reaction is a chemical reaction that happens in a living organism to keep the organism alive. A metabolite is a substance involved in a metabolic reaction.

Water Molecules Have a Simple Structure

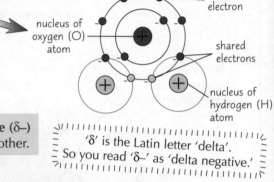

1) A molecule of **water** (H_2O) is **one atom** of **oxygen** (O) joined to **two atoms** of **hydrogen** (H_2) by **shared electrons**.

2) Because the **shared negative** hydrogen electrons are **pulled towards** the oxygen atom, the other side of each hydrogen atom is left with a **slight positive charge**.

3) The **unshared** negative electrons on the oxygen atom give it a **slight negative charge**.

4) This makes water a **polar** molecule — it has a **partial negative** (δ–) charge on one side and a **partial positive** (δ+) charge on the other.

unshared electron

nucleus of oxygen (O) atom

shared electrons

nucleus of hydrogen (H) atom

'δ' is the Latin letter 'delta'. So you read 'δ–' as 'delta negative.'

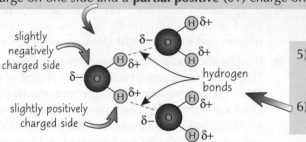

slightly negatively charged side

slightly positively charged side

hydrogen bonds

5) The slightly negatively-charged **oxygen atoms attract** the slightly positively-charged **hydrogen atoms** of other water molecules.

6) This attraction is called **hydrogen bonding** and it gives water some of its useful properties.

Water Has Some Really Useful Properties

Here's a bit more about each of the **useful properties** of **water** that you need to **learn** for your **exam**.

Water is an Important Metabolite

1) Many metabolic reactions involve a **condensation** or **hydrolysis** reaction.

2) A **hydrolysis** reaction requires a **molecule of water** to **break** a **bond**. A **condensation** reaction releases a molecule of water as a **new bond** is formed.

3) For example, **amino acids** are **joined** together to make **polypeptides** (proteins) by **condensation** reactions (see page 8). **Energy** from ATP is released through a **hydrolysis** reaction (see page 22).

Water has a High Latent Heat of Vaporisation

1) It takes a lot of **energy** (heat) to **break** the hydrogen bonds between water molecules.

2) So water has a **high latent heat of vaporisation** — a lot of energy is used up when water **evaporates** (vaporises).

3) This is useful for living organisms because it means they can use water loss through evaporation to **cool down** (e.g. humans **sweat** to cool down) without losing too much water.

Water

Water Can **Buffer** (Resist) Changes in **Temperature**

1) The **hydrogen bonds** between water molecules can **absorb** a **lot** of energy.

2) So water has a **high specific heat capacity** — it takes a lot of energy to heat it up.

3) This is useful for living organisms because it means that water **doesn't** experience **rapid temperature changes**. This makes water a **good habitat** because the temperature **under water** is likely to be **more stable** than on land. The water **inside** organisms also remains at a fairly **stable** temperature — helping them to **maintain** a **constant** internal **body temperature**.

Water is a **Good Solvent**

1) A lot of important substances in metabolic reactions are **ionic** (like **salt**, for example). This means they're made from **one positively charged** atom or molecule and **one negatively charged** atom or molecule (e.g. salt is made from a positive sodium ion and a negative chloride ion).

2) Because water is polar, the **positive end** of a water molecule will be attracted to the **negative ion**, and the **negative end** of a water molecule will be attracted to the **positive ion**.

3) This means the ions will get **totally surrounded** by water molecules — in other words, they'll **dissolve**.

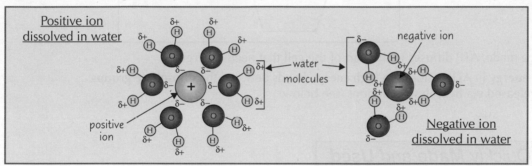

4) So water's **polarity** makes it a useful **solvent**.

There's Strong **Cohesion** Between **Water** Molecules

1) Cohesion is the **attraction** between molecules of the same type (e.g. two water molecules). Water molecules are **very cohesive** (they tend to stick together) because they're **polar**.

2) Strong cohesion helps water to **flow**, making it great for **transporting substances**. For example, it's how water travels in **columns** up the **xylem** (tube-like transport cells) in **plants** (see p. 78).

3) Strong cohesion also means that water has a **high surface tension** when it comes into contact with **air**. This is the reason why sweat forms **droplets**, which evaporate from the skin to cool an organism down. It's also the reason that **pond skaters**, and some other insects, can 'walk' on the surface of a pond.

Practice Questions

Q1 Briefly describe the structure of a water molecule.

Q2 Why is water's high specific heat capacity useful for living organisms?

Q3 Describe how a positive ion dissolves in water.

Exam Question

Q1 In hot temperatures, elephants commonly spray themselves with water.
With reference to the structure and properties of water, explain:

a) why this behaviour acts as a cooling mechanism for the elephant. [3 marks]

b) why water forms droplets when the elephant sprays it from its trunk. [2 marks]

Pssssssssssssssssssssssssssssssssssssssssssssss — need the loo yet?

Water is pretty darn useful really. It looks so, well, dull — but in fact it's scientifically amazing. It's essential for all kinds of jobs — keeping cool, transporting things, enabling reactions, etc. You need to learn all of its properties and functions.

ATP

ATP is an important molecule in all living things. Without it, we wouldn't be able to function. On the plus side, that would mean no exams — but on the other hand, we wouldn't know the great smell of freshly baked bread. Ahh...

ATP is the Immediate Source of Energy in a Cell

1) Plant and animal cells **release energy** from **glucose** — this process is called **respiration**.

2) A cell **can't** get its energy **directly** from glucose.

3) So, in respiration, the **energy released** from glucose is used to **make ATP** (adenosine triphosphate).

4) ATP is made from the nucleotide base **adenine**, combined with a **ribose sugar** and **three phosphate groups**. It's what's known as a **nucleotide derivative** because it's a **modified form** of a **nucleotide**:

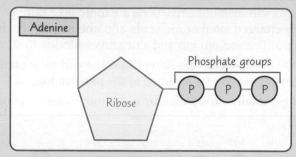

5) Once made, ATP **diffuses** to the **part** of the **cell** that needs **energy**.

6) The **energy** in ATP is stored in **high energy bonds** between the **phosphate groups**. It's released via **hydrolysis reactions** (see below).

ATP is Quickly Made and Used

1) When **energy** is needed by a cell, **ATP** is **broken down** into **ADP** (adenosine diphosphate) and **P$_i$** (inorganic phosphate).

2) This is a **hydrolysis reaction**. A **phosphate bond** is **broken** and **energy** is **released**. The reaction is **catalysed** by the enzyme **ATP hydrolase**.

3) **ATP hydrolysis** can be '**coupled**' to other **energy-requiring reactions** in the cell — this means the energy released can be **used directly** to make the **coupled reaction** happen, rather than being **lost** as heat.

4) The released **inorganic phosphate** can also be put to use — it can be **added** to another **compound** (this is known as **phosphorylation**), which often makes the compound **more reactive**.

5) **ATP** can be **re-synthesised** in a **condensation reaction** between **ADP** and **P$_i$**. This happens during both **respiration** and **photosynthesis**, and is **catalysed** by the enzyme **ATP synthase**.

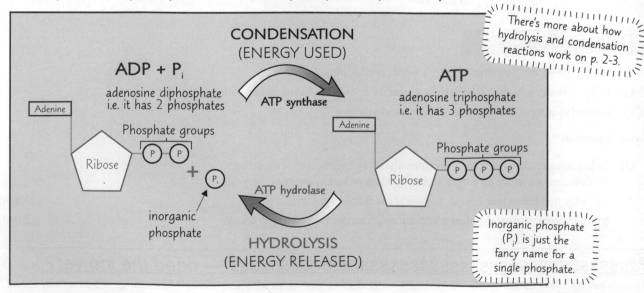

There's more about how hydrolysis and condensation reactions work on p. 2-3.

Inorganic phosphate (P$_i$) is just the fancy name for a single phosphate.

Inorganic Ions

Inorganic Ions Have an Electric Charge

1) An **ion** is an atom (or group of atoms) that has an **electric charge**.
2) An ion with a **positive charge** is called a **cation**.
3) An ion with a **negative charge** is called an **anion**.
4) An **inorganic** ion is one which **doesn't contain carbon** (although there are a few exceptions to this rule).
5) There are inorganic ions, in **solution**, in the **cytoplasms of cells** and in the **body fluids of organisms**. **Each** ion has a **specific role**, depending on its **properties**. An ion's role determines whether it is found in **high** or **low concentrations**.

Iron Ions Are an Important Part of Haemoglobin

See page 68 for more on haemoglobin.

- **Haemoglobin** is a large protein that carries **oxygen** around the **body**, in the **red blood cells**.
- It's made up of **four** different polypeptide chains, each with an **iron ion** (Fe^{2+}) in the centre.
- It's the Fe^{2+} that actually **binds** to the **oxygen** in haemoglobin — so it's a pretty key component.
- When oxygen **is** bound, the Fe^{2+} ion temporarily becomes an Fe^{3+} ion, until oxygen is released.

Hydrogen Ions (H⁺) Determine pH

pH is calculated based on the **concentration** of **hydrogen ions** (H^+) in the environment. The **more** H^+ present, the **lower** the pH (and the more **acidic** the environment). Enzyme-controlled reactions are all affected by pH.

Sodium Ions (Na⁺) Help Transport Glucose and Amino Acids Across Membranes

- **Glucose** and **amino acids** need a bit of help crossing cell membranes.
- A molecule of **glucose** or an **amino acid** can be transported into a cell (across the cell-surface membrane) alongside **sodium** ions (Na^+). This is known as **co-transport** (see pages 42 and 43 for more).

Phosphate Ions Are an Essential Component of ATP and DNA

- When a **phosphate ion** (PO_4^{3-}) is attached to another molecule, it's known as a **phosphate group**.
- **DNA**, **RNA** and **ATP** all contain phosphate groups.
- It's the bonds between **phosphate groups** that store energy in **ATP** (see previous page).
- The phosphate groups in **DNA** and **RNA** allow **nucleotides** to join up to form the **polynucleotides** (see p. 17).

Practice Questions

Q1 Draw a molecule of ATP.
Q2 How many phosphate groups does ADP have?
Q3 How are hydrogen ions related to the pH of an environment?

Exam Questions

Q1 The diagram on the right shows a molecule involved in the synthesis of ATP. Describe how ATP is synthesised from this molecule. [3 marks]

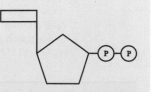

Q2 Free inorganic ions can play very important roles in the body.
a) Describe how iron ions carry oxygen to where it is needed in the body. [3 marks]
b) Explain the role of phosphate ions in providing energy for cellular reactions. [2 marks]

Oh dear, I've used up all my ATP on these two pages...

Well, I won't beat about the bush, some of this ATP stuff is pretty tricky... nearly as hard as a cross between Mr T, Hulk Hogan and Arnie. But, with a little patience and perseverance (and plenty of [chocolate] [coffee] [marshmallows] — delete as you wish), you'll get there. Inorganic ions should provide you with a little light relief at any rate.

Eukaryotic Cells and Organelles

There are two types of cell — prokaryotic and eukaryotic. The next few pages are about eukaryotic cells and their organelles (all the tiny bits and bobs that you can only see in detail with a fancy microscope)...

Organisms can be **Prokaryotes** or **Eukaryotes**

1) Prokaryotic organisms are **prokaryotic cells** (i.e. they're single-celled organisms) and eukaryotic organisms are made up of **eukaryotic cells**.

2) Both types of cells contain **organelles**. Organelles are **parts** of cells — each one has a **specific function**.

1) Eukaryotic cells are **complex** and include all **animal** and **plant** cells, as well as all cells in **algae** and **fungi**.

2) Prokaryotic cells are **smaller** and **simpler**, e.g. bacteria. See page 28 for more.

You Need to Know the Structure of *Eukaryotic Cells*

Eukaryotic cells are generally a **bit more complicated** than prokaryotic cells. You've probably been looking at **animal** and **plant cell** diagrams for years, so hopefully you'll be familiar with some of the bits and pieces...

Animal Cell

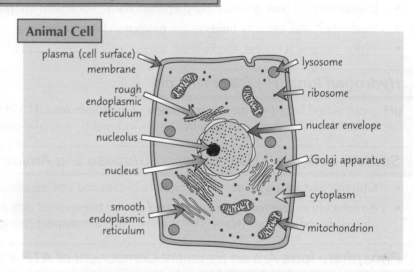

plasma (cell surface) membrane
rough endoplasmic reticulum
nucleolus
nucleus
smooth endoplasmic reticulum
lysosome
ribosome
nuclear envelope
Golgi apparatus
cytoplasm
mitochondrion

Plant Cell

Plant cells have all the **same organelles** as animal cells, but with a few **added extras**:

- a **cellulose cell wall** with **plasmodesmata** ('channels' for exchanging substances with adjacent cells),
- a **vacuole** (compartment that contains cell sap),
- and of course good old **chloroplasts**.

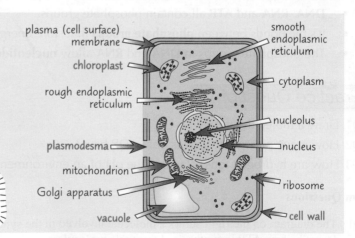

plasma (cell surface) membrane
chloroplast
rough endoplasmic reticulum
plasmodesma
mitochondrion
Golgi apparatus
vacuole
smooth endoplasmic reticulum
cytoplasm
nucleolus
nucleus
ribosome
cell wall

You might also see starch grains in plant cells, although they're not organelles. Plants use starch grains to store excess sugars.

Algal and Fungal Cells

1) **Algal** cells are a lot like **plant cells** — they have all the **same** organelles, including a **cell wall** and **chloroplasts**.

2) **Fungal** cells are also a lot like plant cells, but with two key **differences**:
   - their cell walls are made of **chitin**, not cellulose.
   - they **don't have chloroplasts** (because they don't photosynthesise).

Algae carry out photosynthesis, like plants, but can be single-celled or multicellular. Fungi include mushrooms and yeast.

Eukaryotic Cells and Organelles

Different Organelles have Different Functions

This giant table contains a big list of organelles — you need to know the **structure** and **function** of them all. Sorry.
Most organelles are surrounded by **membranes**, which sometimes causes confusion — don't make the mistake of
thinking that a diagram of an organelle is a diagram of a whole cell. They're not cells — they're **parts of** cells.

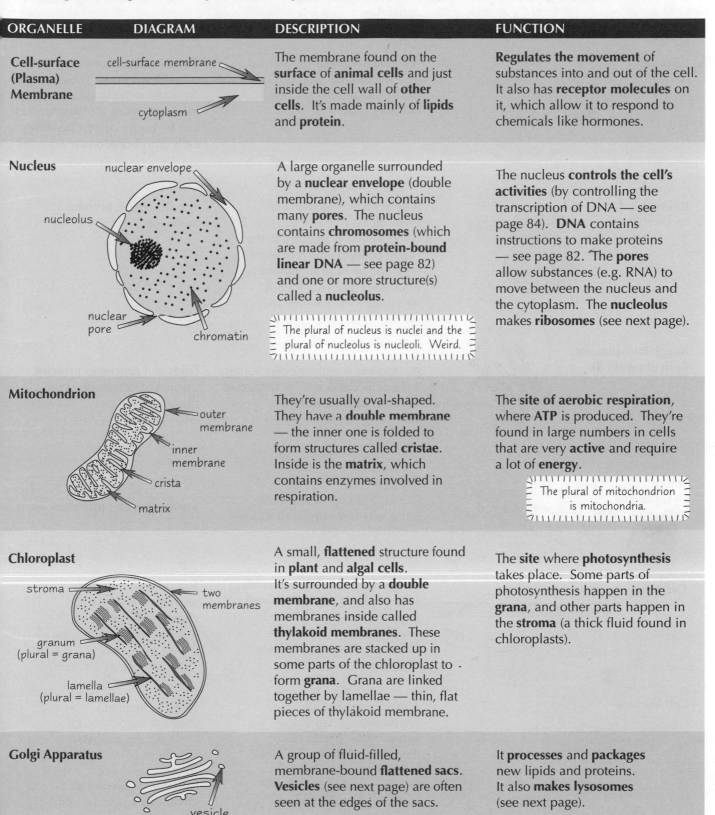

ORGANELLE	DIAGRAM	DESCRIPTION	FUNCTION
Cell-surface (Plasma) Membrane	cell-surface membrane / cytoplasm	The membrane found on the **surface** of **animal cells** and just inside the cell wall of **other cells**. It's made mainly of **lipids** and **protein**.	**Regulates the movement** of substances into and out of the cell. It also has **receptor molecules** on it, which allow it to respond to chemicals like hormones.
Nucleus	nuclear envelope / nucleolus / nuclear pore / chromatin	A large organelle surrounded by a **nuclear envelope** (double membrane), which contains many **pores**. The nucleus contains **chromosomes** (which are made from **protein-bound linear DNA** — see page 82) and one or more structure(s) called a **nucleolus**. *The plural of nucleus is nuclei and the plural of nucleolus is nucleoli. Weird.*	The nucleus **controls the cell's activities** (by controlling the transcription of DNA — see page 84). **DNA** contains instructions to make proteins — see page 82. The **pores** allow substances (e.g. RNA) to move between the nucleus and the cytoplasm. The **nucleolus** makes **ribosomes** (see next page).
Mitochondrion	outer membrane / inner membrane / crista / matrix	They're usually oval-shaped. They have a **double membrane** — the inner one is folded to form structures called **cristae**. Inside is the **matrix**, which contains enzymes involved in respiration.	The **site of aerobic respiration**, where **ATP** is produced. They're found in large numbers in cells that are very **active** and require a lot of **energy**. *The plural of mitochondrion is mitochondria.*
Chloroplast	stroma / two membranes / granum (plural = grana) / lamella (plural = lamellae)	A small, **flattened** structure found in **plant** and **algal cells**. It's surrounded by a **double membrane**, and also has membranes inside called **thylakoid membranes**. These membranes are stacked up in some parts of the chloroplast to form **grana**. Grana are linked together by lamellae — thin, flat pieces of thylakoid membrane.	The **site** where **photosynthesis** takes place. Some parts of photosynthesis happen in the **grana**, and other parts happen in the **stroma** (a thick fluid found in chloroplasts).
Golgi Apparatus	vesicle	A group of fluid-filled, membrane-bound **flattened sacs**. **Vesicles** (see next page) are often seen at the edges of the sacs.	It **processes** and **packages** new lipids and proteins. It also **makes lysosomes** (see next page).

Eukaryotic Cells and Organelles

ORGANELLE	DIAGRAM	DESCRIPTION	FUNCTION
Golgi Vesicle	vesicle	A small **fluid-filled sac** in the cytoplasm, surrounded by a membrane and produced by the **Golgi apparatus**.	**Stores** lipids and proteins made by the Golgi apparatus and **transports** them out of the cell (via the cell-surface membrane).
Lysosome		A **round organelle** surrounded by a **membrane**, with no clear internal structure. It's a type of **Golgi vesicle**.	Contains **digestive enzymes** called **lysozymes**. These are kept separate from the cytoplasm by the surrounding membrane, and can be used to **digest invading cells** or to **break down** worn out components of the cell.
Ribosome	small subunit / large subunit	A **very small organelle** that either **floats free** in the cytoplasm or is attached to the **rough endoplasmic reticulum**. It's made up of **proteins** and **RNA** (see page 16). It's **not** surrounded by a membrane.	The **site** where **proteins** are made.
Rough Endoplasmic Reticulum (RER)	ribosome / fluid	A system of membranes enclosing a fluid-filled space. The surface is **covered with ribosomes**.	**Folds** and **processes proteins** that have been made at the ribosomes.
Smooth Endoplasmic Reticulum (SER)		Similar to rough endoplasmic reticulum, but with no **ribosomes**.	**Synthesises** and **processes lipids**.
Cell Wall	cell-surface membrane / cell wall / cytoplasm	A rigid structure that surrounds cells in **plants**, **algae** and **fungi**. In plants and algae it's made mainly of the carbohydrate **cellulose**. In fungi, it's made of **chitin**.	**Supports** cells and prevents them from **changing shape**.
Cell Vacuole	tonoplast	A membrane-bound organelle found in the **cytoplasm** of **plant cells**. It contains **cell sap** — a weak solution of sugar and salts. The surrounding membrane is called the **tonoplast**.	Helps to maintain **pressure** inside the cell and keep the cell **rigid**. This **stops** plants **wilting**. Also involved in the **isolation** of **unwanted chemicals** inside the cell.

Eukaryotic Cells and Organelles

The Organelles in Specialised Cells Vary

1) In **multicellular** eukaryotic organisms, cells become **specialised** to carry out **specific functions**.

2) A cell's **structure** (i.e. its shape and the organelles it contains) helps it to carry out its **function** — so depending on what job it does, a specialised cell can look very different to the cells you saw on page 24.

3) In the exam, you might get a question where you need to apply your knowledge of **organelles** to explain why a specialised cell is particularly **suited** to its **function**. You'll need to think about **what organelles** the cell **needs** to do its **job** — e.g. if the cell uses a lot of **energy**, it'll need lots of **mitochondria**. If it makes a lot of **proteins** it'll need a lot of **ribosomes**.

Example: **Epithelial cells** in the **small intestine** are specialised to **absorb food efficiently**.

1) The walls of the small intestine have lots of finger-like projections called **villi**. These **increase surface area** for absorption.

2) The **epithelial cells** on the surface of the villi have **folds** in their **cell-surface membranes**, called **microvilli**. Microvilli increase surface area even more.

3) They also have **lots of mitochondria** — to provide **energy** for the transport of digested food molecules into the cell.

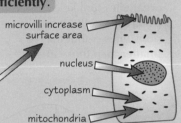

microvilli increase surface area

nucleus

cytoplasm

mitochondria

Specialised Cells are Organised into Tissues, Organs and Organ Systems

1) In multicellular eukaryotic organisms, **specialised cells** are grouped together to form **tissues**.

2) A tissue is a group of cells **working together** to perform a particular **function**.

3) Different **tissues** work together to form **organs**. Different organs make up an **organ system**.

For example...

> **Epithelial cells** make up **epithelial tissue**. Epithelial tissue, **muscular tissue** and **glandular tissue** (which secretes chemicals) all work together to form the **stomach** — an **organ**. The stomach is part of the **digestive system** — this is an **organ system** made up of all the organs involved in the digestion and absorption of food (including the **small intestine**, **large intestine** and **liver**).

Practice Questions

Q1 What is a plant cell wall made of? What about a fungal cell wall?

Q2 What is the function of a mitochondrion?

Q3 What is the function of a ribosome?

Q4 How does the structure of rough endoplasmic reticulum differ from that of smooth endoplasmic reticulum?

Q5 In multicellular organisms, what is a tissue?

Exam Questions

Q1 Plant cells have a vacuole, but animal cells do not.
   a) Give two functions of a plant cell vacuole.   [2 marks]
   b) Name two other organelles found in plant cells but not in animal cells.   [2 marks]

Q2 Cilia are hair-like structures found on lung epithelial cells. Their function is to beat and move mucus out of the lungs. Beating requires energy. Suggest how ciliated cells are adapted to their function in terms of the organelles they contain. Explain your answer.   [2 marks]

Q3 Pancreatic cells make and secrete hormones (made of protein) into the blood.
   From production to secretion, list, in order, four organelles involved in making hormones.   [4 marks]

Organelles — not a church girl band...

Not the most exciting pages in the world, but you need to know what all the organelles listed do. I'm afraid they'll keep popping up throughout the rest of the book — mitochondria are needed for respiration, the cell-surface membrane is essential for controlling the movement of things in and out of the cell, and all the DNA stuff happens in the nucleus.

Prokaryotic Cells and Viruses

Now we're on to prokaryotic cells and viruses. They're much smaller than eukaryotic cells — and, luckily for both of us, so is the section on them in this book. Nevertheless, you need to know everything in it for your exams...

The Structure of **Prokaryotic** Cells is Different to **Eukaryotic** Cells

Remember, prokaryotic cells are **smaller** and **simpler** than eukaryotic cells (see page 24). **Bacteria** are examples of prokaryotic cells. You need to know the **structure** of a prokaryotic cell and what all the different organelles do.

The **cytoplasm** of a prokaryotic cell has **no membrane-bound organelles** (unlike a eukaryotic cell). It has **ribosomes** — but they're **smaller** than those in a eukaryotic cell.

Just like in a eukaryotic cell, the **plasma membrane** is mainly made of lipids and proteins. It controls the movement of substances into and out of the cell.

See pages 25-26 for more on organelles.

The **cell wall supports** the cell and prevents it from changing shape. It's made of a polymer called **murein**. Murein is a **glycoprotein** (a protein with a carbohydrate attached).

The **flagellum** (plural **flagella**) is a long, hair-like structure that rotates to make the prokaryotic cell **move**. **Not all** prokaryotes have a flagellum. **Some** have **more than one**.

Plasmids are **small loops of DNA** that aren't part of the main circular DNA molecule. Plasmids contain genes for things like **antibiotic resistance**, and can be passed between prokaryotes. Plasmids are **not always** present in prokaryotic cells. **Some** prokaryotic cells have **several**.

Unlike a eukaryotic cell, a prokaryotic cell **doesn't** have a nucleus. Instead, the **DNA** floats free in the cytoplasm. It's **circular DNA**, present as one long coiled-up strand. It's **not attached** to any **histone proteins** (see p. 82).

Some prokaryotes, e.g. bacteria, also have a **capsule** made up of secreted **slime**. It helps to **protect** bacteria from attack by cells of the immune system.

Theo went the wrong way about getting practical experience in understanding cell structure.

Viruses are Acellular — They're Not Cells

Viruses are just **nucleic acids** surrounded by **protein** — they're **not even alive**.

- They're even **smaller** than bacteria — e.g. HIV is about 0.1 µm across.
- **Unlike** bacteria, viruses have **no** plasma membrane, **no** cytoplasm and **no** ribosomes.
- **All** viruses invade and reproduce **inside** the cells of **other** organisms. These cells are known as **host cells**.

Viruses contain a **core** of **genetic material** — either **DNA** or **RNA**.

DNA and RNA are nucleic acids — see page 16.

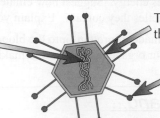

The **protein coat** around the core is called the **capsid**.

Attachment proteins stick out from the edge of the capsid. These let the virus cling on to a suitable host cell.

Prokaryotic Cells and Viruses

Prokaryotic Cells Replicate by Binary Fission

In binary fission, the cell **replicates** (makes copies of) its genetic material, before physically **splitting** into **two daughter cells**:

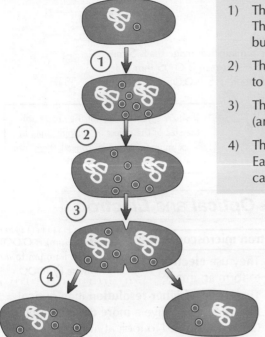

1) The circular DNA and plasmid(s) **replicate**. The main **DNA loop** is only replicated **once**, but **plasmids** can be replicated **loads of times**.

2) The cell gets bigger and the **DNA loops** move to **opposite 'poles'** (ends) of the cell.

3) The **cytoplasm** begins to **divide** (and **new cell walls** begin to form).

4) The cytoplasm **divides** and two **daughter cells** are produced. Each daughter cell has **one copy** of the **circular DNA**, but can have a **variable** number of copies of the **plasmid(s)**.

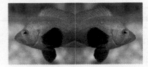

Binary fishin'

Viruses Use Host Cells to Replicate Themselves

1) Viruses use their **attachment proteins** to **bind** to **complementary receptor proteins** on the surface of **host cells**.

2) Different viruses have different attachment proteins and therefore require **different** receptor proteins on host cells. As a result, some viruses can only infect **one type of cell** (others can infect lots of different cells).

3) Because they're not alive, viruses **don't** undergo cell division. Instead, they **inject** their **DNA or RNA** into the host cell — this hijacked cell then uses its own 'machinery' (e.g. enzymes, ribosomes) to do the virus's dirty work and **replicate the viral particles**.

Remember — viruses are <u>acellular</u> — they're not cells.

Practice Questions

Q1 What is a plasmid?

Q2 What is a flagellum?

Q3 What is the protein coat around the core of a virus called?

Exam Question

Q1 Cholera is a disease caused by the prokaryotic organism *Vibrio cholerae*.

  a) Name the polymer that makes up the cell wall of *Vibrio cholerae*. [1 mark]

  b) Outline the process by which *Vibrio cholerae* replicates. [3 marks]

  c) There are different strains of *Vibrio cholerae*. One strain has a capsule. Another does not. Suggest how having a capsule might benefit *Vibrio cholerae*. [1 mark]

Viruses and binary fission — nothing to do with computers...

You need to know the differences between eukaryotic and prokaryotic cells. Make sure you spend plenty of time memorising them (see page 24 for more on eukaryotic cells). Remember that binary fission is only how prokaryotic cells replicate — eukaryotic cells and viruses use different techniques. Remember viruses aren't cells or prokaryotes.

Analysis of Cell Components

You can use microscopes to look at all the lovely organelles you've been learning about...

Magnification *is* Size, Resolution *is* Detail

We all know that microscopes produce a **magnified image** of a sample, but **resolution** is just as important...

1) MAGNIFICATION is how much **bigger** the image is than the specimen (the sample you're looking at). It's calculated using this formula:

$$\text{magnification} = \frac{\text{size of image}}{\text{size of real object}}$$

For example:
If you have a magnified image that's 5 mm wide and your specimen is 0.05 mm wide, the magnification is: 5 ÷ 0.05 = **× 100**.

5 mm

2) RESOLUTION is how **detailed** the image is. More specifically, it's how well a microscope **distinguishes** between **two points** that are **close together**. If a microscope lens can't separate two objects, then increasing the magnification won't help.

If you're given the size of the image and the size of the object in <u>different units</u> in the exam, make sure you <u>convert them</u> into the <u>same units</u> before using the formula.

There are **Two Main Types** of Microscope — **Optical** and **Electron**

Optical (light) microscopes

1) They use **light** to form an image.
2) They have a maximum resolution of about **0.2 micrometres** (μm). This means you can't use an optical microscope to view organelles smaller than 0.2 μm. That includes **ribosomes**, the **endoplasmic reticulum** and **lysosomes**. You may be able to make out **mitochondria** — but not in perfect detail. You can also see the **nucleus**.
3) The maximum useful **magnification** of an optical microscope is about **× 1500**.

Electron microscopes

A micrometre (μm) is 0.001 mm. To convert from μm to mm, divide by 1000.

1) They use **electrons** to form an image.
2) They have a **higher resolution** than optical microscopes so give a **more detailed image** (and can be used to look at more organelles).
3) They have a maximum resolution of about **0.0002 micrometres** (μm). (About 1000 times higher than optical microscopes.)
4) The maximum useful **magnification** of an electron microscope is about **× 1 500 000**.

Electron Microscopes are either **'Scanning'** or **'Transmission'**

Transmission electron microscopes (TEMs)

1) TEMs use **electromagnets** to focus a **beam of electrons**, which is then transmitted **through** the specimen.
2) **Denser** parts of the specimen absorb **more electrons**, which makes them look **darker** on the image you end up with.
3) TEMs are good because they give **high resolution images**, so you see the **internal structure** of **organelles** like chloroplasts.
4) But they can only be used on **thin specimens**.

Scanning electron microscopes (SEMs)

1) SEMs **scan** a beam of electrons across the specimen. This **knocks off** electrons from the **specimen**, which are gathered in a **cathode ray tube** to form an **image**.
2) The images you end up with show the **surface** of the specimen and they can be **3-D**.
3) SEMs are good because they can be used on **thick specimens**.
4) But they give **lower resolution images** than TEMs.

You **View Specimens** Under an **Optical Microscope** Using **Slides**

Here's how to prepare a 'temporary mount' of a specimen on a slide:
- Start by pipetting a small **drop of water** onto the **slide** (a strip of clear glass or plastic). Then use **tweezers** to place a **thin section** of your specimen on **top** of the water drop.
- Add a drop of a **stain**. Stains are used to **highlight objects** in a cell. For example, **eosin** is used to make the **cytoplasm** show up. **Iodine** in **potassium iodide solution** (see p. 4) is used to stain **starch grains** in plant cells.
- Finally, add the **cover slip** (a square of clear plastic that protects the specimen). To do so, stand the slip **upright** on the slide, next to the water droplet. Then carefully **tilt** and lower it so it covers the specimen. Try **not** to get any **air bubbles** under there — they'll obstruct your view of the specimen (see page 35).

Analysis of Cell Components

Cell Fractionation *Separates Organelles*

Suppose you wanted to look at some **organelles** under an **electron microscope**. First you'd need to **separate** them from the **rest of the cell** — you can do this by **cell fractionation**. There are **three** steps to this technique:

1 Homogenisation — Breaking Up the Cells

Homogenisation can be done in several **different ways**, e.g. by vibrating the cells or by grinding the cells up in a blender. This **breaks up** the **plasma membrane** and **releases** the **organelles** into solution. The solution must be kept **ice-cold**, to reduce the activity of enzymes that break down organelles. The solution should also be **isotonic** — this means it should have the **same concentration** of **chemicals** as the cells being broken down, to prevent damage to the organelles through **osmosis**. A **buffer solution** should be added to **maintain** the **pH**.

2 Filtration — Getting Rid of the Big Bits

Next, the homogenised cell solution is **filtered** through a **gauze** to separate any **large cell debris** or **tissue debris**, like connective tissue, from the organelles. The organelles are much **smaller** than the debris, so they pass through the gauze.

3 Ultracentrifugation — Separating the Organelles

After filtration, you're left with a solution containing a **mixture** of organelles. To separate a particular organelle from all the others you use **ultracentrifugation**.

1) The cell fragments are poured into a **tube**. The tube is put into a **centrifuge** (a machine that separates material by spinning) and is spun at a **low speed**. The **heaviest organelles**, like nuclei, get flung to the **bottom** of the tube by the centrifuge. They form a **thick sediment** at the bottom — the **pellet**. The rest of the organelles stay suspended in the fluid above the sediment — the **supernatant**.

2) The supernatant is **drained off**, poured into **another tube**, and spun in the centrifuge at a **higher speed**. Again, the **heaviest organelles**, this time the mitochondria, form a pellet at the bottom of the tube. The supernatant containing the rest of the organelles is drained off and spun in the centrifuge at an **even higher speed**.

3) This process is **repeated** at higher and higher speeds, until all the organelles are **separated out**. Each time, the pellet at the bottom of the tube is made up of lighter and lighter organelles.

As the ride got faster, everyone felt their nuclei sink to their toes...

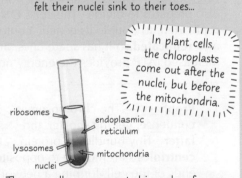

In plant cells, the chloroplasts come out after the nuclei, but before the mitochondria.

The organelles are <u>separated in order of mass</u> (from heaviest to lightest) — this order is usually: nuclei, then mitochondria, then lysosomes, then endoplasmic reticulum, and finally ribosomes.

Practice Questions

Q1 What is meant by a microscope's magnification?

Q2 What is meant by a microscope's resolution?

Exam Questions

organelle	diameter / µm
lysosome	0.1
mitochondrion	2
nucleus	5
ribosome	0.02
vesicle	0.05

Q1 The table shows the dimensions of some different organelles found in animal cells. Name those organelles in the table that would be visible using a good quality light microscope. Explain your answer. [3 marks]

Q2 Explain why a homogenised cell solution should be kept ice-cold and isotonic. [2 marks]

Cell fractionation — sounds more like maths to me...

So, if you fancy getting up close and personal with mitochondria remember to homogenise, filter and ultracentrifuge first. Then decide if you want to use an SEM or TEM to view them, taking into account each of their limitations.

Cell Division — Mitosis

If it wasn't for cell division, we'd still only be one cell big. If it wasn't for pies, my favourite jeans would still fit.

Mitosis is Cell Division that Produces Genetically Identical Cells

There are two types of cell division in **eukaryotes** — **mitosis** and **meiosis** (see pages 88-89 for more on meiosis).

1) In **mitosis** a **parent cell** divides to produce **two genetically identical daughter cells** (they contain an **exact copy** of the **DNA** of the parent cell).

2) Mitosis is needed for the **growth** of multicellular organisms (like us) and for **repairing damaged tissues**.

3) In multicellular organisms, not all cells keep their ability to divide (see next page). The ones that do, follow a **cell cycle**. Mitosis is part of the cell cycle:

The cell cycle consists of a period of **cell growth** and **DNA replication** called **interphase**. Mitosis happens after that. Interphase (cell growth) is subdivided into three separate growth stages. These are called G_1, **S** and G_2.

GAP PHASE 2
cell keeps growing
and proteins
needed for
cell division
are made

SYNTHESIS
cell replicates its DNA,
ready to divide by mitosis

MITOSIS
(the cycle starts
and ends here)

GAP PHASE 1
cell grows and new
organelles and
proteins are made

INTERPHASE

Mitosis has Four Division Stages

Mitosis is really one **continuous process**, but it's described as a series of **division stages** — prophase, metaphase, anaphase and telophase. **Interphase** comes **before** mitosis in the cell cycle.

Interphase — The cell carries out normal functions, but also prepares to divide. The cell's **DNA** is **unravelled** and **replicated**, to double its genetic content. The **organelles** are also **replicated** so it has spare ones, and its ATP content is increased (ATP provides the energy needed for cell division).

Interphase

Cell
Chromosome
Cytoplasm
Nucleus
Centriole

Unravelled DNA
containing two
copies of each
chromosome

1) **Prophase** — The **chromosomes condense**, getting **shorter** and **fatter.** Tiny bundles of protein called **centrioles** start moving to opposite ends of the cell, forming a network of protein fibres across it called the **spindle**. The **nuclear envelope** (the membrane around the nucleus) **breaks down** and chromosomes lie free in the cytoplasm.

Centrioles
move to
opposite
ends of
the cell

Nuclear
envelope
starts to
break down

Centromere

As mitosis begins, the chromosomes are made of two strands joined in the middle by a centromere. The separate strands are called chromatids. There are two strands because each chromosome has already made an identical copy of itself during interphase. When mitosis is over, the chromatids end up as one-strand chromosomes in the daughter cells.

One chromatid
Centromere
Sister
chromatids

2) **Metaphase** — The chromosomes (each with two chromatids) **line up** along the middle of the cell and become **attached** to the **spindle** by their **centromere.**

Spindle
fibres

Centromeres
on spindle
equator

3) **Anaphase** — The **centromeres divide, separating** each pair of sister **chromatids**. The **spindles contract**, pulling chromatids to **opposite poles** (ends) of the **spindle**, centromere first. This makes the chromatids appear **v-shaped.**

Sister chromatids
moving to opposite
poles of the spindle

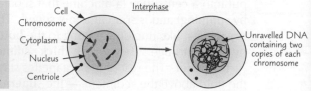
You need to be able to explain the appearance of cells at each stage of mitosis for your exam.

4) **Telophase** — The chromatids reach the **opposite poles** on the spindle. They **uncoil** and become **long** and **thin** again. They're now called **chromosomes** again. A **nuclear envelope** forms around each group of chromosomes, so there are now **two nuclei**. The **cytoplasm divides** (**cytokinesis**) and there are now **two daughter cells** that are **genetically identical** to the original cell and to each other. Mitosis is finished and each daughter cell starts the **interphase** part of the cell cycle to get ready for the next round of mitosis.

Centriole

Cytoplasm
beginning to divide

Cell Division — Mitosis

*The **Time Taken** for Each **Stage** of Mitosis **Varies***

You can **calculate** how long each stage of mitosis lasts if you're given the right information.

> **Example:** A scientist observes a section of growing tissue under the microscope. He counts 100 cells undergoing mitosis. Of those, 10 cells are in metaphase. One complete cell cycle of the tissue lasts 15 hours. How long do the cells spend in metaphase? Give your answer in minutes.

1) The scientist has observed that **10 out of 100 cells** are in **metaphase**. This suggests that the **proportion** of time the cells spend in metaphase must be **10/100th** of the **cell cycle**.

2) You're told that the cell cycle in these cells lasts **15 hours**. That's (15 × 60 =) **900 minutes**.

3) So the cells spend: $\frac{10}{100} \times 900 =$ **90 minutes** in metaphase.

*Cancer is the Result of **Uncontrolled Cell Division***

Mutations are changes in the base sequence of an organism's DNA (see p. 91).

1) **Mitosis** and the **cell cycle** are **controlled by genes**.

2) Normally, when cells have divided enough times to make **enough new cells**, they stop. But if there's a **mutation** in a gene that controls cell division, the cells can **grow out of control**.

3) The cells **keep on dividing** to make more and more cells, which form a **tumour**.

4) **Cancer** is a tumour that **invades** surrounding tissue.

*Some **Cancer Treatments** Target the **Cell Cycle***

Some treatments for cancer are designed to **control** the **rate of cell division** in tumour cells by **disrupting** the **cell cycle**. This **kills** the **tumour cells**. These treatments don't **distinguish** tumour cells from normal cells though — they also **kill normal body cells** that are dividing. However, tumour cells **divide much more frequently** than normal cells, so the treatments are **more likely** to kill tumour cells. Some cell cycle **targets** of cancer treatments include:

1) **G1 (cell growth and protein production)** — Some chemical drugs (chemotherapy) prevent the **synthesis of enzymes** needed for DNA replication. If these aren't produced, the cell is unable to enter the **synthesis phase** (S), disrupting the cell cycle and forcing the cell to **kill itself**.

2) **S phase (DNA replication)** — **Radiation** and some drugs **damage DNA**. At several points in the cell cycle (including just before and during the S phase) the DNA in the cell is **checked** for damage. If severe damage is detected, the **cell** will **kill** itself — **preventing** further **tumour growth**.

Practice Questions

Q1 Give the two main functions of mitosis.

Q2 List the four stages of mitosis.

Q3 Describe how tumours are formed.

Q4 Give one example of how a cancer treatment can target the cell cycle.

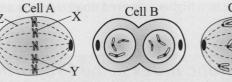

Exam Question

Q1 The diagrams show cells at different stages of mitosis.

    a) For each of the cells A, B and C, name the stage of mitosis.   [3 marks]

    b) Name the structures labelled X, Y and Z in cell A.   [3 marks]

Doctor, I'm getting short and fat — don't worry, it's just a phase...

Quite a lot to learn on these pages — but it's all important stuff, so no slacking. Mitosis is vital — it's how cells multiply and how organisms like us grow. Don't forget — the best way to learn is to get drawing those diagrams.

Cell Division — Investigating Mitosis

It's time to dust off your lab coat and get out your safety specs. Here are all the techniques you need to study mitosis. You'll need to know how to stain root cells on slides and how to use an optical microscope and graticules.

Root Tips Can be Stained and Squashed to Observe Mitosis

You need to know how to **prepare** and **stain** a **root tip** in order to observe the **stages of mitosis**. Make sure you're wearing **safety goggles** and a **lab coat** before you start. You should also wear **gloves** when using **stains**.

1) **Cut 1 cm from the tip** from a **growing root** (e.g. of an onion). It needs to be the **tip** because that's where **growth** occurs (and so that's where **mitosis** takes place).
   If you're using ethano-orcein to stain the cells, the tips will also need to be fixed in ethanoic acid.

2) **Prepare** a boiling tube containing **1 M hydrochloric acid** and put it in a **water bath at 60 °C**.

3) **Transfer** the **root tip** into the **boiling tube** and incubate for about **5 minutes**.

4) Use a pipette to **rinse** the **root tip** well with **cold water**. Leave the tip to **dry** on a **paper towel**.

5) Place the root tip on a **microscope slide** and cut **2 mm** from the **very tip** of it. Get **rid** of the **rest**.

6) Use a **mounted needle** to **break** the tip **open** and **spread** the cells out thinly.

7) **Add** a few drops of **stain** and leave it for a few minutes. The stain will make the **chromosomes easier to see** under a microscope. There are loads of different stains, all with crazy names (**toluidine blue O, ethano-orcein, Feulgen stain...**
   If you're using the Feulgen stain, you'll need an extra rinse.

8) **Place** a **cover slip** over the cells and **push** down firmly to **squash** the tissue. This will make the tissue **thinner** and allow **light** to pass through it. **Don't smear** the cover slip sideways (or you'll damage the chromosomes).

9) Now you can look at all the stages of mitosis under an **optical microscope** (see below). You should see something that looks like the photograph on the right.

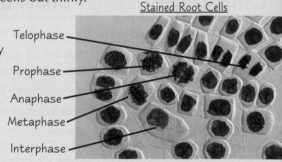

Stained Root Cells

Telophase
Prophase
Anaphase
Metaphase
Interphase

HERVE CONGE, ISM/SCIENCE PHOTO LIBRARY

You need to be able to recognise cells in the different stages of mitosis — see p. 32 for more info.

You Can Observe Cells Using an Optical Microscope

You need to know how to use an optical microscope to **observe** your prepared root tip cells:

1) Start by clipping the **slide** you've prepared onto the **stage**.

2) Select the **lowest-powered objective lens** (i.e. the one that produces the lowest magnification).

3) Use the **coarse adjustment knob** to move the objective lens down to just above the slide.

4) Look down the **eyepiece** (which contains the ocular lens) and adjust the **focus** with the **fine adjustment knob**, until you get a **clear image** of what's on the slide.

5) If you need to see the slide with **greater magnification**, swap to a **higher-powered objective lens** and refocus.

Eyepiece

Coarse adjustment knob

Fine adjustment knob

High and low power objective lenses

Stage

Light

If you're asked to draw cells undergoing mitosis under the microscope, make sure you write down the magnification the specimen was viewed under. You'll also need to label your drawing.

The Mitotic Index Is the Proportion of Cells Undergoing Mitosis

You can **calculate** the **mitotic index** of your cells using this **formula**:

$$\text{mitotic index} = \frac{\text{number of cells with visible chromosomes}}{\text{total number of cells observed}}$$

This lets you work out how quickly the **tissue** is growing and if there's anything **weird** going on. A **plant root tip** is constantly **growing**, so you'd expect a **high mitotic index** (i.e. **lots** of cells in **mitosis**). In other tissue samples, a high mitotic index could mean that **tissue repair** is taking place or that there is **cancerous growth** in the tissue.

Cell Division — Investigating Mitosis

You Can Use A *Graticule* and *Micrometer* to Calculate the *Size* of *Cells*...

1) You need to be able to calculate the **size** of the cells you're looking at.
   That's where the **eyepiece graticule** and **stage micrometer** come in — they're a bit like **rulers**.

2) An **eyepiece graticule** is fitted onto the **eyepiece**. It's like a transparent ruler with **numbers**, but **no units**.

3) The **stage micrometer** is placed on the **stage** — it is a microscope slide with an **accurate scale** (it has units) and it's used to work out the **value** of the divisions on the **eyepiece graticule** at a **particular magnification**.

4) This means that when you take the stage micrometer away and replace it with the slide containing your tissue sample, you'll be able to **measure** the size of the cells. Here's an **example**:

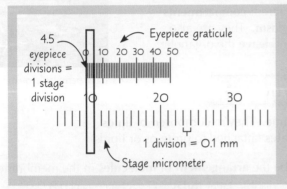

4.5 eyepiece divisions = 1 stage division

Eyepiece graticule

1 division = 0.1 mm

Stage micrometer

1) Line up the **eyepiece** graticule and the **stage** micrometer.

2) Each **division** on the stage micrometer is **0.1 mm** long.

3) At this magnification, **1 division** on the **stage micrometer** is the same as **4.5 divisions** on the **eyepiece graticule**.

4) To work out the size of **1 division** on the **eyepiece graticule**, you need to divide 0.1 by 4.5:
   1 division on eyepiece graticule = 0.1 ÷ 4.5 = **0.022 mm**

5) So if you look at a cell under the microscope at this magnification and it's **4 eyepiece divisions** long, you know it measures:
   4 × 0.022 = **0.088 mm**.

The eyepiece graticule will need to be re-calibrated at different magnifications.

...Or You Can Use This *Formula*...

If you're given an **image** of cells under the microscope in the exam, you can calculate their **actual size** using this **formula**:

$$\text{actual size} = \frac{\text{size of image}}{\text{magnification}}$$

Example: If the image of a cell measures **5 mm** and the magnification is **x 100**, then the **actual** size of the cell will be: 5 ÷ 100 = **0.05 mm**.

Artefacts Can Get in the Way of Your *Observations*

1) Artefacts are things that you can see down the microscope that **aren't** part of the **cell or specimen** that you're looking at.

2) They can be anything from bits of **dust**, **air bubbles** and **fingerprints**, to inaccuracies caused by **squashing** and **staining** your sample.

3) Artefacts are usually made during the **preparation** of your slides and **shouldn't** really be there at all — you'll need to prepare your root tip cells **carefully** to avoid creating artefacts.

The new organelle Steve had discovered looked just like his thumb print.

Artefacts are especially common in **electron micrographs** because specimens need a lot of **preparation** before you can **view** them under an electron microscope. The first scientists to use these microscopes could only **distinguish** between **artefacts** and **organelles** by **repeatedly** preparing specimens in **different ways**. If an object could be seen with **one** preparation technique, but **not another**, it was more likely to be an **artefact** than an **organelle**.

Practice Questions

Q1 Why do you need to squash the tissue when preparing a slide of plant root tip cells?

Exam Question

Q1 A sample of cells was prepared to observe mitosis. In total, 42 cells were observed. 32 of those had visible chromosomes. Calculate the mitotic index for this sample. Give your answer to 2 decimal places. [2 marks]

'Staining your samples' — a common problem at the start of exams...

Wow — I bet you never realised there was so much to know about using a microscope. Still, staining is pretty straightforward and so's preparing a slide. Using a graticule is tricky, but once you get your head round it you'll be fine.

Cell Membrane Structure

You might remember a bit about cell membranes from p. 25. Well now it's time to delve a little deeper...

Membranes Control What Passes Through Them

All cells are surrounded by **membranes**. In **eukaryotic cells**, many of the **organelles** are surrounded by membranes too.

1) **Cell-surface membranes** surround cells. They are a **barrier** between the **cell** and its **environment**, controlling **which substances enter and leave** the cell. They're **partially permeable** — they let some molecules through but not others. Substances can move across the cell-surface membrane by **diffusion**, **osmosis** or **active transport** (see pages 38-43).

2) The membranes around **organelles** divide the cell into different **compartments** — they act as a **barrier** between the **organelle** and the **cytoplasm**. They are also **partially permeable** and control what substances **enter** and **leave** the organelle.

Partially permeable membranes can be useful at sea.

Cell Membranes have a 'Fluid Mosaic' Structure

The basic **structure** of **all cell membranes** is pretty much the same. They're composed of **lipids** (mainly phospholipids — see page 7), **proteins** and **carbohydrates** (attached to proteins or lipids).

1) In 1972, the **fluid mosaic model** was suggested to describe the **arrangement** of **molecules** in the membrane.

2) In the model, **phospholipid molecules** form a continuous, double layer (**bilayer**).

3) This bilayer is '**fluid**' because the phospholipids are **constantly moving**.

The phospholipid bilayer is about 7 nm thick.

4) **Cholesterol** molecules (see below) are present within the bilayer.

5) **Proteins** are scattered through the bilayer, like tiles in a **mosaic**. These include **channel proteins** and **carrier proteins**, which allow **large molecules** and **ions** to pass **through the membrane**. **Receptor proteins** on the cell-surface membrane allow the cell to **detect chemicals** released from other cells. The chemicals **signal** to the cell to **respond** in some way, e.g. the hormone insulin binds to receptor proteins on liver cells, which tells the cells to absorb glucose.

6) Some **proteins** are able to **move sideways** through the bilayer, while others are **fixed** in position.

7) Some **proteins** have a **polysaccharide** (carbohydrate) **chain** attached — these are called **glycoproteins**.

8) Some **lipids** also have a **polysaccharide chain** attached — these are called **glycolipids**.

glycoprotein
glycolipid
phospholipids
protein
cholesterol
protein channel

The Different Components of Cell Membranes have Different Roles

Phospholipids Form a Barrier to Dissolved Substances

1) **Phospholipid molecules** have a 'head' and a 'tail'.

2) The **head** is **hydrophilic** — it **attracts water**. The **tail** is **hydrophobic** — it **repels water**.

3) The molecules automatically **arrange** themselves into a **bilayer** — the **heads face out** towards the water on either side of the membrane.

4) The **centre** of the bilayer is **hydrophobic** so the membrane **doesn't** allow **water-soluble substances** (like ions) through it — it acts as a **barrier** to these dissolved substances.

phospholipid bilayer

phospholipid head
phospholipid tail

Cholesterol Gives the Membrane Stability

1) **Cholesterol** is a type of **lipid**.

2) It's present in **all** cell membranes (except bacterial cell membranes).

3) Cholesterol molecules fit **between** the phospholipids. They bind to the hydrophobic tails of the phospholipids, causing them to pack **more closely together**. This **restricts** the **movement** of the phospholipids, making the membrane **less fluid** and **more rigid**.

4) Cholesterol helps to **maintain** the **shape** of **animal cells** (which don't have cell walls). This is particularly important for cells that **aren't supported by other cells**, e.g. red blood cells, which float free in the blood.

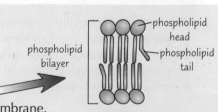

phospholipid
cholesterol

Cell Membrane Structure

The Permeability of the Cell Membrane can be Investigated in the Lab

The permeability of cell membranes is affected by **different conditions**, e.g. **temperature** and **solvent concentration**. You ⬛⬛⬛ate how these things affect permeability by doing an experiment using **beetroot**. Beetroot cells contain a **coloured pigment** that **leaks out** — the **higher** the **permeability** of the membrane, the **more pigment** leaks out of the cell. Here's how you could investigate how **temperature** affects **beetroot membrane permeability**:

1) Use a **scalpel** to carefully cut five **equal sized** pieces of beetroot. (Make sure you do your cutting on a **cutting board**.) **Rinse** the pieces to remove any pigment released during cutting.

2) Add the five pieces to five different **test tubes**, each containing **5 cm³ of water**. Use a **measuring cylinder** or **pipette** to measure the water.

3) Place each test tube in a **water bath** at a **different temperature**, e.g. 10 °C, 20 °C, 30 °C, 40 °C, 50 °C, for the **same length of time** (measured using a **stopwatch**).

4) **Remove** the pieces of beetroot from the tubes, leaving just the **coloured liquid**.

5) Now you need to use a **colorimeter** — a machine that passes **light** through the liquid and measures how much of that light is **absorbed**. The **higher** the absorbance, the **more pigment released**, so the **higher** the **permeability** of the membrane.

Colorimeters need 5 minutes to stabilise before using and calibrating at zero by taking a measurement through pure water.

6) You can connect the colorimeter to a **computer** and use **software** to **collect the data** and draw a **graph** of the results.

Increasing the Temperature Increases Membrane Permeability

Experiments like the one above have shown that membrane permeability **changes** with temperature:

(1) **Temperatures below 0 °C** — the phospholipids don't have much energy, so they can't move very much. They're **packed closely together** and the membrane is **rigid**. But **channel proteins** and **carrier proteins** in the membrane **deform**, **increasing** the **permeability** of the membrane. **Ice crystals** may form and **pierce** the membrane making it **highly permeable** when it thaws.

(2) **Temperatures between 0 and 45 °C** — the phospholipids can **move** around and **aren't** packed as tightly together — the membrane is **partially permeable**. As the temperature **increases** the phospholipids **move more** because they have more energy — this **increases** the **permeability** of the membrane.

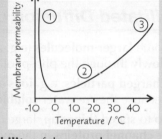

(3) **Temperatures above 45 °C** — the phospholipid bilayer starts to **melt** (break down) and the membrane becomes more **permeable**. **Water** inside the cell **expands**, putting pressure on the membrane. **Channel proteins** and **carrier proteins deform** so they can't control what enters or leaves the cell — this increases the **permeability** of the membrane.

You could also investigate the effect of solvents on the permeability of cell membranes. Surrounding cells in an increasing concentration of a solvent (such as alcohol or acetone) increases membrane permeability because the solvent dissolves the lipids in the cell membrane, causing it to lose its structure.

Practice Questions

Q1 Give three molecules that are present in animal cell membranes.

Q2 What effect does cholesterol have on the cell membrane?

Exam Questions

Q1 Explain why the plasma membrane can be described as having a fluid mosaic structure. [2 marks]

Q2 The table on the right shows the results of an investigation into the effect of alcohol concentration on the permeability of beetroot cell membranes.

a) Suggest a suitable method that could have been used to obtain these results. [4 marks]

b) What conclusion can be drawn from the results? [2 marks]

Alcohol concentration / %	Absorbance
0	0.14
25	0.22
50	0.49
75	1.03
100	1.28

Fluid Mosaic Model — Think I saw one being sold at a craft fair...

It's weird to think that cells are surrounded by a layer that's 'fluid' — it's a good job they are though because if cell membranes were too rigid, a cell wouldn't be able to change shape or stretch without bursting.

Exchange Across Cell Membranes — Diffusion

*Ooooh it's starting to get a bit more exciting... here's how some substances can get across
cell membranes without using energy. Just what you've always wanted to know, I bet.*

Diffusion is the Passive Movement of Particles

1) Diffusion is the net movement of particles (molecules or ions) from an area of
higher concentration to an area of **lower concentration**.

2) Molecules will diffuse **both ways**, but the **net movement** will be to the area of **lower concentration**.
This continues until particles are **evenly distributed** throughout the liquid or gas.

3) The **concentration gradient** is the path from an area of higher concentration to an
area of lower concentration. Particles diffuse **down** a concentration gradient.

4) Diffusion is a **passive process** — **no energy** is needed for it to happen.

5) Particles can diffuse **across cell membranes**, as long as they can
move freely through the membrane.

> *Polar molecules have
> partial positive and negative
> charges (see p. 20).
> Non-polar molecules don't.*

> E.g. **oxygen** and **carbon dioxide** can diffuse easily through cell membranes because they're
> **small**, so they can pass through spaces between the phospholipids. They're also **non-polar**,
> which makes them **soluble in lipids**, so they can **dissolve** in the **hydrophobic bilayer**.

6) When molecules diffuse **directly** through a cell membrane, it's also known as **simple diffusion**.

Facilitated Diffusion uses Carrier Proteins and Protein Channels

1) Some **larger molecules** (e.g. amino acids, glucose) would **diffuse extremely
slowly** through the phospholipid bilayer because they're so **big**.

2) **Charged particles**, e.g. **ions** and **polar molecules**, would also diffuse slowly — that's
because they're **water soluble**, and the **centre** of the **bilayer** is **hydrophobic** (see page 36).

3) So to **speed things up**, large or charged particles diffuse through **carrier proteins**
or **channel proteins** in the membrane instead — this is called **facilitated diffusion**.

4) Like diffusion, facilitated diffusion moves particles **down** a
concentration gradient, from a higher to a lower concentration.

5) It's also a passive process — it **doesn't** use **energy**.

*Andy needed all his
concentration for this
particular gradient...*

Carrier proteins move **large molecules** across
membranes, down their concentration gradient.
Different carrier proteins facilitate the diffusion
of **different molecules**.

1) First, a large molecule **attaches** to a
carrier protein in the membrane.

2) Then, the protein **changes shape**.

3) This **releases** the molecule on the
opposite side of the membrane.

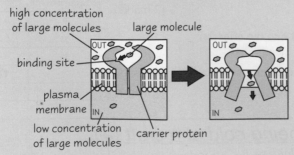

Channel proteins form **pores** in the
membrane for **charged particles** to diffuse
through (down their concentration gradient).
Different channel proteins facilitate the
diffusion of **different charged particles**.

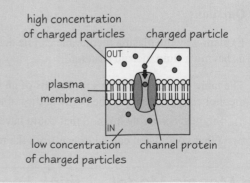

Exchange Across Cell Membranes — Diffusion

The **Rate of Diffusion** Depends on **Several Factors**

The **rate** of **diffusion** across both **external** and **internal cell membranes** can **vary**. Some cells are **adapted** for **rapid transport** across their membranes.

Internal cell membranes are ones surrounding organelles, e.g. the mitochondria.

Simple diffusion depends on...

1) The **concentration gradient** — the **higher** it is, the **faster** the rate of diffusion. As diffusion takes place, the **difference in concentration** between the two sides of the membrane **decreases** until it reaches an **equilibrium** (i.e. the concentration on both sides is equal). This means that diffusion **slows down** over time.

2) The **thickness** of the **exchange surface** — the **thinner** the exchange surface (i.e. the **shorter** the **distance** the particles have to travel), the **faster** the rate of diffusion.

3) The **surface area** — the **larger** the surface area (e.g. of the cell-surface membrane), the **faster** the rate of diffusion.

Microvilli increase the surface area for faster diffusion

Some cells (e.g. epithelial cells in the small intestine) have **microvilli** — projections formed by the cell-surface membrane folding up on itself (see p. 27). Microvilli give the cell a **larger surface area** — in human cells, microvilli can increase the surface area by about **600 times**. A larger surface area means that **more particles** can be **exchanged** in the same amount of time — **increasing** the **rate of diffusion**.

Facilitated diffusion depends on...

1) The **concentration gradient** — the **higher** the **concentration gradient**, the **faster** the **rate** of **facilitated diffusion** (**up to a point**, see point 2 below). As **equilibrium** is reached, the **rate** of facilitated diffusion will **level off**.

2) The **number** of **channel** or **carrier proteins** — once **all** the **proteins** in a membrane are **in use**, facilitated diffusion **can't happen any faster**, even if you increase the concentration gradient. So the **greater the number** of channel or carrier proteins in the cell membrane, the **faster the rate** of facilitated diffusion.

Having more channel proteins increases the rate of facilitated diffusion

Aquaporins are special **channel proteins** that allow the **facilitated diffusion** of **water** through cell membranes. Some **kidney cells** are **adapted** to have **lots** of **aquaporins**. The aquaporins allow the cells to **reabsorb** a lot of the water that would otherwise be **excreted** by the body — about **180 litres** need re-absorbing every day.

Water can also diffuse directly through the membrane, even though it's polar. That's because it's relatively small.

In the exams, you might be asked to calculate the **rate of diffusion** (or any other form of transport across a membrane) from a **graph**. For a straight line graph, this means finding the **gradient** of the line. For a curved graph, it means drawing a **tangent** and finding the gradient of the tangent. There's more on both of these techniques on page 107.

Practice Questions

Q1 Diffusion is a passive process. What does this mean?

Q2 How do microvilli increase the rate of diffusion?

Exam Question

Q1 Chloride ions are transported into a cell across its cell-surface membrane by facilitated diffusion.

a) What type of molecule must be present in a cell membrane for the facilitated diffusion of chloride ions to take place? [1 mark]

b) Explain why the simple diffusion of chloride ions across a cell-surface membrane would be extremely slow. [2 marks]

c) The chloride ions in the cell are not immediately used up. Describe and explain what will happen to the rate of facilitated diffusion of the chloride ions into the cell over time. [2 marks]

All these molecules moving about — you'd think they'd get tired...

Right, I think I get it. If you're a small molecule, like oxygen, you can just cross the membrane by simple diffusion. And if you're a large or charged molecule you have a little help from a channel or carrier protein. As long as you want to go down a concentration gradient. If not, there's always active transport. Luckily that's coming up soon (page 42).

Exchange Across Cell Membranes — Osmosis

These two pages are entirely about the movement of water molecules.
If you've mastered diffusion (see pages 38-39) you'll nail this lot in no time.

Osmosis *is* Diffusion *of* Water Molecules

1) Osmosis is the **diffusion** of **water molecules** across a **partially permeable membrane**, from an area of **higher water potential** (i.e. higher concentration of water molecules) to an area of **lower water potential** (i.e. lower concentration of water molecules).

2) **Water potential** is the potential (likelihood) of water molecules to diffuse out of or into a solution.

3) **Pure water** has the **highest water potential**. All solutions have a **lower** water potential than pure water.

4) If two solutions have the **same water potential**, they're said to be **isotonic**.

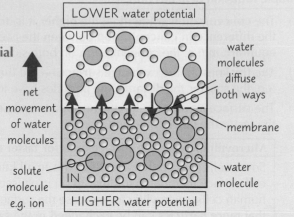

The **Rate** of **Osmosis** Depends on Several **Factors**

The factors affecting the rate of osmosis are similar to those affecting the rate of diffusion (see previous page).

1) The **water potential gradient** — the **higher** the **water potential gradient**, the **faster** the rate of osmosis. As osmosis takes place, the **difference in water potential** on either side of the membrane **decreases**, so the rate of osmosis **levels off** over time.

2) The **thickness** of the **exchange surface** — the **thinner** the **exchange surface**, the **faster** the rate of osmosis.

3) The **surface area** of the **exchange surface** — the **larger** the **surface area**, the **faster** the rate of osmosis.

You can do **Experiments** to Investigate **Water Potential** using **Serial Dilutions**

You can do a **simple experiment**, using potato cylinders, to find out the **water potential** of plant tissue (see next page). First though, you need to make up several solutions of **different, known concentrations** to test the cylinders in. You can do this using a **serial dilution** technique:

> You don't have to dilute solutions by a factor of 2. E.g. to dilute by a factor of 10, take 1 cm³ from your original sample and add it to 9 cm³ of water.

This is how you'd make **five serial dilutions** of a sucrose solution, starting with an initial sucrose concentration of **2 M** and **diluting** each solution by a **factor of 2**...

1) Line up five **test tubes** in a rack.

2) Add **10 cm³** of the initial **2 M sucrose solution** to the first test tube and **5 cm³ of distilled water** to the other four test tubes.

3) Then, using a pipette, draw **5 cm³** of the solution from the **first** test tube, add it to the distilled water in the **second** test tube and **mix** the solution **thoroughly**. You now have **10 cm³** of solution that's **half as concentrated** as the solution in the first test tube (it's **1 M**).

4) Repeat this process **three more times** to create solutions of **0.5 M, 0.25 M** and **0.125 M**.

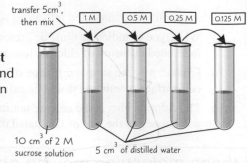

Exchange Across Cell Membranes — Osmosis

You Can Also Make Solutions of Different Concentrations By Finding the Scale Factor

You can make sucrose solutions of **any concentration** by finding the **scale factor**.
For example, if you want to make **15 cm³** of **0.4 M** sucrose solution...

1) Start with a **solution** of a **known concentration**, e.g. **1 M**.

2) Find the **scale factor** by **dividing** the **concentration** of this solution by the **concentration** of the solution **you want to make**. So in this case the scale factor = 1 M ÷ 0.4 M = **2.5**.

3) This means that the solution you want to make is **2.5 times weaker** than the one you have. To make the solution 2.5 times weaker, use 2.5 times less of it, i.e. 15 cm³ ÷ 2.5 = **6 cm³**. **Transfer** this amount to a **clean test tube**.

4) **Top up** the test tube with **distilled water** to get the **volume** you want to make. In this case you want to make 15 cm³ of solution, so you need to add: 15 – 6 = **9 cm³** of distilled water.

Use Your Solutions To Find the Water Potential of Potato Cells

1) Use a cork borer to cut **potatoes** into **identically sized** chips, about 1 cm in diameter.

2) Divide the chips into groups of **three** and measure the **mass** of each **group** using a **mass balance**.

3) Place **one group** into **each** of your **sucrose solutions**.

4) **Leave** the chips in the solutions for **at least** 20 minutes (making sure that they all get the **same amount of time**).

5) Remove the chips and pat dry **gently** with a paper towel.

6) **Weigh** each group again and record your results.

7) Calculate the **% change in mass** for each group.

8) Use the results to make a **calibration curve**, showing **% change in mass** against **sucrose concentration**.

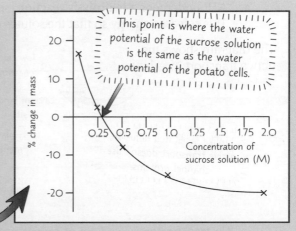

This point is where the water potential of the sucrose solution is the same as the water potential of the potato cells.

The potato chips will **gain water** (and therefore **mass**) in solutions with a **higher water potential** than the chips, and **lose water** in solutions with a **lower** water potential.

The point at which the **curve crosses the x-axis** (where the % change in mass is **0**) is the point at which the **water potential** of the **sucrose solution** is the **same** as the **water potential** of the **potato cells**. Find the **concentration** at this point, then **look up** the **water potential** for that concentration of sucrose solution in, e.g. a textbook.

Practice Questions

Q1 Define osmosis.

Q2 Give two factors that affect the rate of osmosis.

Q3 What are serial dilutions?

Exam Question

Q1 Pieces of potato of equal mass were put into different concentrations of sucrose solution for 24 hours. The difference in mass for each is recorded in the table.

Concentration of sucrose / %	1	2	3	4
Mass difference / g	0.4	0.2	0	– 0.2

   a) Explain why the pieces of potato in 1% and 2% sucrose solutions gained mass. [2 marks]

   b) Suggest a reason why the mass of the piece of potato in 3% sucrose solution stayed the same. [1 mark]

   c) What would you expect the mass difference for a potato in a 5% solution to be? Explain your answer. [2 marks]

I always knew that glass of water had potential...

Osmosis is just a fancy name for the diffusion of water molecules. But whether water moves in or out of a cell depends on the water potential of the surrounding solution. Water potential can be pretty confusing — if you can't make head nor tail of an exam question about it try replacing the word 'potential' with 'concentration' and it'll become clearer.

Exchange Across Cell Membranes — Active Transport

Diffusion and osmosis are passive processes — they don't require energy. So, for those of you feeling a bit more active, here's a page all about... you guessed it... active transport.

Active Transport Needs Energy

Active transport uses **energy** to move **molecules** and **ions** across membranes, usually **against** a **concentration gradient**.

Carrier proteins are involved in active transport. The process is pretty **similar** to **facilitated diffusion** (see p. 38) — a molecule **attaches** to the carrier protein, the protein **changes shape** and this moves the molecule **across** the membrane, **releasing it** on the other side.

There are **two main differences** between active transport and facilitated diffusion though:

1) Active transport usually moves solutes from a **low** to a **high** concentration — in facilitated diffusion, they **always** move from a **high** to a **low** concentration.

2) Active transport requires **energy** — facilitated diffusion **does not**.

   • **ATP** is a common **source of energy** in the cell. It's produced by **respiration**.
   • ATP undergoes a **hydrolysis reaction**, splitting into **ADP** and P_i (inorganic phosphate). This **releases energy** so that the solutes can be transported.

The diagram shows the active transport of **calcium**.

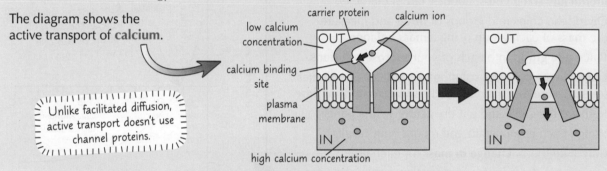

Unlike facilitated diffusion, active transport doesn't use channel proteins.

Co-transporters are a type of **carrier protein**.

1) They bind **two** molecules at a time.

2) The concentration gradient of one of the molecules is used to move the other molecule **against** its own concentration gradient.

The diagram shows the co-transport of **sodium ions** and **glucose**. Sodium ions move into the cell **down** their concentration gradient. This moves glucose into the cell too, **against** its concentration gradient.

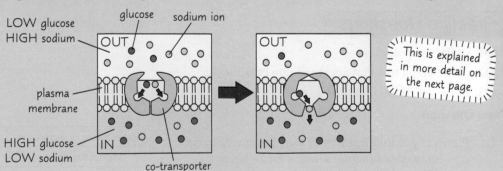

This is explained in more detail on the next page.

Learn these Factors Affecting the Rate of Active Transport

When **active transport** moves molecules and ions **against** their concentration gradient, a **decreasing** concentration gradient **doesn't** affect the **rate** of **active transport**. The rate of active transport is affected by:

1) The **speed** of **individual** carrier **proteins** — the **faster** they **work**, the **faster** the **rate** of active transport.

2) The **number** of **carrier proteins** present — the **more proteins** there are, the **faster** the **rate** of active transport.

3) The rate of **respiration** in the cell and the availability of **ATP**. If respiration is **inhibited**, active transport **can't** take place.

Exchange Across Cell Membranes — Active Transport

Glucose is Absorbed by Co-transport in the Mammalian Ileum

1) **Glucose** is absorbed into the **bloodstream** in the **small intestine**.
2) In the **ileum** (the final part of the small intestine) the **concentration** of glucose is **too low** for glucose to diffuse out into the blood. So glucose is absorbed from the **lumen** (middle) of the **ileum** by **co-transport**.

Glucose enters the ileum epithelium with sodium ions

1) **Sodium ions** are **actively transported out** of the ileum epithelial **cells**, into the **blood**, by the **sodium-potassium pump**. This creates a **concentration gradient** — there's now a higher concentration of sodium ions in the lumen of the ileum than inside the cell.

2) This causes sodium ions to **diffuse** from the lumen of the ileum **into the epithelial cell**, down their concentration gradient. They do this via the **sodium-glucose co-transporter proteins**.

3) The co-transporter carries **glucose** into the cell with the sodium. As a result the concentration of **glucose** inside the cell **increases**.

4) Glucose diffuses out of the cell, into the blood, down its concentration gradient through a protein channel, by **facilitated diffusion**.

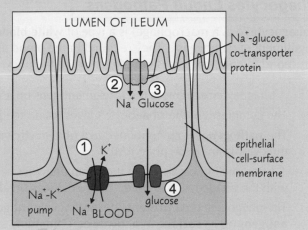

As you can see from this example, the same substance can be transported into or out of a cell in **different ways**. Sometimes **several methods of transport** are needed to move a substance from A to B.

Practice Questions

Q1 Which molecule provides the energy for active transport?

Q2 Describe how carrier proteins actively transport substances across the cell membrane.

Exam Question

Q1 The graph shows the results from an experiment into the uptake of two different solutes (X and Y) by simple bacterial cells.

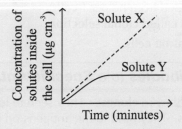

a) Which solute, X or Y, entered the cells by active transport? Give a reason for your answer. [1 mark]

b) Why is energy needed for the active transport of this solute? [1 mark]

c) Describe the process by which energy is released by the cell for active transport. [2 marks]

Revision — like working against a concentration gradient...

Don't worry if it takes you a while to learn these pages — there's quite a lot to cover. It's a good idea to learn it bit by bit. Don't move on to co-transport until you fully understand active transport in normal carrier proteins.

The Immune System

An infectious disease is one that is caused by pathogens, such as bacteria, viruses and fungi. Infectious diseases can be really nasty, but luckily there's an army of cells in the body that helps to protect us — the immune system.

Foreign Antigens Trigger an Immune Response

Antigens are **molecules** (usually proteins) that can **generate** an **immune response** when detected by the body. They are **usually** found on the **surface** of cells and are used by the **immune system** to identify: **pathogens** (organisms that cause disease), **abnormal body cells** (e.g. cancerous or pathogen-infected cells, which have abnormal antigens on their surface), **toxins** and cells from **other individuals** of the **same species** (e.g. organ transplants). There are **four** main stages in the immune response:

1 Phagocytes Engulf Pathogens

A **phagocyte** (e.g. a macrophage) is a type of **white blood cell** that carries out **phagocytosis** (engulfment of pathogens). They're found in the **blood** and in **tissues** and are the first cells to respond to an immune system trigger inside the body. Here's how they work:

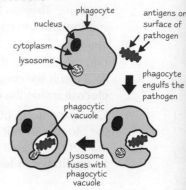

1) A phagocyte **recognises** the foreign **antigens** on a **pathogen**.

2) The cytoplasm of the phagocyte moves round the **pathogen**, **engulfing** it.

3) The **pathogen** is now contained in a **phagocytic vacuole** (a bubble) in the cytoplasm of the phagocyte.

4) A **lysosome** (an organelle that contain enzymes called **lysozymes**) **fuses** with the phagocytic vacuole. The lysozymes **break down** the pathogen.

5) The phagocyte then **presents** the **pathogen's antigens** — it sticks the **antigens** on its **surface** to **activate** other **immune system cells**.

2 Phagocytes Activate T-cells

A **T-cell** (also called a T-lymphocyte) is another type of **white blood cell**. It has **receptor proteins** on its surface that **bind** to **complementary antigens** presented to it by **phagocytes**. This **activates** the T-cell. Different types of T-cells respond in different ways. For example, **helper T-cells** (T_H cells) release chemical signals that activate and **stimulate phagocytes** and **cytotoxic T-cells** (T_C cells), which kill abnormal and foreign cells. T_H cells also activate **B-cells**, which secrete antibodies (see below).

3 T-cells Activate B-cells, Which Divide into Plasma Cells

B-cells (also called B-lymphocytes) are also a type of **white blood cell**. They're covered with **antibodies** — proteins that **bind antigens** to form an **antigen-antibody complex**. Each B-cell has a **different shaped antibody** on its membrane, so different ones bind to **different shaped antigens**.

1) When the antibody on the surface of a B-cell meets a **complementary shaped** antigen, it binds to it.

2) This, together with substances released from helper T-cells, **activates** the B-cell. This process is called **clonal selection**.

3) The activated B-cell **divides** into **plasma cells**.

4 Plasma Cells Make More Antibodies to a Specific Antigen

Plasma cells are **identical** to the B-cell (they're **clones**). They secrete loads of **antibodies** specific to the antigen. These are called **monoclonal antibodies**. They bind to the antigens on the surface of the pathogen to form lots of antigen-antibody complexes.

An **antibody** has **two binding sites**, so can **bind** to **two pathogens** at the **same time**. This means that pathogens become **clumped** together — this is called **agglutination**. **Phagocytes** then bind to the antibodies and phagocytose **many** pathogens at once. This process leads to the **destruction** of **pathogens** carrying this **antigen** in the body.

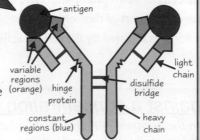

Antibodies are **proteins** — they're made up of chains of amino acids. The **specificity** of an antibody depends on its **variable regions**, which form the **antigen binding sites**. Each antibody has a variable region with a **unique tertiary structure** (due to different amino acid sequences) that's **complementary** to one **specific antigen**. All antibodies have the same **constant regions**.

The Immune System

The **Immune Response** Can be Split into **Cellular** and **Humoral**

Just to add to your fun, the **immune response** is split into **two** — the **cellular response** and the **humoral response**.

1) <u>Cellular</u> — The **T-cells** and **other** immune system **cells** that they **interact** with, e.g. phagocytes, form the cellular response.

2) <u>Humoral</u> — **B-cells**, **clonal selection** and the production of **monoclonal antibodies** form the **humoral response**.

Both types of response are **needed** to remove a pathogen from the body and the responses **interact** with each other, e.g. T-cells help to **activate** B-cells, and antibodies **coat** pathogens making it **easier** for **phagocytes** to **engulf** them.

The **Immune Response** for Antigens can be **Memorised**

The **Primary Immune Response**

1) When an antigen enters the body for the **first time** it activates the immune system. This is called the **primary response**.

2) The primary response is **slow** because there **aren't many B-cells** that can make the antibody needed to bind to it.

Neil's primary response — to his parents.

3) Eventually the body will produce **enough** of the right antibody to overcome the infection. Meanwhile the infected person will show **symptoms** of the disease.

4) After being exposed to an antigen, both T- and B-cells produce **memory cells**. These memory cells **remain in the body** for a **long** time. Memory T-cells remember the **specific antigen** and will recognise it a second time round. Memory B-cells record the specific **antibodies** needed to bind the antigen.

5) The person is now **immune** — their immune system has the **ability** to respond **quickly** to a second infection.

The **Secondary Immune Response**

1) If the **same pathogen** enters the body again, the immune system will produce a **quicker, stronger** immune response — the **secondary response**.

2) **Clonal selection** happens **faster**. Memory B-cells are activated and divide into **plasma cells** that produce the right antibody to the antigen. **Memory T-cells** are activated and divide into the **correct type** of T-cells to kill the cell carrying the antigen.

3) The secondary response often gets rid of the pathogen **before** you begin to show any **symptoms** (you are **immune** to the pathogen).

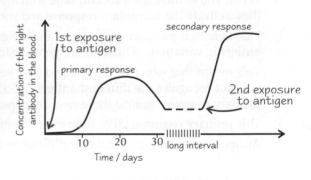

Remember, T-cells and B-cells are also called T-lymphocytes and B-lymphocytes.

Practice Questions

Q1 What are antigens?

Q2 What does the humoral response involve?

Exam Questions

Q1 Describe the function of antibodies. [2 marks]

Q2 Describe and explain how a secondary immune response differs to a primary immune response. [4 marks]

Memory cells — I need a lot more to cope with these pages...

If memory cells are mentioned in the exam, remember that they are still types of T-cells and B-cells. They just hang around a lot longer than most T-cells and B-cells. When the antigen enters the body for a second time they can immediately divide into more of the specific T-cells and B-cells that can kill the pathogen or release antibodies against it.

Immunity and Vaccines

The primary response gives us immunity against a disease, but only after you've become infected. If only there was a way to stimulate memory cell production without getting the disease... well, there is — vaccination.

Vaccines can Protect Individuals and Populations Against Disease

1) While your B-cells are busy **dividing** to build up their numbers to deal with a pathogen (i.e. the **primary response** — see previous page), you **suffer** from the disease. **Vaccination** can help avoid this.

2) Vaccines **contain antigens** that cause your body to **produce memory cells** against a particular pathogen, **without** the pathogen **causing disease**. This means you become **immune** without getting any **symptoms**.

3) Vaccines protect individuals that have them and, because they reduce the **occurrence** of the disease, those **not** vaccinated are also less likely to catch the disease (because there are fewer people to catch it from). This is called **herd immunity**.

4) Vaccines always contain antigens — these may be **free** or **attached** to a **dead** or **attenuated** (weakened) **pathogen**.

The oral vaccine was proving hard to swallow.

5) Vaccines may be **injected** or taken **orally**. The **disadvantages** of taking a vaccine orally are that it could be **broken down** by **enzymes** in the gut or the **molecules** of the vaccine may be **too large** to be **absorbed** into the blood.

6) Sometimes **booster** vaccines are given later on (e.g. after several years) to **make sure** that memory cells are produced.

Antigenic Variation Helps Some Pathogens Evade the Immune System

1) **Antigens** on the surface of pathogens **activate** the **primary response**.

2) When you're **infected** a **second time** with the **same pathogen** (which has the **same antigens** on its surface) they **activate** the **secondary response** and you don't get ill.

3) However, some sneaky pathogens can **change** their surface antigens. This **antigen variability** is called **antigenic variation**. (Different antigens are formed due to changes in the **genes** of a pathogen.)

4) This means that when you're infected for a **second time**, the **memory cells** produced from the **first infection** will **not recognise** the **different antigens**. So the immune system has to start from scratch and carry out a **primary response** against these new antigens.

5) This **primary response** takes **time** to get rid of the infection, which is why you get **ill again**.

6) **Antigenic variation** also makes it **difficult** to develop **vaccines** against some pathogens for the same reason. **Examples** of pathogens that show antigenic variation include **HIV** and the **influenza virus**.

7) Here's how **antigenic variation** affects the production of **vaccines** to help prevent people catching **influenza**:

1) The **influenza (flu) vaccine** changes every year. That's because the **antigens** on the surface of the influenza virus **change regularly**, forming **new strains** of the virus.

2) **Memory cells** produced from **vaccination** with **one strain** of the flu will **not recognise** other strains with **different antigens**. The strains are **immunologically distinct**.

3) Every year there are **different strains** of the influenza virus **circulating** in the **population**, so a **different vaccine** has to be made.

4) **New vaccines** are **developed** and one is chosen **every year** that is the **most effective** against the **recently** circulating influenza viruses.

5) Governments and health authorities then implement a **programme** of **vaccination** using the most **suitable** vaccine.

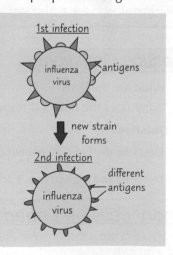

Immunity and Vaccines

Immunity can be Active or Passive

ACTIVE IMMUNITY

This is the type of immunity you get when **your immune system makes its own antibodies** after being **stimulated** by an **antigen**. There are **two** different types of active immunity:

1) **Natural** — this is when you become immune after **catching a disease**.

2) **Artificial** — this is when you become immune after you've been given a **vaccination** containing a harmless dose of antigen.

PASSIVE IMMUNITY

This is the type of immunity you get from being **given antibodies made by a different organism** — your immune system **doesn't** produce any antibodies of its own. Again, there are **two** types:

1) **Natural** — this is when a **baby** becomes immune due to the antibodies it receives from its **mother**, through the **placenta** and in **breast milk**.

2) **Artificial** — this is when you become immune after being **injected** with **antibodies** from **someone else**. E.g. If you contract tetanus you can be injected with antibodies against the tetanus toxin, collected from blood donations.

Active and Passive Immunity Have Contrasting Characteristics

In the exam you might be asked about the **differences** between these types of **immunity**:

Active immunity	Passive immunity
Requires exposure to antigen	Doesn't require exposure to antigen
It takes a while for protection to develop	Protection is immediate
Memory cells are produced	Memory cells aren't produced
Protection is long-term because the antibody is produced (after activation of memory cells) in response to complementary antigen being present in the body	Protection is short-term because the antibodies given are broken down

Practice Questions

Q1 How do vaccines cause immunity?

Q2 Explain what antigenic variability is.

Exam Questions

Q1 Vaccines can be used to protect people against some diseases. Not all individuals in a population must receive the vaccine for a vaccination programme to be successful. Explain why this is the case. [3 marks]

Q2 The influenza virus causes the flu. Explain why it is possible to suffer from the flu more than once. [4 marks]

Q3 Immunity from a disease can be either active or passive.

a) Explain why active immunity offers long-term protection against a disease, whereas passive immunity only offers protection in the short-term. [2 marks]

b) It normally takes 14 days for immunity to develop after receiving a vaccine. Explain why vaccines do not usually offer immediate protection against a disease. [1 mark]

An injection of dead bugs — roll on my next vaccine...

The influenza virus is so clever that it would almost make you think it had a mind of its own. I mean, as soon as we catch up with it and develop a vaccine, off it goes and changes its surface antigens again. Influenza virus: one, humans: nil. This is one of the ways viruses have evolved to avoid your immune system. Well, clever them.

Antibodies in Medicine

Antibodies aren't only great for fighting off infection, they're also excellent tools for use in medical diagnosis and drug development. Let's all give three cheers for antibodies. Without them, we'd all probably be dead by now.

Monoclonal Antibodies can be used to Target Specific Substances or Cells

1) **Monoclonal antibodies** are antibodies **produced** from a **single group of genetically identical B-cells** (plasma cells). This means that they're all **identical** in **structure**.

2) As you know, antibodies are **very specific** because their binding sites have a **unique tertiary structure** (see p.44) that only one particular antigen will fit into (one with a **complementary shape**).

3) You can make monoclonal antibodies **that bind to anything** you want, e.g. a cell antigen or other substance, and they will only bind to (target) this molecule.

EXAMPLE: Targeting drugs to a particular cell type — cancer cells

1) **Different cells** in the body have **different** surface **antigens**.

2) Cancer cells have antigens called **tumour markers** that are **not** found on normal body cells.

3) **Monoclonal antibodies** can be made that will bind to the tumour markers.

4) You can also attach **anti-cancer drugs** to the antibodies.

5) When the antibodies come into **contact** with the cancer cells they will **bind** to the tumour markers.

6) This means the drug will **only accumulate** in the body where there are **cancer cells**.

7) So, the **side effects** of an antibody-based drug are lower than other drugs because they accumulate near **specific cells**.

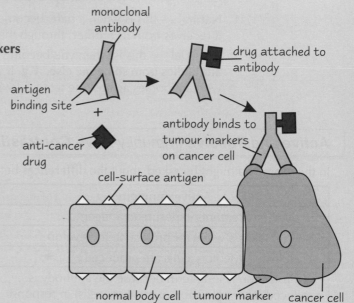

EXAMPLE: Targeting a particular substance for medical diagnosis — pregnancy testing

Pregnancy tests detect the hormone **human chorionic gonadotropin (hCG)** that's found in the **urine** of pregnant women:

1) The application area contains **antibodies for hCG** bound to a **coloured bead** (**blue**).

2) When urine is applied to the application area any hCG will **bind** to the antibody on the beads, forming an **antigen-antibody complex**.

3) The urine **moves** up the stick to the **test strip, carrying** any **beads** with it.

4) The test strip contains **antibodies to hCG** that are stuck in place (**immobilised**).

5) If there **is hCG present** the test strip turns **blue** because the **immobilised** antibody binds to any **hCG** — concentrating the hCG-antibody complex with the **blue beads** attached. If **no hCG** is present, the beads will **pass through** the test area **without** binding to anything, and so it **won't** go blue.

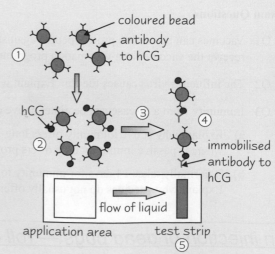

Antibodies in Medicine

The **ELISA Test** is a **Medical Diagnostic** Test that Uses **Antibodies**

1) The **enzyme-linked immunosorbent assay** (ELISA) allows you to see if a patient has any **antibodies** to a certain **antigen** (see example below) or any **antigen** to a certain **antibody**.

2) It can be used to test for **pathogenic infections**, for **allergies** (e.g. to nuts or lactose) and for just about **anything** you can make an **antibody** for.

3) In an ELISA test, an antibody is used which has an **enzyme attached** to it. This enzyme can **react** with a substrate to produce a **coloured product**. This causes the solution in the reaction vessel to **change colour**.

4) If there's a **colour change**, it demonstrates that the **antigen** or **antibody** of interest is **present** in the sample being tested (e.g. blood plasma). In some types of ELISA, the **quantity** of this antigen/antibody can be worked out from the **intensity** of the colour change.

5) There are several **different types** of ELISA. **Direct ELISA** uses a **single** antibody that is complementary to the antigen you're testing for. **Indirect ELISA** is different because it uses **two** different antibodies. This method is outlined below:

EXAMPLE: Using an ELISA as a HIV (Human Immunodeficiency Virus) Test

An **indirect ELISA test** can be used to see if a patient possesses **antibodies** to the HIV virus:

① **HIV antigen** is **bound** to the bottom of a **well** in a **well plate** (a plastic tray with loads of little circular pits in it).

② A sample of the **patient's blood plasma**, which might contain several different antibodies, is **added** to the **well**. If there are any **HIV-specific antibodies** (i.e. antibodies against HIV) these will **bind** to the **HIV antigen** stuck to the bottom of the **well**. The well is then **washed out** to remove any **unbound antibodies**.

③ A **secondary antibody**, that has a specific **enzyme** attached to it, is added to the **well**. This secondary antibody can bind to the **HIV-specific antibody** (which is also called the **primary antibody**). The well is **washed out** again to remove any **unbound secondary antibody**. If there's no primary antibody in the sample, all of the secondary antibody will be **washed away**.

④ A **solution** is added to the **well**. This solution contains a **substrate**, which is able to react with the **enzyme** attached to the secondary antibody and produce a **coloured product**. If the solution **changes colour**, it indicates that the patient has **HIV-specific antibodies** in their blood and is **infected** with HIV.

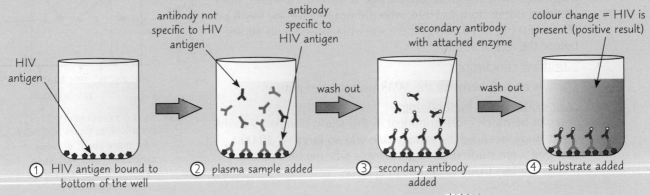

① HIV antigen bound to bottom of the well ② plasma sample added ③ secondary antibody added ④ substrate added

The washing steps are important to make sure unbound antibodies aren't left in the well which could affect the results. E.g. unbound secondary antibodies could cause the test to appear positive when there are no HIV antibodies present.

If the ELISA result was negative, there would be no colour change because there would be no HIV-specific antibodies for the secondary antibodies to bind to.

Practice Questions

Q1 What are monoclonal antibodies?

Exam Question

Q1 Describe how monoclonal antibodies can be used to target a drug to cancer cells. [4 marks]

Antibodies — the multi-tool of the immune system...

Monoclonal antibodies are really useful — they can even be made against other antibodies. For example, people with asthma produce too many of a type of antibody that causes inflammation in the lungs. Monoclonal antibodies can be made to bind this type of antibody, so it can no longer cause inflammation, which can reduce the asthma symptoms.

Interpreting Vaccine and Antibody Data

If someone claims anything about a vaccine or antibody, the claim has to be validated (confirmed) before it's accepted. To do this, you need to evaluate the data used to support the claim and the methodology behind it.

New Knowledge About Vaccines and Antibodies is Validated by Scientists

When a **study** presents evidence for a **new theory** (e.g. a vaccine has a dangerous side effect) it's important that other scientists come up with **more evidence** to **validate** (confirm) the theory. Other scientists may **repeat** the study and try to **reproduce** the results, or **conduct other studies** to try to prove the same theory.

EXAMPLE 1: The MMR Vaccine

1) In 1998, a study was published about the **safety of the measles, mumps and rubella (MMR) vaccine**. The study was based on **12 children** with **autism** (a life-long developmental disability) and concluded that there may be a **link** between the MMR vaccine and autism.

2) Not everyone was convinced by this study because it had a **very small sample size** of 12 children, which increased the likelihood of the results being due to **chance**. The study may have been **biased** because one of the scientists was helping to gain evidence for a **lawsuit** against the MMR vaccine manufacturer. Also, studies carried out by different scientists found no link between autism and the MMR vaccine.

3) There have been **further scientific studies** to sort out the **conflicting** evidence. In **2005**, a **Japanese** study was published about the incidence of autism in Yokohama (an area of Japan). They looked at the medical records of **30 000 children** born between **1988 and 1996** and counted the number of children that developed **autism** before the age of seven. The **MMR jab** was first **introduced in Japan in 1989** and was **stopped in 1993**. During this time the MMR vaccine was administered to children at **12 months old**. The graph shows the results of the study.

4) In the exam you could be asked to **evaluate evidence** like this.

   - <u>You might be asked to **describe the data**...</u>
     The graph shows that the number of children diagnosed with autism continued to **rise** after the MMR vaccine was **stopped**. For example, from all the children born in 1992, who did receive the MMR jab, about 60 out of 10 000 were diagnosed with autism before the age of seven. However, from all the children born in 1994, who did not receive the MMR jab, about 160 out of 10 000 of them were diagnosed with autism before the age of seven.

   - <u>...or draw conclusions</u>
     There is **no link** between the MMR vaccine and autism.

   - <u>... or evaluate the methodology</u>
     You can be much more confident in this study, compared to the 1998 study, because the **sample size** was so **large** — 30 000 children were studied. A larger sample size means that the results are less likely to be due to **chance**.

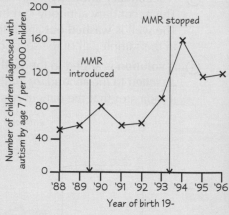

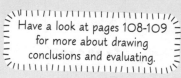

> Have a look at pages 108-109 for more about drawing conclusions and evaluating.

EXAMPLE 2: Herceptin® — Monoclonal Antibodies

About **20%** of **women with breast cancer** have tumours that produce more than the usual amount of a **receptor** called **HER2**. **Herceptin®** is a **drug** used to treat this type of breast cancer — it contains **monoclonal antibodies** that **bind the HER2 receptor** on a **tumour cell** and **prevent** the cells from growing and dividing.

In **2005**, a study **tested** Herceptin® on women who had already undergone **chemotherapy** for HER2-type **breast cancer**. **1694** women took the **drug** for a **year** after chemotherapy and another **1694** women were **observed** for the **same time** (the control group). The results are shown in the graph on the right.

<u>**Describe the data:**</u> Almost **twice as many** women in the **control group** developed breast cancer again or died **compared** to the group taking Herceptin®.

<u>**Draw conclusions:**</u> A **one-year treatment** with Herceptin®, after chemotherapy, **increases** the disease-free survival rate for women with HER2-type breast cancer.

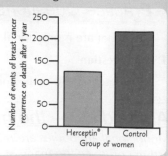

Interpreting Vaccine and Antibody Data

Use of Vaccines and Antibodies Raises Ethical Issues

Ethical issues surrounding vaccines include:

1) All vaccines are **tested on animals** before being tested on humans — some people **disagree** with animal testing. Also, **animal based substances** may be used to **produce** a vaccine, which some people disagree with.

2) **Testing** vaccines on **humans** can be **tricky**, e.g. volunteers may put themselves at **unnecessary risk** of contracting the disease because they think they're fully protected (e.g. they might have unprotected sex because they have had a new HIV vaccine and think they're protected — and the vaccine might not work).

3) Some people **don't** want to take the vaccine due to the **risk** of **side effects**, but they are **still protected** because of **herd immunity** (see p. 46) — other people think this is **unfair**.

4) If there was an **epidemic** of a **new disease** (e.g. a new influenza virus) there would be a rush to **receive** a vaccine and **difficult decisions** would have to be made about **who** would be the **first** to receive it.

Ethical issues surrounding monoclonal antibody therapy often involve animal rights issues. **Animals** are used to **produce the cells** from which the monoclonal antibodies are produced. Some people **disagree** with the use of animals in this way.

Practice Questions

Q1 Suggest one ethical issue surrounding vaccines.

Q2 Suggest one ethical issue surrounding monoclonal antibodies.

Exam Question

Q1 The graph below shows the number of laboratory reports of *Haemophilus influenzae* type b (Hib), in England and Wales, from 1990 to 2004. Hib affects children and can lead to meningitis and pneumonia.

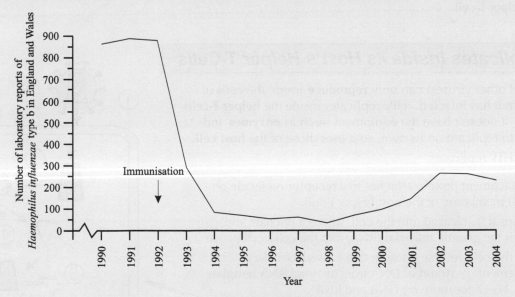

a) Explain how immunisation could have caused the sharp decrease in Hib cases after 1992. [2 marks]

b) Suggest a possible explanation for the increase in Hib cases after 1998. [1 mark]

Some scientists must have to validate the taste of chocolate — nice job...

After the 1998 study, some parents were worried about giving their kids the MMR vaccine, so the number of children given the vaccine fell. With fewer children in each community protected by the vaccine, herd immunity decreased. This meant that more people were vulnerable to measles, mumps and rubella, so the number of cases of went up.

HIV and Viruses

Viruses aren't cells like bacteria. They're not even living things — they can only reproduce inside the cells of another organism (called the host). All viruses cause disease, and you need to know all about one particularly nasty blighter...

HIV is the Virus That Causes AIDS

1) **HIV (Human Immunodeficiency Virus)** is a virus that affects the **immune system**. It eventually leads to **acquired immune deficiency syndrome (AIDS)**.

2) **AIDS** is a condition where the immune system **deteriorates** and eventually **fails**. This makes someone with AIDS more **vulnerable** to **other infections**, like pneumonia (see next page).

3) **HIV** infects (and eventually kills) **helper T-cells**, which act as the **host cells** (see p. 28) for the virus. Remember, helper T-cells send chemical signals that **activate phagocytes**, **cytotoxic T-cells** and **B-cells** (see p. 44) so they're **hugely important cells** in the **immune response**. Without enough helper T-cells, the immune system is **unable** to mount an **effective** response to **infections** because other immune system cells **don't behave** how they **should**.

4) People infected with HIV develop **AIDS** when the **helper T-cell numbers** in their body reach a critically **low** level.

HIV has a Spherical Structure

You might get asked about the structure of HIV in your exam.

1) A **core** that contains the **genetic material** (RNA) and some **proteins** (including the enzyme **reverse transcriptase**, which is needed for virus replication).

2) An **outer coating** of protein called a **capsid**.

3) An **extra outer layer** called an **envelope**. This is made of **membrane** stolen from the cell membrane of a previous host cell.

4) Sticking out from the envelope are **loads of copies** of an **attachment protein** that help HIV **attach** to the **host helper T-cell**.

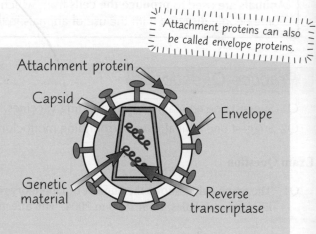

Attachment protein, Capsid, Envelope, Genetic material, Reverse transcriptase

HIV Replicates Inside its Host's Helper T-Cells

HIV (and all other viruses) can only **reproduce** inside the cells of the organism it has infected. HIV replicates inside the **helper T-cells** of the host. It doesn't have the equipment (such as **enzymes** and **ribosomes**) to replicate on its own, so it uses those of the **host cell**. Here's how **HIV** replicates:

1) The attachment protein **attaches** to a **receptor molecule** on the cell membrane of the host helper T-cell.

2) The capsid is released into the cell, where it **uncoats** and releases the **genetic material** (RNA) into the cell's cytoplasm.

3) Inside the cell, reverse transcriptase is used to make a **complementary strand** of DNA from the **viral RNA template** (see p. 16-17 for more on DNA and RNA).

4) From this, **double-stranded DNA** is made and **inserted** into the human DNA.

5) Host cell enzymes are used to make **viral proteins** from the **viral DNA** found within the human DNA.

6) The viral proteins are **assembled** into **new viruses**, which **bud** from the cell and go on to infect other cells.

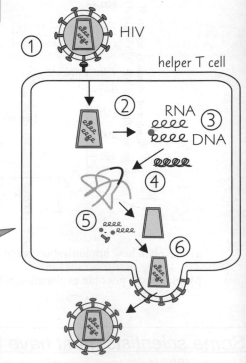

HIV, helper T cell, RNA, DNA

During the initial infection period, HIV replicates rapidly and the infected person may experience severe flu-like symptoms. After this period, HIV replication drops to a lower level. This is the **latency period**. During the latency period (which can last for years), the infected person **won't experience** any **symptoms**.

HIV and Viruses

People with **AIDS** are **Susceptible** to a Range of **Illnesses**

People with HIV are classed as having AIDS when **symptoms** of their **failing immune system** start to **appear** or their **helper T-cell count drops** below a certain level. People with AIDS generally develop diseases that **wouldn't** cause serious problems in people with a **healthy** immune system. The length of time between **infection** with HIV and the **development** of AIDS **varies** between individuals but without treatment it's usually around **10 years**.

1) The **initial symptoms** of AIDS include **minor infections** of mucous membranes (e.g. the inside of the nose, ears and genitals), and recurring respiratory infections.

2) As AIDS **progresses** the number of **immune system cells decreases** further. Patients become susceptible to **more serious infections** including chronic diarrhoea, severe bacterial infections and tuberculosis.

3) During the **late stages** of AIDS patients have a very **low number** of immune system cells and can develop a **range of serious infections** such as toxoplasmosis of the brain (a parasite infection) and candidiasis of the respiratory system (fungal infection). It's these serious infections that kill AIDS patients, not HIV itself.

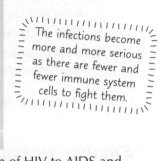
The infections become more and more serious as there are fewer and fewer immune system cells to fight them.

The length of time that people survive with AIDS varies a lot. Factors that affect progression of HIV to AIDS and survival time with AIDS include **existing infections**, the **strain of HIV** they're infected with, **age** and access to **healthcare**.

Antibiotics **Don't Work** Against **Viruses**

1) Antibiotics kill **bacteria** by **interfering** with their metabolic reactions. They target the **bacterial enzymes** and **ribosomes** used in these reactions.

2) Bacterial enzymes and ribosomes are **different** from **human** enzymes and ribosomes. Antibiotics are designed to **only target** the bacterial ones so they don't damage human cells. Makes sense.

3) Viruses **don't have their own** enzymes and ribosomes — they use the ones in the host's cells. So because human viruses use human enzymes and ribosomes to replicate, antibiotics **can't** inhibit them because they **don't** target human processes.

4) Most **antiviral drugs** are designed to target the few **virus-specific enzymes** (enzymes that only the virus uses) that exist. For example, HIV uses **reverse transcriptase** to replicate (see previous page). Human cells **don't** use this enzyme so drugs can be designed to inhibit it **without affecting** the host cell. These drugs are called reverse-transcriptase inhibitors.

There's **No Cure** for **HIV**

1) There's currently **no cure** or **vaccine** for HIV but **antiviral** drugs can be used to **slow down** the **progression** of HIV infection and AIDS in an infected person.

2) The best way to control HIV infection in a population is by **reducing** its **spread**. HIV can be **spread** via **unprotected sexual intercourse**, through **infected bodily fluids** (e.g. like blood from sharing contaminated needles) and from a HIV-positive **mother** to her **fetus**. Not all babies from HIV-positive mothers are born infected with HIV and taking antiviral drugs during pregnancy can reduce the chance of the baby being HIV-positive.

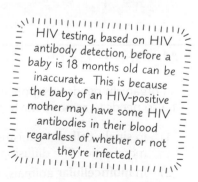
HIV testing, based on HIV antibody detection, before a baby is 18 months old can be inaccurate. This is because the baby of an HIV-positive mother may have some HIV antibodies in their blood regardless of whether or not they're infected.

Practice Questions

Q1 What type of cell does HIV replicate in?
Q2 Why can't antibiotics be used to treat HIV?

Exam Question

Q1 HIV is the virus that eventually causes AIDS. Describe the structure of HIV. [4 marks]

Viruses can be dangerous and hard to treat — they're just not funny...

Well, apart from rhinoviruses, which cause colds, but they're only funny because of the name. It's actually quite a logical name — rhino is from the Greek for nose. They're literally nose viruses. If I was a virus I'd choose somewhere better to infect. Anyway, you need to learn this stuff. Scribble everything down and see what you remember.

Size and Surface Area

Exchanging things with the environment is pretty easy if you're a single-celled organism, but if you're multicellular it all gets a bit more complicated... and it's all down to this 'surface area to volume ratio' malarkey.

Organisms Need to **Exchange Substances** with their **Environment**

Every organism, whatever its size, needs to exchange things with its environment.
Otherwise there'd be no such thing as poop scoops...

1) Cells need to take in **oxygen** (for aerobic respiration) and **nutrients**.

2) They also need to excrete **waste products** like **carbon dioxide** and **urea**.

3) Most organisms need to stay at roughly the **same temperature**,
so **heat** needs to be exchanged too.

Raj was glad he'd exchanged
his canoe for a bigger boat.

How easy the exchange of substances is depends on the organism's **surface area to volume ratio**.

Smaller Animals have *Higher Surface Area : Volume Ratios*

A mouse has a bigger surface area **relative to its volume** than a hippo. This can be hard to imagine, but you can prove it mathematically. Imagine these animals as cubes:

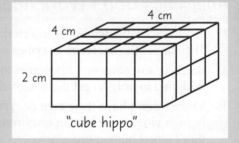

The hippo could be represented by a block measuring
2 cm × 4 cm × 4 cm.

Its **volume** is $2 \times 4 \times 4 = \textbf{32 cm}^3$

Its **surface area** is $2 \times 4 \times 4 = 32$ cm² (top and bottom surfaces of cube)
　　　　　　　　　$+ 4 \times 2 \times 4 = 32$ cm² (four sides of the cube)

Total surface area = **64 cm²**

So the hippo has a **surface area : volume ratio** of 64 : 32 or **2 : 1**.

"cube hippo"

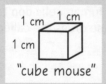

"cube mouse"

Compare this to a cube mouse measuring 1 cm × 1 cm × 1 cm.

Its **volume** is $1 \times 1 \times 1 = \textbf{1 cm}^3$

Its **surface area** is $6 \times 1 \times 1 = \textbf{6 cm}^2$

So the mouse has a **surface area : volume ratio** of **6 : 1**.

The cube mouse's surface area is six times its volume, but the cube hippo's surface area is only twice its volume. Smaller animals have a bigger surface area compared to their volume.

Multicellular Organisms need *Exchange Organs* and *Mass Transport Systems*

An organism needs to supply **every one of its cells** with substances like **glucose** and **oxygen** (for respiration). It also needs to **remove waste products** from every cell to avoid damaging itself.

1) In **single-celled** organisms, these substances can **diffuse directly** into (or out of) the cell across the cell-surface membrane. The diffusion rate is quick because of the small distances the substances have to travel (see p. 39).

2) In **multicellular** animals, diffusion across the outer membrane is **too slow**, for two reasons:

   • Some cells are **deep within the body** — there's a big distance between them and the **outside environment**.

   • Larger animals have a **low surface area to volume ratio** — it's difficult to exchange **enough** substances to supply a **large volume of animal** through a relatively **small outer surface**.

So rather than using straightforward diffusion to absorb and excrete substances, multicellular animals need specialised **exchange organs** (like lungs — see p. 58).

They also need an efficient system to carry substances to and from their individual cells — this is **mass transport**. In mammals, 'mass transport' normally refers to the **circulatory system** (see p. 70), which uses **blood** to carry glucose and oxygen around the body. It also carries **hormones**, **antibodies** (p. 44) and **waste** like CO_2. Mass transport in **plants** involves the transport of **water** and **solutes** in the **xylem** and **phloem** (see pages 78 and 80).

Size and Surface Area

Body Size and *Shape* Affect *Heat Exchange*

As well as creating **waste products** that need to be transported away, the metabolic activity inside cells creates **heat**. Staying at the right temperature is difficult, and it's pretty heavily influenced by your **size** and **shape**...

Size

The **rate of heat loss** from an organism depends on its **surface area**. If an organism has a large volume, e.g. a hippo, its surface area is relatively **small**. This makes it **harder** for it to lose heat from its body. If an organism is small, e.g. a mouse, its relative surface area is **large**, so heat is lost more **easily**. This means **smaller** organisms need a relatively **high metabolic rate**, in order to **generate** enough **heat** to stay warm.

Shape

1) Animals with a **compact** shape have a **small surface area** relative to their volume
   — **minimising heat loss** from their surface.

2) Animals with a **less compact** shape (those that are a bit **gangly** or have **sticky outy** bits) have a **larger surface area** relative to their volume — this **increases heat loss** from their surface.

3) Whether an animal is compact or not depends on the **temperature** of its **environment**. Here's an example:

Arctic fox	African bat-eared fox	European fox
Body temperature 37 °C	Body temperature 37 °C	Body temperature 37 °C
Average outside temperature 0 °C	Average outside temperature 25 °C	Average outside temperature 12 °C

The Arctic fox has **small ears** and a **round head** to **reduce** its SA : V ratio and heat loss.	The African bat-eared fox has **large ears** and a more **pointed nose** to **increase** its SA : V ratio and heat loss.	The European fox is **intermediate** between the two, matching the temperature of its environment.

Organisms have **Behavioural** *and* **Physiological Adaptations** *to Aid Exchange*

Not all organisms have a body size or shape to suit their climate — some have **other adaptations** instead...

1) Animals with a high SA : volume ratio tend to **lose more water** as it evaporates from their surface. Some **small desert mammals** have **kidney structure adaptations** so that they produce **less urine** to compensate.

2) To support their **high metabolic rates**, small mammals living in **cold regions** need to eat large amounts of **high energy foods** such as seeds and nuts.

3) Smaller mammals may have thick layers of **fur** or **hibernate** when the weather gets really cold.

4) **Larger organisms** living in **hot regions**, e.g. elephants and hippos, find it hard to keep cool as their heat loss is relatively slow. **Elephants** have developed **large flat ears** to **increase** their **surface area**, allowing them to lose more heat. **Hippos** spend much of the day in the **water** — a **behavioural adaptation** to help them lose heat.

Practice Questions

Q1 Give four things that organisms need to exchange with their environment.
Q2 Describe how body shape affects heat exchange.

Exam Question

Q1 Explain why a small mammal needs a relatively high metabolic rate compared to a large mammal.   [3 marks]

Cube animals indeed — it's all gone a bit Picasso...

You need to know how size and surface area to volume ratio are related, as well as what adaptations multicellular organisms have to help with exchange and transport. Don't panic, there are more adaptations coming up next...

Gas Exchange

Lots of organisms have developed adaptations to improve their rate of gas exchange. It's a tricky business if you're an insect or a plant though — you've got to exchange enough gas but avoid losing all your water and drying to a crisp...

Gas Exchange Surfaces have **Two** Major **Adaptations**

Most gas exchange surfaces have two things in common:

1) They have a **large surface area**.
2) They're **thin** (often just one layer of epithelial cells)
   — this provides a **short diffusion pathway** across the gas exchange surface.

The organism also maintains a **steep concentration gradient** of gases across the exchange surface.

> All these features **increase** the **rate of diffusion** — see page 39.

Single-celled **Organisms** Exchange Gases across their **Body Surface**

1) Single-celled organisms absorb and release gases by **diffusion** through their **outer surface**.

2) They have a relatively **large surface area**, a **thin surface** and a **short diffusion pathway** (oxygen can take part in **biochemical reactions** as soon as it **diffuses** into the cell) — so there's **no need** for a gas exchange system.

Fish Use a **Counter-Current System** for Gas Exchange

There's a **lower concentration** of oxygen in water than in air. So **fish** have special **adaptations** to get enough of it.

1) Water, containing oxygen, enters the fish through its **mouth** and passes out through the gills.

2) Each gill is made of lots of **thin plates** called **gill filaments**, which give a **big surface area** for **exchange** of **gases**.

3) The gill filaments are covered in lots of tiny structures called **lamellae**, which **increase** the **surface area** even more.

4) The lamellae have lots of **blood capillaries** and a thin surface layer of cells to speed up diffusion.

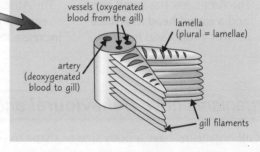
vessels (oxygenated blood from the gill)
lamella (plural = lamellae)
artery (deoxygenated blood to gill)
gill filaments

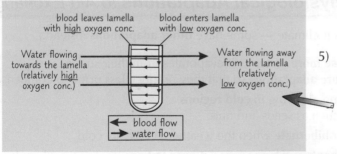
blood leaves lamella with <u>high</u> oxygen conc.
blood enters lamella with <u>low</u> oxygen conc.
Water flowing towards the lamella (relatively <u>high</u> oxygen conc.)
Water flowing away from the lamella (relatively <u>low</u> oxygen conc.)
← blood flow
→ water flow

5) **Blood** flows through the lamellae in one direction and **water** flows over in the opposite direction. This is called a **counter-current system**. It maintains a **large concentration gradient** between the water and the blood. The **concentration of oxygen** in the **water** is always **higher** than that in the **blood**, so as much oxygen as possible diffuses from the water into the blood.

oxygen concentration
water
blood
distance along gill plate

Insects use **Tracheae** to **Exchange Gases**

1) Insects have microscopic air-filled pipes called **tracheae** which they use for gas exchange.

2) Air moves into the tracheae through pores on the surface called **spiracles**.

3) **Oxygen** travels down the **concentration gradient** towards the **cells**.

4) The tracheae branch off into smaller **tracheoles** which have **thin, permeable walls** and go to individual cells. This means that oxygen diffuses directly into the respiring cells — the insect's circulatory system doesn't transport O_2.

5) **Carbon dioxide** from the cells moves down its own concentration gradient towards the **spiracles** to be **released** into the atmosphere.

6) Insects use **rhythmic abdominal movements** to move air in and out of the spiracles.

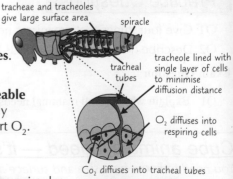
tracheae and tracheoles give large surface area
spiracle
tracheal tubes
tracheole lined with single layer of cells to minimise diffusion distance
O_2 diffuses into respiring cells
CO_2 diffuses into tracheal tubes

Gas Exchange

Dicotyledonous Plants Exchange Gases at the Surface of the Mesophyll Cells

1) Plants need CO_2 for **photosynthesis**, which produces O_2 as a waste gas. They need O_2 for **respiration**, which produces CO_2 as a waste gas.

2) The main gas exchange surface is the **surface of the mesophyll cells** in the leaf. They're well adapted for their function — they have a **large surface area**.

3) The mesophyll cells are inside the leaf. Gases move in and out through special pores in the **epidermis** called **stomata** (singular = stoma).

4) The stomata can **open** to allow exchange of gases, and **close** if the plant is losing too much water. **Guard cells** control the opening and closing of stomata.

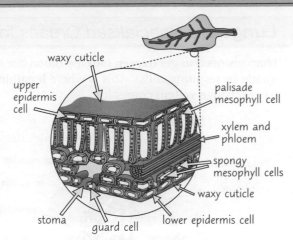

Insects and Plants can Control Water Loss

Exchanging gases tends to make you **lose water** — there's a sort of **trade-off** between the two. Luckily for plants and insects though, they've evolved **adaptations** to **minimise water loss** without reducing gas exchange too much.

1) If **insects** are losing too much water, they **close** their **spiracles** using muscles. They also have a **waterproof, waxy cuticle** all over their body and **tiny hairs** around their spiracles, both of which **reduce evaporation**.

2) Plants' stomata are usually kept **open** during the day to allow **gaseous exchange**. Water enters the guard cells, making them **turgid**, which **opens** the stomatal pore. If the plant starts to get **dehydrated**, the guard cells lose water and become **flaccid**, which **closes** the pore.

3) Some plants are specially adapted for life in **warm**, **dry** or **windy** habitats, where **water loss** is a problem. These plants are called **xerophytes**.

See p. 78 for more on water loss in plants.

Examples of **xerophytic adaptations** include:

- **Stomata** sunk in **pits** that trap moist air, reducing the concentration gradient of water between the leaf and the air. This reduces the amount of water diffusing out of the leaf and evaporating away.

- A layer of 'hairs' on the epidermis — again to trap moist air round the stomata.

- **Curled leaves** with the **stomata inside**, protecting them from wind (windy conditions increase the rate of diffusion and evaporation).

- A **reduced number of stomata**, so there are fewer places for water to escape.

- **Waxy, waterproof cuticles** on leaves and stems to reduce evaporation.

Practice Questions

Q1 How are single-celled organisms adapted for efficient gas exchange?

Q2 What is the advantage to fish of having a counter-current system in their gills?

Q3 What are an insect's spiracles?

Q4 Through which pores are gases exchanged in plants?

Exam Questions

Q1 Describe, using an example, one way that gas exchange organs are adapted to their function. [2 marks]

Q2 Explain why plants that live in the desert often have sunken stomata or stomata surrounded by hairs. [2 marks]

Keep revising and you'll be on the right trachea...

There's a pretty strong theme on these pages — whatever organism it is, to exchange gases efficiently it needs exchange organs with a large surface area, a thin exchange surface and a high concentration gradient. Just don't you forget that.

Gas Exchange in Humans

In humans, gas exchange takes place in the lungs. You need to know the structure of the lungs as well as how they're ventilated... take a deep breath...

Lungs are Specialised Organs for Gas Exchange

Humans need to get **oxygen** into the blood (for respiration) and they need to **get rid** of **carbon dioxide** (made by respiring cells). This is where **breathing** (or **ventilation** as it's sometimes called) and the **gas exchange system** comes in.

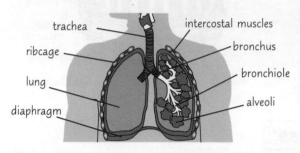

Human Gas Exchange System

trachea
ribcage
lung
diaphragm
intercostal muscles
bronchus
bronchiole
alveoli

1) As you breathe in, air enters the **trachea** (windpipe).

2) The trachea splits into two **bronchi** — one **bronchus** leading to each lung.

3) Each bronchus then branches off into smaller tubes called **bronchioles**.

4) The bronchioles end in small 'air sacs' called **alveoli** (this is where gases are exchanged — see next page).

5) The **ribcage**, **intercostal muscles** and **diaphragm** all work together to move air in and out (see below).

There are actually three layers of intercostal muscles. You need to know about two of them (the internal and external intercostal muscles — see below) for your exam. We've only shown one layer here for simplicity.

Ventilation is Breathing In and Out

Ventilation consists of **inspiration** (breathing in) and **expiration** (breathing out). It's controlled by the movements of the **diaphragm**, **internal** and **external intercostal muscles** and **ribcage**.

Inspiration

1) The **external intercostal** and **diaphragm muscles contract**.

2) This causes the **ribcage** to move **upwards and outwards** and the **diaphragm** to **flatten**, **increasing the volume** of the **thoracic cavity** (the space where the lungs are).

3) As the volume of the thoracic cavity increases, the **lung pressure decreases** (to below atmospheric pressure).

4) Air will always flow from an area of **higher pressure** to an area of **lower pressure** (i.e. down a pressure gradient) so air flows down the trachea and **into the lungs**.

5) Inspiration is an **active process** — it requires **energy**.

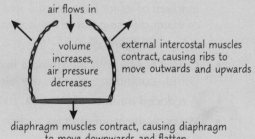

air flows in

volume increases, air pressure decreases

external intercostal muscles contract, causing ribs to move outwards and upwards

diaphragm muscles contract, causing diaphragm to move downwards and flatten

Expiration

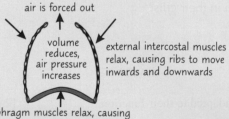

air is forced out

volume reduces, air pressure increases

external intercostal muscles relax, causing ribs to move inwards and downwards

diaphragm muscles relax, causing diaphragm to become curved again

1) The **external intercostal** and **diaphragm muscles relax**.

2) The **ribcage** moves **downwards and inwards** and the **diaphragm** becomes **curved** again.

3) The **volume** of the thoracic cavity **decreases**, causing the **air pressure to increase** (to above atmospheric pressure).

4) Air is forced down the pressure gradient and **out of the lungs**.

5) Normal expiration is a **passive process** — it **doesn't** require energy.

6) Expiration can be **forced** though (e.g. if you want to blow out the candles on your birthday cake).

7) During forced expiration, the external intercostal muscles relax and **internal** intercostal muscles **contract, pulling** the **ribcage further down** and **in**. During this time, the movement of the two sets of intercostal muscles is said to be **antagonistic** (opposing).

Gas Exchange in Humans

In Humans Gaseous Exchange Happens in the Alveoli

Lungs contain millions of microscopic air sacs where gas exchange occurs — called **alveoli**.
Each **alveolus** is made from a **single layer** of **thin**, **flat cells** called **alveolar epithelium**.

Epithelial tissue is pretty common in the body. It's usually found on exchange surfaces.

1) There's a huge number of alveoli in the lungs, which means there's a **big surface area** for exchanging oxygen (O_2) and carbon dioxide (CO_2).

2) The alveoli are surrounded by a network of **capillaries**.

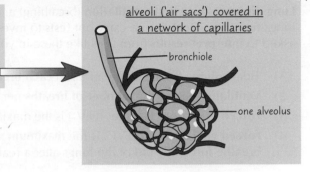

alveoli ('air sacs') covered in a network of capillaries

bronchiole

one alveolus

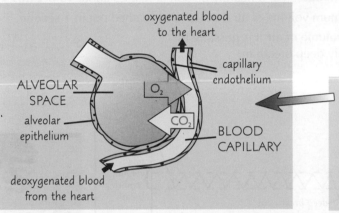

oxygenated blood to the heart

capillary endothelium

ALVEOLAR SPACE

O_2

CO_2

alveolar epithelium

BLOOD CAPILLARY

deoxygenated blood from the heart

3) O_2 diffuses **out of** the alveoli, across the **alveolar epithelium** and the **capillary endothelium** (a type of epithelium that forms the capillary wall), and into **haemoglobin** (see p. 68) in the **blood**.

4) CO_2 diffuses **into** the alveoli from the blood, and is breathed out.

So, **in summary**: **oxygen** from the **air** moves down the **trachea**, **bronchi** and **bronchioles** into the **alveoli**. This movement happens **down** a **pressure gradient**. Once in the alveoli, the oxygen **diffuses** across the **alveolar epithelium**, then the **capillary endothelium**, ending up in the capillary itself. This movement happens **down** a **diffusion gradient**.

The Alveoli are Adapted for Gas Exchange

Alveoli have features that **speed up** the **rate of diffusion** so gases can be exchanged quickly:

1) **A thin exchange surface** — the **alveolar epithelium** is only **one cell thick**. This means there's a **short diffusion pathway** (which speeds up diffusion).

2) **A large surface area** — the **large number** of alveoli means there's a large surface area for gas exchange.

See pages 38 and 39 for more on diffusion.

There's also a **steep concentration gradient** of oxygen and carbon dioxide between the alveoli and the capillaries, which increases the rate of diffusion. This is constantly maintained by the **flow of blood** and **ventilation**.

Practice Questions

Q1 Describe the structure of the human gas exchange system.

Q2 How is normal expiration different to forced expiration?

Q3 Describe the movement of carbon dioxide and oxygen across the alveolar epithelium.

Exam Questions

Q1 Describe two ways in which lungs are adapted for efficient gas exchange. [2 marks]

Q2 Describe the process of inspiration. [4 marks]

Alveoli — useful things... always make me think about pasta...

A mammal's lungs act as an interface with the environment — they take in air and give out waste gases. Ventilation moves these gases into and out of the lungs, but the alveoli have the task of getting them in and out of the bloodstream. Luckily, like many other biological structures, they're well adapted for doing their job.

The Effects of Lung Disease

It's all very well when your lungs are working perfectly, but some pathogens (and even your lifestyle) can muck them up good and proper. This can make it more difficult to breathe and reduce the rate of gas exchange.

Measures of Lung Function Can Help to Diagnose Lung Diseases

Lung diseases affect both **ventilation** (breathing) and **gas exchange** in the lungs — in other words, how well the lungs **function**. Doctors can carry out **tests** to investigate lung function and diagnose a lung disease. You might be asked to **interpret results** from tests like these in your exams. Here are some **terms** you might come across:

1) **Tidal volume** is the volume of air in **each breath** — usually between **0.4 dm³** and **0.5 dm³** for adults.
2) **Ventilation rate** is the **number of breaths per minute**. For a healthy person at rest it's about **15 breaths**.
3) **Forced expiratory volume₁ (FEV₁)** is the maximum volume of air that can be breathed out in **1 second**.
4) **Forced vital capacity (FVC)** is the **maximum volume of air** it is possible to breathe forcefully out of the lungs after a really deep breath in.

You can figure out **tidal volume**, **ventilation rate** and other measures of breathing from the graph produced from a **spirometer** (a fancy machine that scientists and doctors use to measure the volume of air breathed in and out):

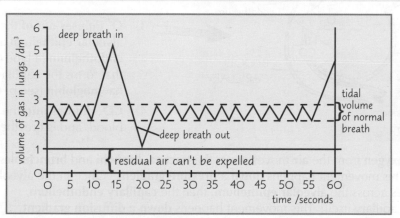

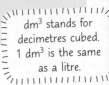

dm³ stands for decimetres cubed. 1 dm³ is the same as a litre.

Measuring tidal volume is one of the hardest jobs in the world.

Different Diseases Affect the Lungs in Different Ways

Here are some examples of different **lung diseases** and how they affect breathing.

Pulmonary Tuberculosis (TB)

1) When someone becomes infected with **tuberculosis bacteria**, immune system cells build a **wall** around the bacteria in the **lungs**. This forms small, hard lumps known as **tubercles**.
2) Infected tissue within the tubercles **dies** and the **gaseous exchange surface** is **damaged**, so **tidal volume** is **decreased**.
3) Tuberculosis also causes **fibrosis** (see below), which further **reduces** the **tidal volume**.
4) A reduced tidal volume means **less air** can be **inhaled** with each breath. In order to take in enough oxygen, patients have to **breathe faster**, i.e. **ventilation rate** is **increased**.
5) Common symptoms include a persistent **cough**, coughing up **blood** and **mucus**, **chest pains**, **shortness of breath** and **fatigue**.

Fibrosis

1) Fibrosis is the formation of **scar tissue** in the lungs. This can be the result of an **infection** or exposure to substances like **asbestos** or **dust**.
2) Scar tissue is **thicker** and **less elastic** than normal lung tissue.
3) This means that the lungs are **less able to expand** and so **can't hold as much air** as normal — **tidal volume** is **reduced**, and so is **FVC** (i.e. a smaller volume of air can be forcefully breathed out).
4) There's a **reduction** in the rate of **gaseous exchange** — diffusion is **slower** across a **thicker** scarred membrane.
5) Symptoms of fibrosis include **shortness of breath**, a **dry cough**, **chest pain**, **fatigue** and **weakness**.
6) Fibrosis sufferers have a **faster ventilation rate** than normal — to get enough air into their lungs to **oxygenate** their blood.

The Effects of Lung Disease

Asthma

1) Asthma is a respiratory condition where the airways become **inflamed** and **irritated**. The causes vary from case to case but it's usually because of an **allergic reaction** to substances such as **pollen** and **dust**.

2) During an asthma attack, the **smooth muscle** lining the **bronchioles contracts** and a large amount of **mucus** is produced.

3) This causes **constriction** of the airways, making it difficult for the sufferer to **breathe properly**. Air flow in and out of the lungs is **severely reduced**, so less oxygen enters the alveoli and moves into the blood. Reduced air flow means that FEV_1 is severely **reduced** (i.e. less air can be breathed out in 1 second).

4) Symptoms include **wheezing**, a **tight chest** and **shortness of breath**. During an attack the symptoms come on very suddenly. They can be relieved by **drugs** (often in **inhalers**) which cause the muscle in the bronchioles to **relax**, opening up the airways.

Emphysema

1) Emphysema is a lung disease caused by **smoking** or long-term exposure to **air pollution** — foreign particles in the smoke (or air) become **trapped** in the alveoli.

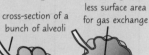
See p. 44 for more on phagocytes.

2) This causes **inflammation**, which attracts **phagocytes** to the area. The phagocytes produce an **enzyme** that breaks down **elastin** (a protein found in the **walls** of the **alveoli**).

3) Elastin is **elastic** — it helps the alveoli to **return** to their **normal shape** after inhaling and exhaling air.

4) Loss of elastin means the alveoli **can't recoil** to **expel air** as well (it remains **trapped** in the alveoli).

5) It also leads to **destruction** of the **alveoli walls**, which **reduces** the surface area of the alveoli, so the rate of **gaseous exchange** decreases.

6) Symptoms of emphysema include **shortness of breath** and **wheezing**. People with emphysema have an **increased ventilation rate** as they try to increase the amount of air (containing oxygen) reaching their lungs.

cross-section of a bunch of alveoli

less surface area for gas exchange

cross-section of damaged alveoli in a person suffering from emphysema

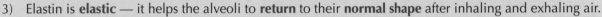

TB, fibrosis, asthma and emphysema all **reduce the rate of gas exchange** in the alveoli. Less oxygen is able to diffuse into the bloodstream, the body cells **receive less oxygen** and the rate of **aerobic respiration** is **reduced**. This means **less energy is released** and sufferers often feel **tired** and **weak**.

Practice Questions

Q1 What is tidal volume?

Q2 What happens to the lung tissue of someone with TB?

Q3 What happens to the alveoli of someone who suffers from emphysema?

Exam Question

Q1 FVC (forced vital capacity) is the maximum amount of air it is possible to expel from the lungs after a deep breath in. A hospital patient has emphysema. The patient has a lower FVC than normal.

a) Explain how emphysema could reduce FVC. [2 marks]

FEV_1 is the maximum volume of air that can be breathed out in 1 second. FEV_1 is around 80% of FVC in a healthy adult. The emphysema patient has an FVC of 3.2 dm³ and a FEV_1 of 1.7 dm³.

b) Calculate FEV_1 as a percentage of FVC in the emphysema patient. [1 mark]

c) In a fibrosis patient, FEV_1 is close to 80% of FVC even though FVC is reduced. Suggest an explanation for this. [1 mark]

Spirometers — they're not machines for measuring spirals...

The examiners like to mix things up a bit, so you could get asked questions about a lung disease you've not come across before or a measure of lung function you've not heard of. If so, take a deep breath and don't panic — the question should give you all the information you need, then it's just a case of applying what you already know to answer it.

TOPIC 3A — EXCHANGE AND TRANSPORT SYSTEMS

Interpreting Lung Disease Data

It's very possible that you could be asked to interpret some data on lung disease in the exam. So being my usual nice self, I've given you some examples to show you how to do it. I know it looks a bit dull but believe me, it'll really help.

You Need to be Able to Interpret Data on Risk Factors and Lung Disease

1) All diseases have factors that will **increase** a person's **chance** of getting that disease. These are called **risk factors**. For example, it's widely known that if you **smoke** you're more likely to get **lung cancer** (smoking is a risk factor for lung cancer).

2) This is an example of a **correlation** — a link between two things (see page 108). However, a correlation doesn't always mean that one thing **causes** the other. Smokers have an **increased risk** of getting cancer but that doesn't necessarily mean smoking **causes** the disease — there are lots of other factors to take into consideration.

3) You need to be able to describe and analyse data given to you in your exams.
   Here's an example of the sort of thing you might get:

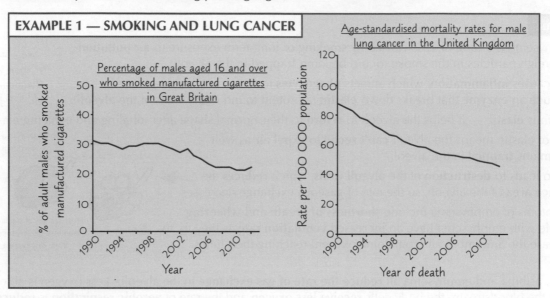

EXAMPLE 1 — SMOKING AND LUNG CANCER

You might be asked to:

1) **Describe the data** — The graph on the left shows that the **number** of adult males in Great Britain who **smoke decreased** between 1990 and 2012. The graph on the right shows that the male lung cancer **mortality (death) rate decreased** between 1990 and 2012 in the United Kingdom.

2) **Draw conclusions** — You need to be careful what you say here. There's a **correlation** (link) between the **number** of males **who smoked** and the **mortality rate** for male lung cancer. But you **can't** say that one **caused** the other. There could be **other reasons** for the trend, e.g. deaths due to lung cancer may have decreased because less asbestos was being used in homes (not because fewer people were smoking).

Other points to consider — The graph on the right shows mortality (**death**) rates. The rate of **cases** of lung cancer **may have been increasing** but medical advances may mean more people were **surviving** (so only mortality was decreasing).

You might also need to **evaluate** the way in which **scientific data** has led to **government restrictions** on the **sources** of risk factors. E.g.

Responses to data

Medical studies in 1950s and 1960s documented the **link** between **smoking** and various forms of **cancer**, particularly lung cancer. The evidence prompted the first **voluntary agreement** between the UK government and tobacco companies in 1971, which stated that tobacco products and adverts should carry a **health warning label**. As of October 2008, **picture health warnings** were made **compulsory** on all UK boxes of cigarettes after studies suggested they were more effective than written warnings alone.

Interpreting Lung Disease Data

EXAMPLE 2 — AIR POLLUTION AND ASTHMA

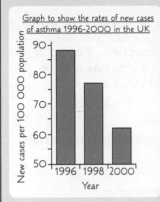

Graph to show the rates of new cases of asthma 1996-2000 in the UK

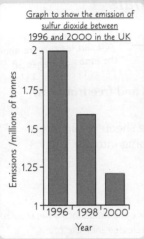

Graph to show the emission of sulfur dioxide between 1996 and 2000 in the UK

The **top graph** shows the number of **new cases of asthma** per 100 000 of the population diagnosed in the UK from 1996 to 2000. The **bottom graph** shows the **emissions** (in millions of tonnes) of **sulfur dioxide** (an **air pollutant**) from 1996 to 2000 in the UK.

You might be asked to describe the data...

1) The **top graph** shows that the number of **new cases of asthma** in the UK **fell** between 1996 and 2000, from 87 to 62 per 100 000 people.

2) The **bottom graph** shows that the **emissions of sulfur dioxide** in the UK **fell** between 1996 and 2000, from 2 to 1.2 million tonnes.

... or draw conclusions

1) Be careful what you say when drawing conclusions. Here there's a **link** between the **number** of new cases of **asthma** and **emissions** of **sulfur dioxide** in the **UK** — the rate of new cases of asthma has **fallen** as sulfur dioxide emissions have **fallen**. You **can't** say that one **causes** the other though because there could be **other reasons** for the trend, e.g. the number of new cases of asthma could be falling due to the **decrease** in the number of people **smoking**.

2) You can't say the **reduction** in asthma cases is **linked** to a **reduction in air pollution** (in general) either as **only** sulfur dioxide levels were studied.

Other points to consider:

1) The top graph shows **new cases** of asthma. The rate of new cases may be **decreasing** but existing cases may be becoming **more severe**.

2) The emissions were for the whole of the UK but air pollution **varies from area to area**, e.g. **cities** tend to be **more polluted**.

3) The asthma data doesn't take into account any **other factors** that may **increase** the risk of developing asthma, e.g. allergies, smoking, etc.

Responses to data

In response to **studies** connecting **air pollution** to various **diseases**, the EU adopted the **National Emissions Ceilings Directive**. This set **upper limits** on the total emissions of **four major pollutants** in the **atmosphere**, to be achieved by **2010**. **New limits** are being agreed on for **2020**. The EU also introduced the **Clean Power for Transport Package** to promote **cleaner fuels** for vehicles, and the UK **taxes car owners** according to their car's **emissions**.

Practice Question

Q1 Give an example of where scientific data has led to restrictions on the source of a risk factor in lung disease.

Exam Question

Q1 In early December 1952, a dense layer of cold air trapped pollutants close to ground level in London. The graph opposite shows daily deaths and levels of sulfur dioxide and smoke between 1st and 15th December.

a) Describe the changes in the daily death rate and the levels of pollutants over the days shown. [3 marks]

b) What conclusion can be drawn from this graph? [1 mark]

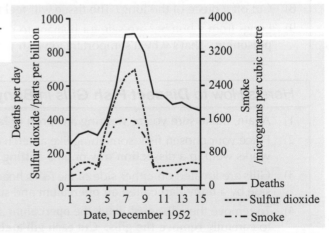

Drawing conclusions — you'll need your wax crayons and some paper...

These pages give examples to help you deal with what the examiners are sure to hurl at you — and boy, do they like throwing data around. There's some important advice here (even if I say so myself) — it's easy to leap to a conclusion that isn't really there — stick to your guns about the difference between correlation and cause and you'll be just fine.

Dissecting Gas Exchange Systems

After learning all about how different organisms are adapted for efficient gas exchange, you might be wondering what those structures really look like. Well, here are some lovely dissections that you might do. How exciting.

You Need to be Able to **Carry Out Dissections**

1) As part of your AS or A level in Biology, you're expected to carry out at least one **dissection**. It could be a dissection of a **gaseous exchange system** or a **mass transport system** (or an organ within one of those systems) in either an **animal** or a **plant**. You could also be asked about dissections in your exams.

2) There's an example of a **plant dissection** that you could do on page 79.
   These two pages cover some **animal dissections** that you could do as well or instead.

3) Whether it's a plant or animal dissection, you're expected to know how to carry it out **safely** and **ethically**. You might also need to **record** your **observations** using **labelled diagrams**.

You Can **Dissect** the **Gaseous Exchange Systems** of **Animals**

Lungs Can be **Dissected** To Show the Main **Structures**

You can learn more about the lungs on pages 58-59.

1) First up, lung dissection is **messy**, so make sure you're wearing a **lab coat**. Your **dissecting tools** (e.g. scalpels, dissecting scissors) should all be **clean**, **sharp** and **free from rust** — blunt tools **don't cut well** and can be **dangerous**.

2) Lay the **lungs** your teacher has given you on a **cutting board**. They'll probably be sheep or pig lungs from a butcher's shop. You should be able to see the **trachea** and two **bronchi** going into the lungs.

3) To see the **lungs inflate**, attach a piece of **rubber tubing** to the **trachea** and pump air into the lungs using a **foot** or **bicycle pump**. The lungs will **deflate** by themselves because of the **elastin** in the walls of the **alveoli** (see p. 61).

   Never blow down the tube to inflate the lungs — you could end up sucking up stale air from inside the lungs into your mouth. Pop the lungs in a clear plastic bag before you start to stop bacteria inside the lungs from being released into the room.

4) Once you've seen the lungs inflate, you can examine the different **tissue types** in the lungs.

5) The **trachea** is supported by **C-shaped rings** of **cartilage**. A **cross-section** of the trachea looks like this:

   smooth muscle

   C-shaped cartilage

   If you do cut the cartilage be careful — you need to wear goggles to protect your eyes.

6) **Cartilage** is **tough**, so if you want to **open up** the **trachea**, it's best to cut it **lengthways**, down the **gap** in the **C-shaped rings**. Use **dissecting scissors** or a **scalpel** to make the cut. If using a scalpel, **cut downwards** (not towards you) and **don't apply** too much **pressure** to the blade.

7) Continue cutting down one of the **bronchi**. You should be able to see the **bronchioles** branching off.

8) Cut off a piece of the lung. The tissue will **feel spongy** because of the air trapped in all the **alveoli**.

9) Lungs from a butcher are safe for humans to handle, but they could still contain **bacteria** that cause **food poisoning**. That's why it's important to **wash your hands** after the dissection and **disinfect work surfaces**.

Here's How to **Dissect Fish Gills** in **Bony Fish**

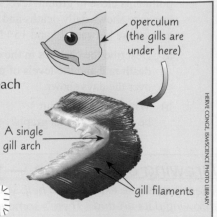

1) Again, make sure you're wearing an **apron** or **lab coat**.

2) Place your chosen fish (something like a perch or salmon works well) in a **dissection tray** or on a **cutting board**.

3) Gills are located on either side of the fish's head. They're protected on each side by a **bony flap** called an **operculum** and supported by **gill arches**.

4) To remove the gills, **push back** the **operculum** and use **scissors** to carefully **remove the gills**. Cut each **gill arch** through the bone at the **top** and **bottom**. They should look a bit like this:

   operculum (the gills are under here)

   A single gill arch

   gill filaments

5) If you look closely, you should be able to see the **gill filaments**.

   For more information about the structure and function of fish gills, see page 56.

HERVE CONGE, ISM/SCIENCE PHOTO LIBRARY

Dissecting Gas Exchange Systems

You Can **Dissect** the **Gaseous Exchange System** in **Insects** too

You can find more information about the gas exchange systems of insects on page 56.

Big insects like **grasshoppers** or **cockroaches** are usually **best** for dissecting because they're easier to handle. For dissection, you'll need to use an insect that's been humanely killed **fairly recently**.

1) First fix the insect to a **dissecting board**. You can put **dissecting pins** through its legs to hold it in place.

2) To examine the **tracheae**, you'll need to carefully **cut** and **remove** a piece of **exoskeleton** (the insect's hard outer shell) from along the length of the insect's **abdomen**.

3) Use a syringe to fill the abdomen with **saline solution**. You should be able to see a network of **very thin, silvery-grey tubes** — these are the **tracheae**. They look silver because they're **filled** with **air**.

4) You can examine the tracheae under an **optical microscope** using a **temporary mount slide** (see p. 30). Again, the tracheae will appear silver or grey. You should also be able to see **rings** of **chitin** in the walls of the **tracheae** — these are there for **support** (like the rings of cartilage in a human trachea).

Some live insects, e.g. grasshoppers, can cause allergic reactions in some people. They need to be handled very carefully.

There are Some **Ethical Issues** Involved in **Dissecting Animals**

Dissecting animals (including **fish** and **insects**) can give you a **better understanding** of their anatomy. However, there are some **ethical issues** involved. Here are some points to think about:

1) Some people argue that it is **morally wrong** to **kill** animals **just for dissections**, as it is **unnecessary** killing. However many dissections that are carried out in schools involve animals that have **already been killed** for their **meat**, e.g. the sheep's lung dissection on the previous page. (Some people disagree with killing animals altogether though.)

2) There are concerns that the animals used for dissections arc **not** always **raised in a humane way** — they may be subject to **overcrowding, extremes of temperature** or **lack of food** — and they may **not** be **killed humanely** either. If animals (e.g. insects) are raised in school for dissection, it's important to make sure they are **looked after properly** and killed humanely to **minimise** any **suffering** or **distress**.

Practice Questions

Q1 Why is it important that dissecting tools are sharp?

Q2 Describe how to remove the gills in a bony fish.

Exam Questions

Q1 A student is examining grasshopper tracheae under the microscope. The tracheae were taken from a preserved grasshopper specimen. The grasshopper was killed some time ago and kept in a liquid preservative. The tracheae do not appear silver under the microscope. Instead they are a dark grey. Suggest why this is the case. [1 mark]

Q2 A student is performing a dissection of a pig's lungs.
  a) The student cuts off a piece of lung tissue and drops it into a beaker of water. The lung tissue floats in the water. Explain why it floats. [1 mark]
  b) Give one safety precaution the student should take when carrying out this dissection. [1 mark]

Dissection tools should be like your mind — clean and sharp...

Well, that's another topic over and done with anyway. Dissections are all about cutting open organisms, so you can see everything you've been learning about and hopefully understand it better. You should be able to apply your knowledge of gas exchange systems (see pages 56-59) to any dissections you get asked about in the exams.

Digestion and Absorption

The whole point of digestion is to break down the food you eat into small molecules that your cells can absorb.
As you might imagine, this involves loads of different chemical reactions and our old friends, enzymes.

Food is **Broken Down** into **Smaller Molecules** During **Digestion**

1) The **large biological molecules** (e.g. starch, proteins) in food are **too big** to cross **cell membranes**. This means they **can't be absorbed** from the gut into the blood.

2) During digestion, these large molecules are **broken down** into **smaller molecules** (e.g. glucose, amino acids), which **can** move across cell membranes. This means they can be **easily absorbed** from the gut into the blood, to be **transported** around the body for use by the body cells.

3) You might remember from Topic 1A, that most **large biological molecules** are **polymers**, which can be **broken down** into **smaller** molecules (**monomers**) using **hydrolysis reactions**. Hydrolysis reactions **break bonds** by **adding water**.

4) During hydrolysis, **carbohydrates** are broken down into **disaccharides** and then **monosaccharides**. Fats are broken down into **fatty acids** and **monoglycerides**. Proteins are broken down into **amino acids**.

Digestive Enzymes are Used to **Break Down Biological Molecules** in **Food**

1) A variety of different **digestive enzymes** are produced by **specialised cells** in the **digestive systems** of mammals. These enzymes are then released into the gut to mix with food.

2) Since enzymes only work with **specific substrates** (see page 11), **different enzymes** are needed to **catalyse** the breakdown of **different food molecules**.

Carbohydrates are Broken Down by **Amylase** and **Membrane-Bound Disaccharidases**

1) **Amylase** is a digestive enzyme that catalyses the conversion of **starch** (a polysaccharide) into the smaller sugar **maltose** (a disaccharide). This involves the **hydrolysis** of the **glycosidic bonds** in starch.

2) Amylase is produced by the **salivary glands** (which release amylase into the **mouth**) and also by the **pancreas** (which releases amylase into the **small intestine**).

3) **Membrane-bound disaccharidases** are enzymes that are attached to the **cell membranes** of **epithelial cells** lining the **ileum** (the final part of the small intestine). They help to break down **disaccharides** (e.g. maltose, sucrose and lactose) into **monosaccharides** (e.g. glucose, fructose and galactose). Again, this involves the hydrolysis of glycosidic bonds.

There's more on polysaccharides, disaccharides and monosaccharides on pages 2-5.

Disaccharide	Disaccharidase	Monosaccharide Products
maltose	maltase	glucose + glucose
sucrose	sucrase	glucose + fructose
lactose	lactase	glucose + galactose

4) **Monosaccharides** can be transported across the cell membranes of the ileum epithelial cells via specific **transporter proteins** (see next page).

Lipids are Broken Down by **Lipase** (with the Help of **Bile Salts**)

1) **Lipase** enzymes catalyse the breakdown of **lipids** into **monoglycerides** and **fatty acids**. This involves the **hydrolysis** of the **ester bonds** in lipids.

2) Lipases are made in the **pancreas**. They work in the **small intestine**.

A monoglyceride is a glycerol molecule with one fatty acid attached.

3) **Bile salts** are produced by the **liver** and **emulsify** lipids — this means they cause the lipids to form **small droplets**.

4) Bile salts are really important in the process of lipid digestion. **Several small lipid droplets** have a **bigger surface area** than a **single large droplet** (for the same volume of lipid). So the formation of small droplets greatly increases the surface area of lipid that's available for **lipases** to work on.

5) Once the lipid has been broken down, the **monoglycerides** and **fatty acids** stick with the **bile salts** to form tiny structures called **micelles**.

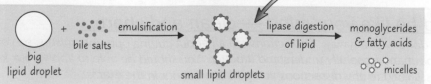

Digestion and Absorption

Proteins are Broken Down by Endopeptidases and Exopeptidases

Proteins are broken down by a combination of different **proteases** (or **peptidases**). These are enzymes that catalyse the conversion of **proteins** into **amino acids** by **hydrolysing** the **peptide bonds** between amino acids. You need to know about **endopeptidases** and **exopeptidases** (including **dipeptidases**):

Endopeptidases

- Endopeptidases act to hydrolyse peptide bonds **within** a protein.
- **Trypsin** and **chymotrypsin** are two examples of endopeptidases. They're synthesised in the **pancreas** and secreted into the **small intestine**.
- **Pepsin** is another endopeptidase. It's released into the **stomach** by cells in the **stomach lining**. Pepsin only works in **acidic conditions** — these are provided by **hydrochloric acid** in the **stomach**.

Remember: endopeptidases break bonds inside the protein.

Exopeptidases

- Exopeptidases act to hydrolyse peptide bonds **at the ends** of protein molecules. They remove **single amino acids** from proteins.
- **Dipeptidases** are exopeptidases that work specifically on **dipeptides**. They act to separate the two amino acids that make up a dipeptide by **hydrolysing** the **peptide bond** between them.
- Dipeptidases are often located in the **cell-surface membrane** of **epithelial cells** in the **small intestine**.

The Products of Digestion are Absorbed Across Cell Membranes

The products of digestion are absorbed across the **ileum epithelium** into the bloodstream.

Monosaccharides

- **Glucose** is absorbed by **active transport** with **sodium ions** via a **co-transporter protein** (see page 43). **Galactose** is absorbed in the same way using the same co-transporter protein.
- **Fructose** is absorbed via **facilitated diffusion** through a different transporter protein.

Monoglycerides and fatty acids

Micelles (see previous page) help to **move** monoglycerides and fatty acids **towards** the **epithelium**. Because micelles constantly break up and reform they can 'release' monoglycerides and fatty acids, allowing them to be absorbed — whole micelles are **not** taken up across the epithelium. **Monoglycerides** and **fatty acids** are **lipid-soluble**, so can **diffuse** directly across the epithelial cell membrane.

Amino acids

Amino acids are absorbed in a similar way to glucose and galactose. **Sodium ions are actively transported** out of the epithelial cells into the ileum itself. They then **diffuse** back into the cells through **sodium-dependent transporter proteins** in the epithelial cell membranes, carrying the amino acids with them.

Practice Questions

Q1 What is the function of amylase in digestion?
Q2 Describe the role of bile salts in lipid digestion.

Exam Question

Q1 Some people suffer from lactose intolerance.
This can be caused by an inability to break down lactose in the upper small intestine.
a) Suggest which disaccharidase enzyme is deficient or missing in people who are lactose-intolerant. [1 mark]
b) How are the digestion products of lactose absorbed across the epithelial cells of the ileum? [2 marks]

Crikey, this all looks a bit tricky to digest... belch...

Don't panic. There's a lot to take in here but as long as you break it down a bit (ha, just like digestion) then it's not too bad. You can't escape learning what all the enzymes act on, but helpfully their names are usually linked to what they do — maltase breaks down maltose, dipeptidases break down dipeptides. See, it's not as bad as it looks...

Haemoglobin

Haemoglobin's a protein that carries oxygen around the body. Different species have different versions of it depending on where each species lives. All of which adds up to two pages of no-holds-barred fun...

Oxygen is Carried Round the Body by Haemoglobin

1) **Red blood cells** contain **haemoglobin** (Hb).

2) Haemoglobin is a large **protein** with a **quaternary** structure (see p. 8 for more) — it's made up of **more than one** polypeptide chain (**four** of them in fact).

3) Each chain has a **haem group**, which contains an **iron ion** (see page 23) and gives haemoglobin its **red** colour.

4) Haemoglobin has a **high affinity for oxygen** — each molecule can carry **four oxygen molecules**.

5) In the lungs, oxygen **joins** to haemoglobin in red blood cells to form **oxyhaemoglobin**.

6) This is a **reversible reaction** — when oxygen leaves oxyhaemoglobin (**dissociates** from it) near the body cells, it turns back to haemoglobin.

> 'Affinity' for oxygen means 'tendency to combine with' oxygen.

$$Hb + 4O_2 \rightleftharpoons HbO_8$$
$$\text{haemoglobin} + \text{oxygen} \rightleftharpoons \text{oxyhaemoglobin}$$

There are many **chemically similar** types of haemoglobin found in many different organisms, all of which carry out the **same function**. As well as being found in all vertebrates, haemoglobin is found in earthworms, starfish, some insects, some plants and even in some bacteria.

Haemoglobin Saturation Depends on the Partial Pressure of Oxygen

1) The **partial pressure** of **oxygen** (pO_2) is a measure of **oxygen concentration**. The **greater** the concentration of dissolved oxygen in cells, the **higher** the partial pressure.

2) Similarly, the **partial pressure** of **carbon dioxide** (pCO_2) is a measure of the concentration of CO_2 in a cell.

3) Haemoglobin's **affinity** for oxygen **varies** depending on the **partial pressure** of **oxygen**:

> Oxygen **loads onto** haemoglobin to form oxyhaemoglobin where there's a **high pO_2**. Oxyhaemoglobin **unloads** its oxygen where there's a **lower pO_2**.

4) Oxygen enters blood capillaries at the **alveoli** in the **lungs**. Alveoli have a **high pO_2** so oxygen **loads onto** haemoglobin to form oxyhaemoglobin.

5) When **cells respire**, they use up oxygen — this **lowers the pO_2**. Red blood cells deliver oxyhaemoglobin to respiring tissues, where it unloads its oxygen.

6) The haemoglobin then returns to the lungs to pick up more oxygen.

There was no use pretending — the partial pressure of CH_4 had just increased, and Keith knew who was to blame.

Dissociation Curves Show How Affinity for Oxygen Varies

A **dissociation curve** shows how **saturated** the haemoglobin is with oxygen at any given partial pressure.

> 100% saturation means every haemoglobin molecule is carrying the maximum of 4 molecules of oxygen.

> 0% saturation means none of the haemoglobin molecules are carrying any oxygen.

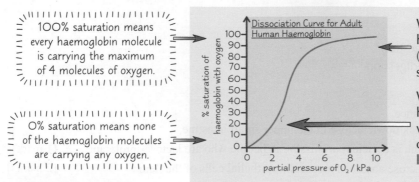

Dissociation Curve for Adult Human Haemoglobin

% saturation of haemoglobin with oxygen

partial pressure of O_2 / kPa

Where pO_2 is high (e.g. in the lungs), haemoglobin has a **high affinity** for oxygen (i.e. it will **readily combine** with oxygen), so it has a **high saturation** of oxygen.

Where pO_2 is low (e.g. in respiring tissues), haemoglobin has a **low affinity** for oxygen, which means it **releases oxygen** rather than combines with it. That's why it has a **low saturation** of oxygen.

The graph is '**S-shaped**' because when haemoglobin (Hb) combines with the **first O_2 molecule**, its **shape alters** in a way that makes it **easier** for other molecules to join too. But as the Hb starts to become saturated, it gets **harder** for more oxygen molecules to join. As a result, the curve has a **steep** bit in the middle where it's really easy for oxygen molecules to join, and **shallow** bits at each end where it's harder. When the curve is steep, a **small change in pO_2** causes a **big change** in the **amount of oxygen** carried by the Hb.

Haemoglobin

Carbon Dioxide Concentration Affects Oxygen Unloading

To complicate matters, haemoglobin gives up its oxygen **more readily** at **higher partial pressures of carbon dioxide** (pCO_2). It's a cunning way of getting more oxygen to cells during activity.

1) When cells respire they produce carbon dioxide, which **raises the pCO_2**.

2) This increases the rate of **oxygen unloading** (i.e. the rate at which oxyhaemoglobin **dissociates** to form haemoglobin and oxygen) — so the dissociation curve '**shifts**' right. The saturation of blood with oxygen is **lower** for a given pO_2, meaning that **more oxygen** is being **released**.

3) This is called the **Bohr effect**.

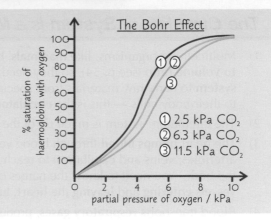

The Bohr Effect

① 2.5 kPa CO_2
② 6.3 kPa CO_2
③ 11.5 kPa CO_2

% saturation of haemoglobin with oxygen

partial pressure of oxygen / kPa

Haemoglobin is Different in Different Organisms

Different organisms have different **types** of haemoglobin with different **oxygen transporting capacities**. Having a particular type of haemoglobin is an **adaptation** that helps the organism to **survive** in a **particular environment**.

1) Organisms that live in environments with a **low concentration of oxygen** have haemoglobin with a **higher affinity** for oxygen than human haemoglobin — the dissociation curve is to the **left** of ours.

2) Organisms that are very **active** and have a **high oxygen demand** have haemoglobin with a **lower affinity** for oxygen than human haemoglobin — the curve is to the **right** of the human one.

A = animal living in depleted oxygen environment, e.g. a lugworm.
B = animal living at high altitude where the partial pressure of oxygen is lower, e.g. a llama in the Andes.
C = human dissociation curve.
D = active animal with a high respiratory rate living where there's plenty of available oxygen, e.g. a hawk.

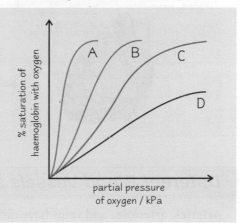

% saturation of haemoglobin with oxygen

partial pressure of oxygen / kPa

Practice Questions

Q1 How many oxygen molecules can each haemoglobin molecule carry?

Q2 Where in the body would you find a low partial pressure of oxygen?

Q3 Why are oxygen dissociation curves S-shaped?

Exam Question

Q1 a) Haemoglobin is a protein with a quaternary structure. Explain what this means. [1 mark]

b) The graph shows the normal oxygen dissociation curve for human haemoglobin.

i) On the graph, sketch the curve you would expect to see for a human in a high carbon dioxide environment. Explain the position of your sketched curve. [3 marks]

ii) Earthworms live in a low oxygen environment. On the graph, sketch the curve you would expect to see for an earthworm. [1 mark]

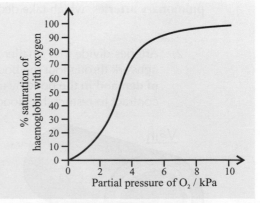

% saturation of haemoglobin with oxygen

Partial pressure of O_2 / kPa

There's more than partial pressure on you to learn this stuff...

Well, I don't know about you but after these pages I need a sit down. Most people get their knickers in a twist over partial pressure — it's not the easiest thing to understand. Whenever you see it written down just pretend it says concentration instead (cross it out and write concentration if you like) and everything should become clearer. Honest.

The Circulatory System

As the name suggests, the circulatory system is responsible for circulating stuff around the body — blood, to be specific. Most multicellular organisms (mammals, insects, fish) have a circulatory system of some type.

The **Circulatory System** is a **Mass Transport System**

1) Multicellular organisms, like **mammals**, have a **low surface area to volume ratio** (see p. 54), so they need a specialised **transport system** to carry raw materials from specialised **exchange organs** to their body cells — this is the **circulatory system**.

2) The circulatory system is made up of the **heart** and **blood vessels**.

3) The heart **pumps blood** through blood vessels (arteries, arterioles, veins and capillaries) to reach different parts of the body. You need to **know** the names of **all** the blood vessels **entering** and **leaving** the **heart**, **lungs** and **kidneys**. ➞

4) Blood transports **respiratory gases**, products of **digestion**, **metabolic wastes** and **hormones** round the body.

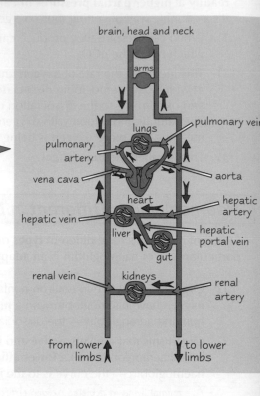

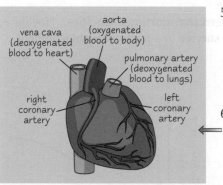

5) There are **two circuits**. One circuit takes blood from the **heart** to the **lungs**, then **back to the heart**. The other loop takes blood around the **rest of the body**.

6) The heart has its own blood supply — the left and right **coronary arteries**.

Different Blood Vessels are Adapted for **Different Functions**

Arteries, **arterioles** and **veins** have different **characteristics**, and you need to know **why**...

1) **Arteries** carry blood **from** the heart **to** the rest of the body. Their walls are thick and **muscular** and have elastic tissue to **stretch** and **recoil** as the heart beats, which helps **maintain** the **high pressure**. The inner lining (**endothelium**) is **folded**, allowing the artery to **stretch** — this also helps it to maintain high pressure. All arteries carry **oxygenated** blood except for the **pulmonary arteries**, which take deoxygenated blood to the lungs.

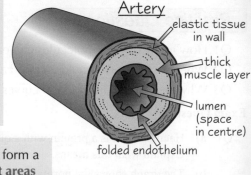

2) Arteries divide into smaller vessels called **arterioles**. These form a network throughout the body. Blood is directed to different **areas of demand** in the body by **muscles** inside the arterioles, which contract to restrict the blood flow or relax to allow full blood flow.

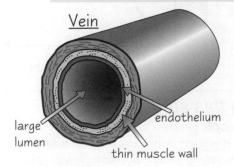

3) **Veins** take blood back **to the heart** under **low pressure**. They have a **wider lumen** than equivalent arteries, with **very little elastic** or **muscle tissue**. Veins contain **valves** to stop the blood flowing backwards. Blood flow through the veins is helped by contraction of the **body muscles** surrounding them. All veins carry **deoxygenated** blood (because oxygen has been used up by body cells), except for the **pulmonary veins**, which carry oxygenated blood to the heart from the lungs.

The Circulatory System

Substances are Exchanged between Blood and Body Tissues at Capillaries

Arterioles branch into **capillaries**, which are the **smallest** of the blood vessels. Substances (e.g. glucose and oxygen) are **exchanged** between cells and capillaries, so they're adapted for **efficient diffusion**.

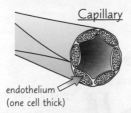
Capillary
endothelium
(one cell thick)

1) They're always found very **near cells in exchange tissues** (e.g. alveoli in the lungs), so there's a **short diffusion pathway**.

2) Their walls are only **one cell thick**, which also shortens the diffusion pathway.

3) There are a large number of capillaries, to **increase surface area** for exchange. Networks of capillaries in tissue are called **capillary beds**.

Tissue Fluid is Formed from Blood

Tissue fluid is the fluid that **surrounds cells** in tissues. It's made from **small molecules** that leave the blood plasma, e.g. oxygen, water and nutrients. (Unlike blood, tissue fluid **doesn't** contain **red blood cells** or **big proteins**, because they're **too large** to be pushed out through the capillary walls.) Cells take in oxygen and nutrients from the tissue fluid, and release metabolic waste into it. In a **capillary bed**, substances move out of the capillaries, into the tissue fluid, by **pressure filtration**:

1) At the **start** of the capillary bed, nearest the arteries, the **hydrostatic (liquid) pressure** inside the capillaries is **greater** than the hydrostatic pressure in the tissue fluid.

2) This **difference** in hydrostatic pressure means an overall outward pressure **forces fluid out** of the **capillaries** and into the **spaces** around the cells, forming **tissue fluid**.

3) As fluid leaves, the hydrostatic pressure **reduces** in the **capillaries** — so the hydrostatic pressure is much **lower** at the **venule end** of the capillary bed (the end that's nearest to the veins).

4) Due to the fluid loss, and an increasing concentration of plasma proteins (which don't leave the capillaries), the **water potential** at the **venule end** of the capillary bed is **lower** than the water potential in the **tissue fluid**.

5) This means that some **water re-enters** the capillaries from the tissue fluid at the venule end by **osmosis** (see p. 40 for more on osmosis).

Any **excess** tissue fluid is drained into the **lymphatic system** (a network of tubes that acts a bit like a drain), which transports this excess fluid from the tissues and dumps it back into the circulatory system.

red blood cell
blood plasma
capillary
tissue cell
tissue fluid

Blood from arteriole
capillary bed
tissue
Blood to venule

water

High blood pressure means a high hydrostatic pressure in the capillaries, which can lead to an accumulation of tissue fluid in the tissues.

Practice Questions

Q1 Name all the blood vessels entering and leaving the heart.

Q2 List four types of blood vessel.

Q3 Explain why water returns to the capillary at the venule end of the capillary bed.

Exam Questions

Q1 Describe two structural features of an artery and explain how each feature relates to its function. [4 marks]

Q2 At the arteriole end of a capillary bed the hydrostatic pressure is 5.1 kPa in a capillary and 0.13 kPa in the space around the cells. Explain the effect this has on the movement of fluid between the capillary and cell space. [2 marks]

If blood can handle transport this efficiently, the trains have no excuse...

Four hours I was waiting at the train station this weekend. Four hours! Anyway, you may have noticed that biologists are obsessed with the relationship between structure and function, so whenever you're learning the structure of something, make sure you know how this relates to its function. Veins, arteries and capillaries are good examples.

The Heart

As I'm sure you know already, your heart is the 'pump' that gets oxygenated blood to your cells. It's very important, so unsurprisingly, you need to know how it works. You'll find that these pages definitely get to the heart of it... groan.

The **Heart** Consists of **Two Muscular Pumps**

1) The diagram on the right shows the **internal structure** of the heart.

2) The **right side** pumps **deoxygenated blood** to the **lungs** and the **left side** pumps **oxygenated blood** to the **whole body**.

3) Note — the **left and right sides** are **reversed** on the diagram, cos it's the left and right of the person that the heart belongs to.

The diagram is a good reminder that veins carry blood into the heart (vena cava and pulmonary vein) and arteries carry blood away from it (pulmonary artery and aorta).

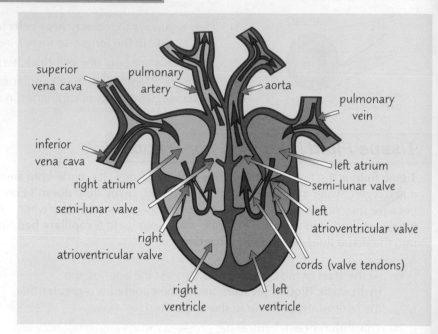

You Need to Know What the Different Parts of the Heart Do

Each bit of the heart is adapted to do its job effectively.

1) The **left ventricle** of the heart has **thicker**, more muscular walls than the **right ventricle**, because it needs to contract powerfully to pump blood all the way round the body. The right side only needs to get blood to the lungs, which are nearby.

2) The **ventricles** have **thicker walls** than the **atria**, because they have to push blood out of the heart whereas the atria just need to push blood a short distance into the ventricles.

3) The **atrioventricular (AV) valves** link the atria to the ventricles and **stop blood flowing back** into the atria when the ventricles contract.

4) The **semi-lunar (SL) valves** link the ventricles to the pulmonary artery and aorta, and **stop blood flowing back** into the heart after the ventricles contract.

5) The **cords** attach the atrioventricular valves to the ventricles to stop them being forced up into the atria when the ventricles contract.

Captain Jeff reckoned the lock gates were just like a big heart valve — with enough pressure he would be able to force his way through.

The **valves** only **open one way** — whether they're open or closed depends on the relative **pressure** of the heart chambers. If there's higher pressure **behind** a valve, it's forced **open**, but if pressure is higher **in front** of the valve it's forced **shut**. This means blood only flows in **one direction** through the heart.

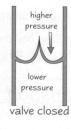

The Heart

The *Cardiac Cycle* Pumps Blood Round the Body

The cardiac cycle is an ongoing sequence of **contraction** and **relaxation** of the atria and ventricles that keeps blood **continuously** circulating round the body. The **volume** of the atria and ventricles **changes** as they contract and relax. **Pressure** changes also occur, due to the changes in chamber volume (e.g. decreasing the volume of a chamber by contraction will increase the pressure in a chamber). The cardiac cycle can be simplified into three stages:

① Ventricles relax, atria contract

The **ventricles are relaxed**. The **atria contract**, decreasing the volume of the chambers and **increasing** the **pressure** inside the chambers. This **pushes** the blood into the **ventricles**. There's a slight **increase** in **ventricular pressure** and **chamber volume** as the **ventricles receive the ejected blood** from the contracting atria.

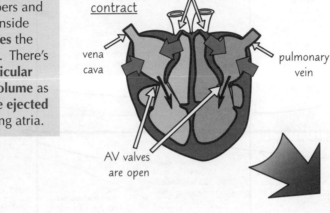

Cardiac contraction is also called systole and relaxation is called diastole.

② Ventricles contract, atria relax

The **atria relax**. The **ventricles contract** (decreasing their volume), **increasing** their **pressure**. The pressure becomes **higher** in the ventricles than the atria, which forces the **AV valves shut** to prevent back-flow. The **pressure** in the **ventricles** is also **higher** than in the **aorta** and **pulmonary artery**, which forces **open** the **SL valves** and blood is forced out into these arteries.

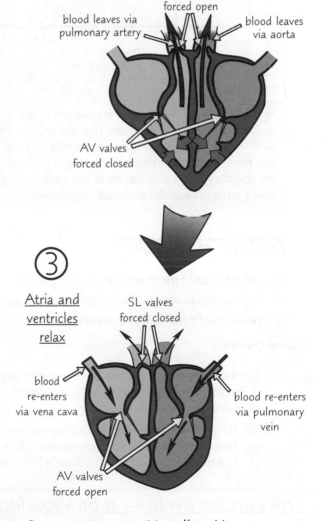

③ Ventricles relax, atria relax

The **ventricles and the atria both relax**. The higher pressure in the pulmonary artery and aorta closes the SL valves to prevent back-flow into the ventricles. Blood returns to the heart and the **atria fill again** due to the higher pressure in the vena cava and pulmonary vein. In turn this starts to **increase** the **pressure** of the atria. As the ventricles continue to **relax**, their **pressure falls below the pressure of the atria** and so the **AV valves open**. This allows blood to flow **passively** (without being pushed by atrial contraction) into the ventricles from the atria. The atria contract, and the whole process begins again.

There's a bit about interpreting cardiac cycle data on the next page. So turn over now — it's well exciting...

The Heart

You Might be Asked to **Interpret Data** on the **Cardiac Cycle**

You may well be asked to analyse or interpret **data** about the changes in **pressure** and **volume** during the cardiac cycle. Here are two examples of the kind of things you might get:

Example 1

① Ventricles relaxed Atria contract

② Ventricles contract Atria relax

③ Ventricles relax Atria relaxed

KEY
— ventricles
— atria

pressure increase due to contraction

pressure increase due to contraction

pressure decrease as ventricles relax

A

pressure decrease as atria relax

pressure increase as atria fill

pressure decrease as some blood passively moves from atria into ventricle

pressure increase as atria continue to fill

slight increase due to passive filling

C

pressure increase as ventricles fill

Pressure / mmHg

ventricles stretch while filling

volume decrease due to contraction

atria expand as they relax and fill with blood

B

some blood passively moves from atria to ventricle as AV valves open

ventricles expand as they relax and fill with blood

Volume / ml

Time / s

If you get a graph you could be asked **questions** like this:

1) **When** does blood start flowing into the **aorta**? At **point A**, the ventricles are **contracting** (and the AV valves are shut), forcing blood into the aorta.

2) Why is **ventricular volume decreasing** at **point B**? The ventricles are **contracting, reducing** the volume of the chamber.

3) Are the **semi-lunar valves** open or closed at **point C**? **Closed.** The ventricles are **relaxed** and **refilling**, so the pressure is **higher** in the **pulmonary artery** and **aorta**, forcing the SL valves **closed**.

Example 2

You may have to describe the changes in pressure and volume shown by a **diagram**, like the one on the right. In this diagram the **AV valves** are **open**. So you know that the **pressure** in the **atria** is **higher** than in the **ventricles**. So you also know that the **atria are contracting** because that's what causes the **increase** in **pressure**.

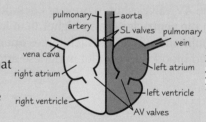

pulmonary artery — — aorta
— SL valves — pulmonary vein
vena cava —
right atrium — — left atrium
right ventricle — — left ventricle
— AV valves

The left ventricle has a thicker wall than the right ventricle and so it contracts more forcefully. This means the pressure is higher in the left ventricle (and in the aorta compared to the pulmonary artery).

Practice Questions

Q1 Which side of the heart carries oxygenated blood?

Q2 Explain the purpose of the semi-lunar valves.

Q3 Name the blood vessel that carries blood from the lungs to the heart.

Exam Question

Q1 The table opposite shows the blood pressure in two heart chambers at different times during part of the cardiac cycle. Use the data in the table to answer the following questions.

| | Blood pressure / kPa | |
Time / s	Left atrium	Left ventricle
0.0	0.6	0.5
0.1	1.3	0.8
0.2	0.4	6.9
0.3	0.5	16.5
0.4	0.9	7.0

a) Between what times are the AV valves shut? [1 mark]

b) Between what times do the ventricles start to relax? [1 mark]

c) Calculate the percentage increase in left ventricle blood pressure between 0.0 s and 0.3 s. [1 mark]

The cardiac cycle — a bewilderingly complicated pump-action bicycle...

Three whole pages to learn here, all full of really important stuff. If you understand all the pressure and volume changes then whether you get a diagram, graph or something else in the exam, you'll be able to interpret it, no probs.

Cardiovascular Disease

Diseases associated with your heart and blood vessels are called cardiovascular diseases (cardio = heart, vascular = blood vessels — geddit?). There are certain factors that increase the risk of developing cardiovascular disease.

Most **Cardiovascular Disease** Starts with **Atheroma** Formation

1) The wall of an artery is made up of **several layers** (see p. 70).
2) The **endothelium** (inner lining) is usually smooth and unbroken.
3) If **damage** occurs to the endothelium (e.g. by high blood pressure) **white blood cells** (mostly macrophages) and **lipids** (fat) from the blood, clump together under the lining to form **fatty streaks**.
4) Over time, more white blood cells, lipids and **connective tissue** build up and harden to form a **fibrous plaque** called an **atheroma**.
5) This plaque **partially blocks** the lumen of the **artery** and **restricts blood flow**, which causes **blood pressure** to **increase**.
6) **Coronary heart disease (CHD)** is a type of cardiovascular disease. It occurs when the coronary arteries have **lots of atheromas** in them, which **restricts blood flow** to the **heart** muscle. It can lead to **myocardial infarction** (see below).

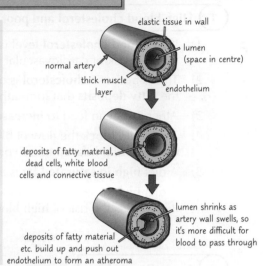

elastic tissue in wall
lumen (space in centre)
normal artery
thick muscle layer
endothelium

deposits of fatty material, dead cells, white blood cells and connective tissue

lumen shrinks as artery wall swells, so it's more difficult for blood to pass through

deposits of fatty material etc. build up and push out endothelium to form an atheroma

Atheromas Increase the **Risk** of **Aneurysm** and **Thrombosis**

Two types of **disease** that affect the **arteries** are:

Aneurysm — a **balloon-like swelling** of the artery.

1) Atheroma plaques **damage** and **weaken arteries**. They also **narrow** arteries, **increasing blood pressure**.
2) When **blood** travels through a weakened artery at **high pressure**, it may **push** the **inner layers** of the artery **through the outer elastic layer** to form a **balloon-like swelling** — an **aneurysm**.
3) This aneurysm may **burst**, causing a **haemorrhage** (bleeding).

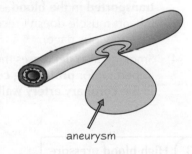

aneurysm

Thrombosis — formation of a **blood clot**.

1) An atheroma plaque can **rupture** (burst through) the **endothelium** (inner lining) of an artery.
2) This **damages** the artery wall and leaves a **rough** surface.
3) **Platelets** and **fibrin** (a protein) accumulate at the site of damage and form a **blood clot** (a thrombus).
4) This blood clot can cause a complete **blockage** of the artery, or it can become **dislodged** and block a blood vessel elsewhere in the body.
5) **Debris** from the rupture can cause another blood clot to form further down the artery.

Interrupted Blood Flow to the **Heart** can Cause a **Myocardial Infarction**

1) The **heart muscle** is supplied with **blood** by the **coronary arteries**.
2) This blood contains the **oxygen** needed by heart muscle cells to carry out **respiration**.
3) If a coronary artery becomes **completely blocked** (e.g. by a **blood clot**) an area of the heart muscle will be totally **cut off** from its blood supply, receiving **no oxygen**.
4) This causes a **myocardial infarction** — more commonly known as a **heart attack**.
5) A heart attack can cause **damage** and **death** of the **heart muscle**.
6) **Symptoms** include **pain** in the chest and upper body, **shortness of breath** and **sweating**.
7) If **large areas** of the heart are affected complete **heart failure** can occur, which is often **fatal**.

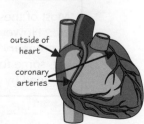

outside of heart
coronary arteries

Cardiovascular Disease

Some *Factors Increase* the *Risk* of *Cardiovascular Disease*

Some of the most common risk factors for cardiovascular disease are:

1) High blood cholesterol and poor diet

1) If the **blood cholesterol level** is **high** (above 240 mg per 100 cm³) then the risk of cardiovascular disease is increased.

2) This is because **cholesterol** is one of the main constituents of the **fatty deposits** that form **atheromas** (see previous page).

3) Atheromas can lead to **increased blood pressure** and **blood clots**.

4) This could **block** the flow of blood to **coronary arteries**, which could cause a **myocardial infarction** (see previous page for details).

5) A diet **high in saturated fat** is associated with high blood cholesterol levels.

6) A diet **high in salt** also **increases** the **risk** of cardiovascular disease because it increases the risk of **high blood pressure** (see below).

John decided to live on the edge and ordered a fry-up.

2) Cigarette smoking

1) Both **nicotine** and **carbon monoxide**, found in **cigarette smoke**, increase the risk of cardiovascular disease.

2) **Nicotine** increases the risk of **high blood pressure** (see below).

3) **Carbon monoxide** combines with **haemoglobin** and **reduces** the amount of **oxygen transported** in the **blood**, and so reduces the amount of oxygen available to tissues. If heart muscle doesn't receive enough oxygen it can lead to a **heart attack** (see previous page).

4) Smoking also **decreases** the **amount of antioxidants** in the blood — these are important for **protecting cells** from damage. Fewer antioxidants means **cell damage** in the **coronary artery walls** is more likely, and this can lead to **atheroma formation**.

3) High blood pressure

1) High blood pressure **increases** the **risk** of **damage** to the **artery walls**.

2) Damaged walls have an **increased risk** of atheroma formation, causing a further increase in blood pressure.

3) Atheromas can also cause **blood clots** to form (see previous page).

4) A blood clot could **block flow** of **blood** to the heart muscle, possibly resulting in **myocardial infarction**.

5) So **anything** that **increases** blood pressure also increases the risk of **cardiovascular disease**, e.g. being **overweight**, **not exercising** and excessive **alcohol** consumption.

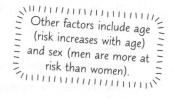

Other factors include age (risk increases with age) and sex (men are more at risk than women).

Most of these factors are within our **control** — a person can **choose** to smoke, eat fatty foods, etc. However, some risk factors can't be controlled, such as having a **genetic predisposition** to coronary heart disease or having high blood pressure as a result of **another condition**, e.g. some forms of diabetes. Even so, the risk of developing cardiovascular disease can be reduced by removing as many **risk factors** as you possibly can.

Cardiovascular Disease

You May Have to *Interpret* Data on *Risk Factors* and *Cardiovascular Disease*

Example: The graph shows the results of a study involving **27 939 American women**. The **LDL cholesterol level** was **measured** for each woman. These women were then **followed** for an average of **8 years** and the **occurrence** of **cardiovascular events** (e.g. heart attack, surgery on coronary arteries) or **death** from cardiovascular diseases was **recorded**. The **relative risk** of a cardiovascular event, **adjusted** for other factors that can affect cardiovascular disease, was then calculated.

Here are some of the things you might be asked to do:

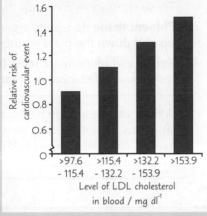

1) <u>Describe the data</u> — The **relative risk** of a cardiovascular event **increases** as the level of **LDL** cholesterol in the blood **increases**.

2) <u>Draw conclusions</u> — The graph shows a **positive correlation** between the **relative risk** of a cardiovascular event and the level of **LDL cholesterol** in the blood.

3) <u>Check any conclusions are valid</u> —
Make sure any conclusions **match** the data, e.g.
- This data only looked at **women** — no males were involved, so you can't say that this trend is true for **everyone**.
- You can't say that a high LDL cholesterol level is **correlated with** an increased risk of **heart attacks**, because the data shows **all** first cardiovascular events, including surgery on coronary arteries.
- Also, you can't conclude that a high LDL cholesterol level **caused** the increased relative risk of a cardiovascular event — there may be other reasons for the trend.

There's more on correlation and cause on page 108.

4) <u>Other things to think about</u> — A **large sample size** was used (27 939). Data based on large samples is **better** than data based on small samples. This is because a large sample is **more representative** of the whole population (i.e. it shares more of the various **characteristics** of the population).

You might also have to evaluate **conflicting evidence** associated with risk factors affecting cardiovascular disease. E.g. one study might conclude that a factor <u>isn't</u> a health risk, whereas another study might conclude that the **same** factor <u>is</u> a health risk.

1) If two studies have produced conflicting results, think about **why** that might be. Was it to do with **study design**? Was one study based on a **small sample size**? Did both studies take into account **other risk factors** (variables) that could have affected the results? Knowing whether both studies used **similar groups** can be helpful, e.g. same age, gender, etc.

2) Sometimes, the only way to **resolve** the problem of conflicting evidence is to **carry out more studies** and **collect more results**. Results need to be **reproduced** by **other scientists** before they're accepted.

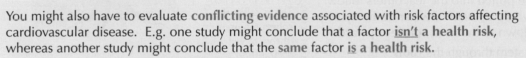

The way in which information is collected can also be important. Some studies rely on the results of questionnaires (e.g. asking people how many cigarettes they smoke). Questionnaires can be unreliable as people can tell fibs or give inaccurate information.

Practice Questions

Q1 Give three factors that can increase the risk of developing cardiovascular disease.

Exam Question

Q1 The results of a study involving 168 000 people in 63 countries have shown a strong correlation between waist measurement and risk of cardiovascular disease. Analysis of the results has shown that waist circumference is independently associated with cardiovascular disease.

    a) Give two reasons why the study provides strong evidence for a link between waist measurement and risk of cardiovascular disease.   **[2 marks]**

    b) Suggest why waist measurement might be related to risk of cardiovascular disease.   **[3 marks]**

Revision — increasing my risk of headache, stress, boredom...

There's a lot to take in on these pages... but make sure you understand the link between atheromas, thrombosis and heart attacks — basically an atheroma forms, which can cause thrombosis, which can lead to a heart attack. Anything that increases the chance of an atheroma forming (high blood pressure, smoking, fatty diet) is bad news for your heart...

Transport in Plants — Xylem

Transport in plants isn't really roads and railways, but I guess it's a bit like a flowing river that's carrying stuff around in a network of tubes. When you consider the movement of water, it's all about the xylem. It's pretty exciting stuff...

Two Types of Tissue are Involved in Transport in Plants

1) **Xylem tissue** transports **water** and **mineral ions** in solution. These substances move **up** the plant from the roots to the leaves.

2) **Phloem tissue** transports organic substances like **sugars** (also in solution) both **up and down** the plant — there's more about the phloem on pages 80-81.

3) Xylem and phloem are **mass transport systems** (see page 54) — they move substances over **large distances**.

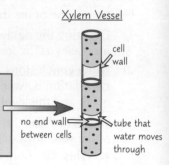

Xylem Vessel

cell wall

no end wall between cells

tube that water moves through

> **Xylem vessels** are the part of the xylem tissue that actually transports the water and ions. Xylem vessels are very **long, tube-like** structures formed from dead cells (vessel elements) joined end to end. There are **no end walls** on these cells, making an **uninterrupted tube** that allows water to pass up through the middle easily.

Water Moves Up a Plant Against the Force of Gravity

Cohesion and **tension** help water move up plants, from roots to leaves, against the force of gravity.

1) Water **evaporates** from the **leaves** at the 'top' of the xylem (this is transpiration — see below).

2) This creates **tension** (**suction**), which pulls more water into the leaf.

3) Water molecules are **cohesive** (they **stick together** — see page 21) so when some are pulled into the leaf others follow. This means the whole **column** of water in the **xylem**, from the leaves down to the roots, **moves upwards**.

4) **Water** enters the stem through the **roots**.

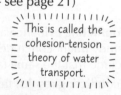

This is called the cohesion-tension theory of water transport.

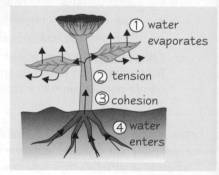

① water evaporates

② tension

③ cohesion

④ water enters

Transpiration is Loss of Water from a Plant's Surface

Transpiration is the **evaporation** of **water** from a plant's surface, especially the **leaves**.

1) Water **evaporates** from the moist cell walls and accumulates in the spaces between cells in the leaf.

2) When the **stomata** open (see page 57), it moves out of the leaf down the **concentration gradient** (there's more water inside the leaf than in the air outside).

Transpiration's really a side effect of photosynthesis — the plant needs to open its stomata to let in CO_2 so that it can produce glucose, but this also lets water out.

Four Main Factors Affect Transpiration Rate

1) **Light** — the **lighter** it is the **faster** the **transpiration rate** (i.e. there's a **positive correlation** between light intensity and transpiration rate). This is because the **stomata open** when it gets **light** to let in CO_2 for **photosynthesis**. When it's **dark** the stomata are usually **closed**, so there's little transpiration.

2) **Temperature** — the **higher the temperature** the **faster** the **transpiration rate**. Warmer water molecules have more energy so they **evaporate** from the cells inside the leaf **faster**. This **increases** the **concentration gradient** between the inside and outside of the leaf, making water **diffuse out** of the leaf **faster**.

3) **Humidity** — the **lower** the **humidity**, the **faster** the **transpiration rate** (i.e. there's a **negative correlation** between humidity and transpiration rate). If the air around the plant is **dry**, the **concentration gradient** between the leaf and the air is **increased**, which increases transpiration.

4) **Wind** — the **windier** it is, the **faster** the **transpiration rate**. Lots of air movement **blows away** water molecules from around the stomata. This **increases** the **concentration gradient**, which increases the rate of transpiration.

Transport in Plants — Xylem

A Potometer can be Used to Estimate Transpiration Rate

A **potometer** is a special piece of apparatus used to **estimate transpiration rates**. It actually measures **water uptake** by a plant, but it's **assumed** that water uptake by the plant is **directly related** to **water loss** by the **leaves**. You can use it to estimate how different factors **affect** the transpiration rate.

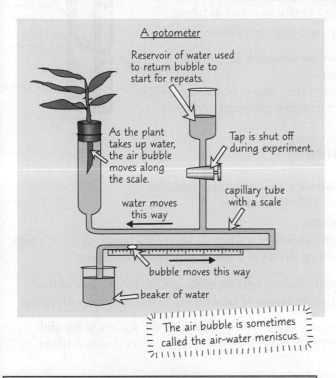

A potometer

Reservoir of water used to return bubble to start for repeats.

As the plant takes up water, the air bubble moves along the scale.

water moves this way

Tap is shut off during experiment.

capillary tube with a scale

bubble moves this way

beaker of water

The air bubble is sometimes called the air-water meniscus.

Here's what you'd do:

1) **Cut** a **shoot underwater** to prevent air from entering the xylem. Cut it at a **slant** to increase the surface area available for water uptake.

2) Assemble the potometer **in water** and insert the shoot **underwater**, so no air can enter.

3) Remove the apparatus from the water but keep the **end of the capillary tube submerged** in a beaker of water.

4) Check that the apparatus is **watertight** and **airtight**.

5) **Dry** the leaves, allow time for the shoot to **acclimatise**, and then **shut the tap**.

6) Remove the end of the capillary tube from the beaker of water until **one air bubble** has formed, then put the end of the tube back into the water.

7) Record the **starting position** of the **air bubble**.

8) Start a **stopwatch** and record the **distance** moved by the bubble **per unit time**, e.g. per hour. The **rate** of **air bubble movement** is an estimate of the **transpiration rate**.

9) Remember, only change **one variable** (e.g. temperature) at a time. All other **conditions** (e.g. light, humidity) must be kept **constant**.

You Might Have to Dissect Plants

You can **look at xylem** or **phloem** in **plant tissue** (e.g. part of a plant stem) under a **microscope**, and then **draw** them. But first you need to **dissect** the plant and **prepare** a section of the tissue. You can do this using the following method:

1) Use a **scalpel** (or razor blade) to cut a **cross-section** of the stem. Cut the sections as **thinly** as possible — thin sections are better for viewing under a microscope.

2) Use **tweezers** to gently place the cut sections in **water** until you come to use them. This stops them from **drying out**.

3) Transfer each section to a dish containing a **stain**, e.g. **toluidine blue O (TBO)**, and leave for one minute. TBO stains the **lignin** in the walls of the xylem vessels **blue-green**. This will let you see the **position** of the xylem vessels and examine their **structure**.

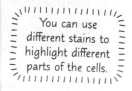

You can use different stains to highlight different parts of the cells.

4) **Rinse off** the sections in water and **mount** each one onto a slide (see page 30).

Practice Questions

Q1 What is the function of xylem tissue?

Q2 Give four factors that affect transpiration rate.

Q3 Name a piece of apparatus used to measure transpiration rate.

Exam Question

Q1 a) What is meant by the term transpiration? [1 mark]

    b) Describe how the cohesion-tension theory helps explain water movement in plants. [3 marks]

Xylem — not to be confused with Wylam, a small village in Northumberland...

So, one of the key things you need to take away from these pages is that xylem is the plant tissue that water is transported through. Water can make its way from the root to the leaves in the lovely xylem tissue and then some of it will end up being lost into the air from the plant's surfaces (particularly the leaves) via good ol' transpiration.

Transport in Plants — Phloem

Next up, it's time to look at phloem. I know, I almost can't contain my excitement. When it comes to the phloem it's all about moving dissolved organic substances around the plant, so it's a bit different to xylem.

Phloem Tissue is Adapted for Transporting Solutes

1) **Solutes** are **dissolved substances**. Phloem tissue **transports solutes** (mainly sugars like sucrose) round plants. Like xylem, phloem is formed from cells arranged in **tubes**.

2) **Sieve tube elements** and **companion cells** are important cell types in phloem tissue:

   - **Sieve tube elements** are living cells that form the **tube** for transporting solutes. They have no nucleus and few organelles, so...
   - ...there's a **companion cell** for each sieve tube element. They carry out living functions for sieve cells, e.g. providing the **energy** needed for the **active transport** of solutes.

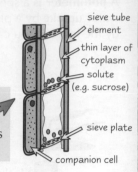

sieve tube element

thin layer of cytoplasm

solute (e.g. sucrose)

sieve plate

companion cell

Translocation is the Movement of Solutes

1) **Translocation** is the **movement** of solutes (e.g. sugars like sucrose, and amino acids) to **where they're needed** in a plant. Solutes are sometimes called **assimilates**.

2) It's an **energy-requiring** process that happens in the **phloem**.

3) Translocation moves solutes from '**sources**' to '**sinks**'. The **source** of a solute is **where it's made** (so it's at a **high concentration** there). The **sink** is the area where it's **used up** (so it's at a **lower concentration** there).

   E.g. the **source** for **sucrose** is usually the **leaves** (where it's made), and the **sinks** are the **other parts** of the plant, especially the **food storage organs** and the **meristems** (areas of growth) in the roots, stems and leaves.

4) **Enzymes** maintain a **concentration gradient** from the source to the sink by **changing** the solutes at the **sink** (e.g. by breaking them down or making them into something else). This makes sure there's always a **lower concentration** at the sink than at the source.

   E.g. in **potatoes**, **sucrose** is converted to **starch** in the **sink** areas, so there's always a **lower concentration** of sucrose **at the sink** than inside the phloem. This makes sure a **constant supply** of new sucrose reaches the sink from the phloem.

The *Mass Flow Hypothesis* Best Explains *Phloem Transport*

Scientists still aren't certain **exactly how** the solutes are transported from source to sink by **translocation**. The best supported theory is the **mass flow hypothesis**:

1
1) Active transport (see p. 42) is used to **actively load** the solutes (e.g. sucrose from photosynthesis) from **companion cells** into the **sieve tubes** of the phloem at the **source** (e.g. the **leaves**).

2) This **lowers** the **water potential** inside the sieve tubes, so water **enters** the tubes by **osmosis** from the **xylem** and **companion cells**.

3) This creates a **high pressure** inside the sieve tubes at the **source end** of the phloem.

2
1) At the **sink** end, **solutes** are removed from the phloem to be used up.

2) This **increases** the **water potential** inside the sieve tubes, so water also **leaves** the tubes by **osmosis**.

3) This **lowers the pressure** inside the sieve tubes.

3
1) The result is a **pressure gradient** from the **source** end to the **sink** end.

2) This gradient pushes solutes along the sieve tubes **towards the sink**.

3) When they reach the sink the solutes will be **used** (e.g. in respiration) or **stored** (e.g. as starch).

① SOURCE
low water potential, high pressure

water flow
solute flow

Water enters from xylem

companion cell

HIGH   Pressure gradient forces solutes down.

sieve plate

LOW   down.

plasmodesma

solute (e.g. sucrose)

Water flows to xylem

② SINK
high water potential, low pressure

Experiments have shown that some sucrose is transported also through the cell walls of the phloem.

The higher the **concentration of sucrose** at the source, the higher the **rate of translocation**.

Transport in Plants — Phloem

You Need to be Able to *Evaluate Evidence* For and Against *Mass Flow*

Supporting evidence

1) If a **ring** of **bark** (which includes the phloem, but not the xylem) is removed from a woody stem, a **bulge forms above** the ring. The fluid from the bulge has a **higher concentration** of **sugars** than the fluid from below the ring — this is evidence that there's a **downward flow** of sugars.

2) A **radioactive tracer** such as radioactive carbon (^{14}C) can be used to **track** the movement of organic substances in a plant (see below).

3) Pressure in the phloem can be investigated using **aphids** (they pierce the phloem, then their bodies are removed leaving the mouthparts behind, which allows the sap to flow out... gruesome). The sap flows out **quicker nearer the leaves** than further down the stem — this is evidence that there's a **pressure gradient**.

4) If a **metabolic inhibitor** (which stops ATP production) is put into the **phloem**, then **translocation stops** — this is evidence that **active transport** is involved.

Objections

1) Sugar travels to **many different sinks**, not just to the one with the **highest water potential**, as the model would suggest.

2) The **sieve plates** would create a **barrier** to mass flow. A **lot of pressure** would be needed for the solutes to get through at a reasonable rate.

> You could get asked about correlations and casual relationships in data relating to mass transport in plants. There's loads on correlation and cause on p. 108.

The *Translocation* of *Solutes* Can be *Demonstrated Experimentally*

Translocation of solutes in plants can be modelled in an experiment using **radioactive tracers**.

1) This can be done by supplying part of a plant (often a **leaf**) with an **organic substance** that has a **radioactive label**. One example is **carbon dioxide** containing the radioactive isotope ^{14}C. This radioactively-labelled CO_2 can be supplied to a single leaf by being pumped into a container which completely surrounds the leaf.

2) The radioactive carbon will then be **incorporated** into organic substances produced by the leaf (e.g. sugars produced by **photosynthesis**), which will be moved around the plant by **translocation**.

> Photosynthesis produces glucose. This is converted to sucrose for transport around the plant.

3) The movement of these substances can be tracked using a technique called **autoradiography**. To reveal where the radioactive tracer has **spread to** in a plant, the plant is killed (e.g. by freezing it using liquid nitrogen) and then the whole plant (or sections of it) is placed on **photographic film** — the radioactive substance is present wherever the film turns **black**.

4) The results demonstrate the translocation of substances from **source** to **sink** over time — for example, autoradiographs of plants **killed** at **different times** show an overall movement of solutes (e.g. products of photosynthesis) from the leaves **towards the roots**.

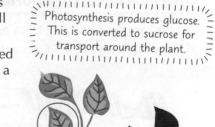

Leaf exposed to $^{14}CO_2$ gas

Autoradiograph of plant showing how radioactivity has spread from the leaf.

Practice Questions

Q1 According to the mass flow hypothesis, how is a pressure gradient set up in the phloem?

Exam Question

Q1 A scientist is investigating where the products of photosynthesis are translocated to in a plant. To do this several upper leaves of a plant were exposed to a radioactive tracer in the form of radioactively-labelled CO_2. The plant was then left for 24 hours before an autoradiograph of the whole plant was taken.

a) Explain how the leaves of the plant can act as a source in translocation. [1 mark]

b) The autoradiograph showed radioactivity in the roots and fruits.
   Explain why radioactivity was seen in the fruits. [1 mark]

Human mass flow — running out of the hall at the end of an exam...

The mass flow hypothesis is just the best theory that scientists have come up with so far. If other evidence came along, a different theory could be developed based on the new findings. It could happen tomorrow, you never know...

DNA, Genes and Chromosomes

DNA can be cruel — it gave me two feet, but made me bad at football... OK, maybe that's not completely DNA's fault. These pages give you plenty of info on how DNA is packaged, what genes are and how they code for stuff.

DNA is **Stored Differently** in Different Organisms

Although the **structure** of DNA is the same in all organisms, **eukaryotic** and **prokaryotic** cells store DNA in slightly different ways. (For a recap on the differences between prokaryotic and eukaryotic cells see pages 24 and 28.)

Nuclear Eukaryotic DNA is **Linear** and Associated with **Proteins**

1) Eukaryotic cells contain **linear** DNA molecules that exist as **chromosomes** — thread-like structures, each made up of **one long molecule** of DNA. Chromosomes are found in the **nucleus**.

2) The DNA molecule is **really long** so, it has to be **wound up** so it can **fit** into the nucleus.

3) The DNA molecule is wound around **proteins** called **histones**.

4) Histone proteins also help to **support** the DNA.

5) The DNA (and protein) is then coiled up **very tightly** to make a **compact chromosome**.

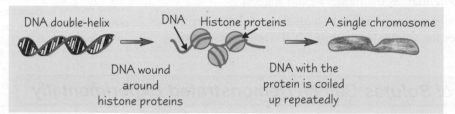

DNA double-helix   DNA   Histone proteins   A single chromosome

DNA wound around histone proteins

DNA with the protein is coiled up repeatedly

Eukaryotic cells include animal and plant cells. Prokaryotic cells are generally bacteria.

6) The **mitochondria** and **chloroplasts** in eukaryotic cells also have their **own** DNA. This is pretty similar to prokaryotic DNA (see below) because it's **circular** and **shorter** than DNA molecules in the nucleus. It's **not associated** with **histone proteins**.

DNA Molecules are **Shorter** and **Circular** in **Prokaryotes**

1) Prokaryotes also carry DNA as **chromosomes** — but the DNA molecules are **shorter** and **circular**.

2) The DNA **isn't** wound around histones — it condenses to fit in the cell by **supercoiling**.

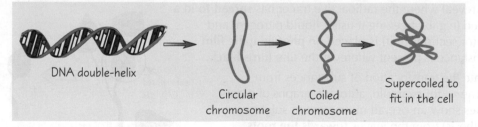

DNA double-helix

Circular chromosome

Coiled chromosome

Supercoiled to fit in the cell

If one more person confused Clifford with supercoiled DNA, he'd have 'em.

DNA Contains **Genes**

1) A **gene** is a **sequence** of **DNA bases** (see p. 16) that codes for either a **polypeptide** or **functional RNA** (see below).

2) The sequence of **amino acids** in a polypeptide forms the **primary structure** of a **protein** (see p. 8).

3) Different polypeptides have a **different number** and **order** of amino acids. It's the **order** of **bases** in a gene that determines the **order of amino acids** in a particular **polypeptide**.

4) Each amino acid is coded for by a sequence of **three bases** in a gene called a **triplet**. ⟹

5) To make a **polypeptide**, DNA is first copied into **messenger RNA** (mRNA). This is the first stage of **protein synthesis** (see p. 84).

6) Genes that don't code for a polypeptide code for **functional RNA** instead. Functional RNA is RNA molecules other than mRNA, which perform **special tasks** during protein synthesis, e.g. **tRNA** (see p. 84) and **ribosomal RNA** (rRNA), which forms part of ribosomes.

Bases on DNA
G T C T G A
DNA triplet = one amino acid

> A cell's **GENOME** is the **complete** set of **genes** in the cell.
> A cell's **PROTEOME** is the **full range** of **proteins** that the cell is able to produce.

DNA, Genes and Chromosomes

Most DNA in Eukaryotic Cells Doesn't Code for Polypeptides

1) **Some** genes don't code for **polypeptides** at all — they code for **functional RNA** (see previous page).

2) In **eukaryotic** DNA, genes that do code for **polypeptides** contain **sections** that **don't code** for amino acids.

3) These sections of DNA are called **introns**. There can be several introns within a gene.

4) All the bits of a gene that do code for amino acids are called **exons**.

5) **Introns** are **removed** during **protein synthesis** — so they **don't** affect the amino acid **order**. Their purpose isn't known for sure. (Prokaryotic DNA **doesn't** have introns.)

6) Eukaryotic DNA also contains regions of **multiple repeats** outside of genes.

7) These are DNA sequences that **repeat** over and over. For example: CCTTCCTTCCTT.

8) These areas **don't code** for amino acids either, so they're called **non-coding repeats**.

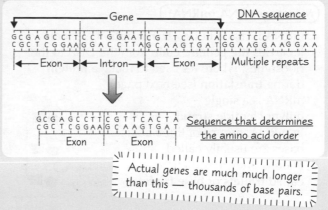

Genes Can Exist in Different Forms Called Alleles

1) A gene can exist in more than one form. These forms are called **alleles**.

2) The order of bases in each allele is slightly different, so they code for **slightly different versions** of the **same polypeptide**. For example, the gene that determines **blood type** exists as one of three alleles — one determines type O, another type A and the other type B.

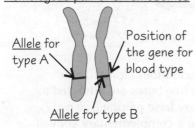

Homologous pair of chromosomes

Allele for type A

Position of the gene for blood type

Allele for type B

In a **eukaryotic** cell nucleus, DNA is stored as **chromosomes**. Humans have **23 pairs** of chromosomes, 46 in total — two number 1s, two number 2s, two number 3s, etc. Pairs of matching chromosomes (e.g. the 1s) are called **homologous pairs**.

In a homologous pair, both chromosomes are the same size and have the **same genes**, although they could have **different alleles**. Alleles coding for the same characteristic will be found at the same **fixed position (locus)** on each chromosome in a homologous pair.

Practice Questions

Q1 What is a DNA triplet?

Q2 What is an intron?

Q3 What are non-coding repeats?

Q4 What is a locus?

Exam Questions

Q1 Describe how DNA is stored in eukaryotic cells. [5 marks]

Q2 A scientist is studying a DNA sequence that is made up of 3800 nucleotide pairs. Exons account for 672 of the nucleotide pairs. Introns account for 3128 of the nucleotide pairs. The sequence codes for a section of a polypeptide. How many amino acids will make up this section of the polypeptide? [2 marks]

Exons stay in, introns go out, in, out, in, out, and shake it all about...

Quite a few terms to learn here, I'm afraid. Some are a bit confusing too. Just try to remember which way round they go. Introns are the non-coding regions, but exons are extremely important — they actually code for the polypeptide.

RNA and Protein Synthesis

Protein synthesis involves two stages — transcription and translation. They both involve RNA.

There's **More Than One** Type of **RNA**

Remember, RNA is a **single** polynucleotide strand and it contains **uracil** (**U**) as a base instead of thymine (see p. 16). Uracil **always pairs** with **adenine** during protein synthesis. RNA isn't all the same though. You need to know about:

Messenger RNA (mRNA)

mRNA is made during **transcription** (see below). It **carries the genetic code** from the DNA to the ribosomes, where it's used to make a **protein** during **translation** (see next page). mRNA is a **single polynucleotide strand**. In mRNA, groups of three adjacent bases are usually called **codons** (they're sometimes called **triplets** or **base triplets**).

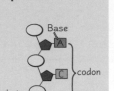

Base
A
C } codon
Phosphate
Ribose sugar
U

Transfer RNA (tRNA)

tRNA is involved in **translation**. It **carries** the amino acids that are used to make **proteins** to the **ribosomes**. tRNA is a **single polynucleotide strand** that's folded into a **clover shape**. **Hydrogen bonds** between **specific base pairs** hold the molecule in this shape. Every tRNA molecule has a **specific sequence** of **three bases** at one end called an **anticodon**. They also have an **amino acid binding site** at the other end.

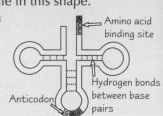

Amino acid binding site
Hydrogen bonds between base pairs
Anticodon

First Stage *of Protein Synthesis — Transcription*

During transcription, an **mRNA copy** of a gene is made from **DNA**. In **eukaryotic** cells, transcription takes place in the **nucleus**. (Prokaryotes don't have a nucleus, so transcription takes place in the cytoplasm.)

1) Transcription starts when **RNA polymerase** (an **enzyme**) **attaches** to the **DNA** double-helix at the **beginning** of a **gene**.

2) The **hydrogen bonds** between the two DNA strands in the gene **break**, **separating** the strands, and the DNA molecule **uncoils** at that point, **exposing** some of the **bases**.

3) **One** of the strands is then used as a **template** to make an **mRNA copy**.

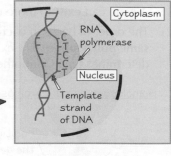

Cytoplasm
RNA polymerase
Nucleus
Template strand of DNA

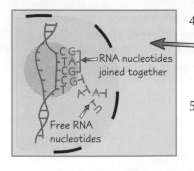

RNA nucleotides joined together
Free RNA nucleotides

4) The RNA polymerase lines up **free RNA nucleotides** alongside the exposed bases on the template strand. The free bases are **attracted** to the exposed bases. Specific, **complementary base pairing** (see p. 17) means that the mRNA strand ends up being a **complementary copy** of the DNA template strand (except the base **T** is replaced by **U** in **RNA**).

5) Once the RNA nucleotides have **paired up** with their **specific bases** on the DNA strand, they're **joined together** by **RNA polymerase**, forming an **mRNA** molecule.

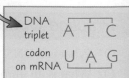

DNA triplet A T C
codon on mRNA U A G

6) The RNA polymerase moves **along** the DNA, separating the strands and **assembling** the mRNA strand.

7) The **hydrogen bonds** between the uncoiled strands of DNA **re-form** once the RNA polymerase has passed by and the strands **coil back into a double-helix**.

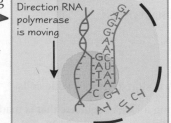

Direction RNA polymerase is moving

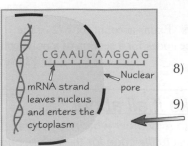

CGAAUCAAGGAG
mRNA strand leaves nucleus and enters the cytoplasm
Nuclear pore

8) When RNA polymerase reaches a particular sequence of DNA called a **stop signal**, it stops making mRNA and **detaches** from the DNA.

9) In eukaryotes, **mRNA** moves **out** of the **nucleus** through a nuclear pore and attaches to a **ribosome** in the cytoplasm, where the next stage of protein synthesis takes place (see next page).

RNA and Protein Synthesis

Transcription Makes Different Products in Eukaryotes and Prokaryotes

1) In **eukaryotes**, the **introns** and **exons** are **both copied** into mRNA during transcription. mRNA strands containing introns and exons are called **pre-mRNA**. A process called **splicing** then occurs — **introns** are removed and the **exons** joined together — forming **mRNA** strands. This takes place in the **nucleus**. The mRNA then **leaves** the nucleus for the next stage of protein synthesis (**translation**).

2) In **prokaryotes**, mRNA is produced **directly** from the DNA — **without** splicing taking place. (There's no need for splicing because there are no introns in prokaryotic DNA.)

Turn to page 83 for more on introns and exons.

Second Stage of Protein Synthesis — Translation

In both eukaryotes and prokaryotes, translation occurs at the **ribosomes** in the **cytoplasm**. During **translation**, **amino acids** are **joined together** to make a **polypeptide chain** (protein), following the sequence of **codons** (triplets) carried by the mRNA.

1) The **mRNA attaches** itself to a **ribosome** and **transfer RNA** (**tRNA**) molecules **carry amino acids** to it. **ATP** provides the energy needed for the **bond** between the **amino acid** and the **tRNA** molecule to form.

2) A **tRNA** molecule (carrying an amino acid), with an **anticodon** that's **complementary** to the **first codon** on the mRNA, attaches itself to the mRNA by **specific base pairing**.

anticodon on tRNA U A C
codon on mRNA A U G

3) A second tRNA molecule attaches itself to the **next codon** on the mRNA in the **same way**.

4) The two amino acids attached to the tRNA molecules are **joined** by a **peptide bond**. The first tRNA molecule **moves away**, leaving its amino acid behind.

5) A third tRNA molecule binds to the **next codon** on the mRNA. Its amino acid **binds** to the first two and the second tRNA molecule **moves away**.

Protein synthesis is also called polypeptide synthesis.

6) This process continues, producing a chain of linked amino acids (a **polypeptide chain**), until there's a **stop signal** on the mRNA molecule.

7) The polypeptide chain **moves away** from the ribosome and translation is complete.

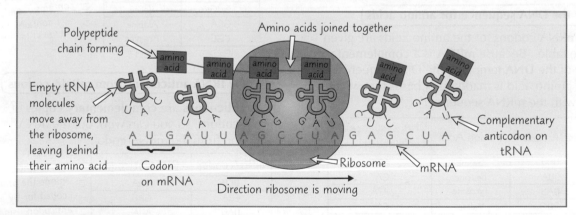

Polypeptide chain forming

Amino acids joined together

Empty tRNA molecules move away from the ribosome, leaving behind their amino acid

Codon on mRNA

Ribosome

mRNA

Complementary anticodon on tRNA

Direction ribosome is moving

Practice Questions

Q1 Describe the structure of tRNA.

Q2 Where does transcription take place in eukaryotes?

Exam Question

Q1 A drug that inhibits cell growth is found to be able to bind to DNA, preventing RNA polymerase from binding. Explain how this drug will affect protein synthesis. [2 marks]

The only translation I'm interested in is a translation of this page into English

So you start off with DNA, lots of cleverness happens and bingo... you've got a protein. Only problem is, you need to know the cleverness in quite a bit of detail. So scribble it down, recite it to yourself, explain it to your best mate or do whatever else helps you remember the joys of protein synthesis. And then think how clever you must be to know it all.

The Genetic Code and Nucleic Acids

The genetic code is exactly as it sounds — a code found in your genes that tells your body how to make proteins. It can be interpreted, just like any other code, which is exactly what you might have to do in your exam...

The Genetic Code is **Non-Overlapping**, **Degenerate** and **Universal**

1) The genetic code is the **sequence of base triplets** (codons) in **mRNA** which **code** for specific **amino acids**.

2) In the genetic code, each base triplet is **read** in sequence, **separate** from the triplet **before** it and **after** it. Base triplets **don't share** their **bases** — the code is **non-overlapping**.

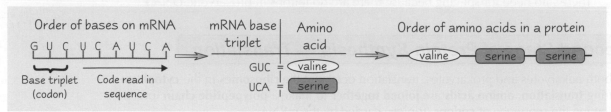

Order of bases on mRNA

G U C U C A U C A

Base triplet (codon) Code read in sequence

mRNA base triplet | Amino acid

GUC = valine
UCA = serine

Order of amino acids in a protein

valine — serine — serine

3) The genetic code is also **degenerate** — there are **more** possible combinations of **triplets** than there are amino acids (20 amino acids but 64 possible triplets). This means that some **amino acids** are coded for by **more than one** base triplet, e.g. tyrosine can be coded for by UAU or UAC.

4) Some triplets are used to tell the cell when to **start** and **stop** production of the protein — these are called **start** and **stop** signals (or **codons**). They're found at the **beginning** and **end** of the mRNA. E.g. UAG is a stop signal.

5) The genetic code is also **universal** — the **same** specific base triplets code for the **same** amino acids in **all living things**. E.g. UAU codes for tyrosine in all organisms.

You need to be able to **Interpret Data** about **Nucleic Acids**

The table on the right shows the **mRNA codons** (triplets) for some amino acids. You might have to **interpret** information like this in the exam. For example, using the table, you could be asked to...

mRNA codon	Amino Acid
UCU	Serine
CUA	Leucine
UAU	Tyrosine
GUG	Valine
GCA	Alanine
CGC	Arginine

When interpreting data on nucleic acids remember that DNA contains T and RNA contains U.

...give the DNA sequence for amino acids

The mRNA codons for the amino acids are given in the table. Because **mRNA** is a **complementary copy** of the **DNA** template, the DNA sequence for each amino acid is made up of bases that would **pair** with the mRNA sequence:

mRNA codon	Amino Acid	DNA sequence (of template strand)
UCU	Serine	AGA
CUA	Leucine	GAT
UAU	Tyrosine	ATA
GUG	Valine	CAC
GCA	Alanine	CGT
CGC	Arginine	GCG

You could also be asked to work out the amino acids from a given DNA sequence and a table.

...give the tRNA anticodons from mRNA codons

tRNA anticodons are **complementary copies** of **mRNA codons**, so you can work out the tRNA anticodon from the mRNA codon:

mRNA codon	tRNA anticodon
UCU	AGA
CUA	GAU
UAU	AUA
GUG	CAC
GCA	CGU
CGC	GCG

You might be asked to name the amino acid coded for by a tRNA anticodon using a table like the one above.

...write the amino acid sequence for a section of mRNA

To **work out** the sequence of **amino acids** from some mRNA, you need to break the genetic code into **codons** and then use the information in the table to work out what **amino acid** they code for.

You might have to work out the sequence of some mRNA from a sequence of amino acids and a table.

Example

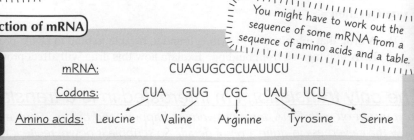

mRNA: CUAGUGCGCUAUUCU

Codons: CUA GUG CGC UAU UCU

Amino acids: Leucine Valine Arginine Tyrosine Serine

The Genetic Code and Nucleic Acids

You Might Have to *Interpret Data* About The *Role* of *Nucleic Acids*

In the exam you might have to **interpret data** from experiments done to **investigate nucleic acids** and their **role** in **protein synthesis**. Here's an example (you **don't** need to **learn** it):

Investigating the effect of new drugs on nucleic acids

1) To investigate **how** two new drugs affect **nucleic acids** and their **role** in protein synthesis, **bacteria** were **grown** in **normal conditions** for a few generations, then moved to media containing the drugs.

2) After a short period of time, the **concentration** of **protein** and **complete strands** of **mRNA** in the bacteria were analysed. The results are shown in the **bar graph**.

3) Both mRNA **and** protein concentration were **lower** in the presence of **drug 1 compared** to the **no-drug control**. This suggests that drug 1 **affects the production** of **full length mRNA**, so there's no mRNA for protein synthesis during **translation**.

4) **mRNA production** in the presence of **drug 2** was **unaffected**, but **less protein** was produced — **3 mg cm⁻³** compared to **8 mg cm⁻³**. This suggests that drug 2 **interferes** with **translation**. **mRNA was produced**, but **less protein** was **translated** from it.

5) **Further tests** to establish the **nature** of the two drugs were carried out.

6) **Drug 1** was found to be a **ribonuclease** (an enzyme that **digests RNA**). This could **explain** the results of the first experiment — **any strands** of **mRNA** produced by the cell would be **digested** by drug 1, so **couldn't** be used in **translation** to make proteins.

7) **Drug 2** was found to be a **single-stranded**, **clover-shaped** molecule capable of binding to the **ribosome**. Again, this helps to **explain** the **results** from the first experiment — drug 2 could work by **binding** to the ribosome, **blocking tRNAs** from binding to it and so **preventing translation**.

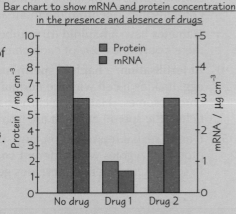
Bar chart to show mRNA and protein concentration in the presence and absence of drugs

A molecule capable of binding to mRNA would have had a similar effect to drug 1, since it would have prevented mRNA being read by the ribosomes and stopped it being translated.

Transcription and translation are on pages 84-85.

Practice Questions

Q1 What is the genetic code?
Q2 Why is the genetic code described as degenerate?
Q3 Why is the genetic code described as universal?

mRNA codon	amino acid
UGU	Cysteine
CGC	Arginine
GGG	Glycine
GUG	Valine
GCA	Alanine
UUG	Leucine
UUU	Phenylalanine

Exam Questions

Q1 The table shows the mRNA codons for some amino acids. Show your working for the following questions.
   a) Give the amino acid sequence for the mRNA sequence: GUGUGUCGCGCA. [2 marks]
   b) Give the DNA template strand sequence that codes for the amino acid sequence: valine, arginine, alanine. [3 marks]

Q2 An artificial mRNA was synthesised to code for a particular polypeptide. Part of the mRNA sequence was: UUGUGUGGGUUUGCAGCA. This produced the following sequence of amino acids: Leucine–Cysteine–Glycine–Phenylalanine–Alanine–Alanine. Use the table above to help you answer the following questions.
   a) Explain how the result suggests that the genetic code is based on triplets of nucleotides in mRNA. [2 marks]
   b) Explain how the result suggests that the genetic code is non-overlapping. [2 marks]

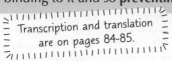

Yay — a page with slightly fewer confusing terms and a lot less to remember. The key to the genetic code is to be able to interpret it, so if you know how DNA, mRNA and tRNA work together to make a protein you should be able to handle any data they can throw at you. Remember, C pairs with G, A pairs with T. Unless it's RNA — then it's U.

Meiosis and Genetic Variation

Ahh, now on to some really exciting stuff — the production of gametes (sex cells to you and me).
This is how we end up different from our parents and our siblings — and yet, in some ways, strangely alike...

DNA from One Generation is Passed to the Next by Gametes

1) **Gametes** are the **sperm** cells in males and **egg** cells in females. They join together at **fertilisation** to form a **zygote**, which divides and develops into a **new organism**.

2) Normal **body cells** have the **diploid number (2n)** of chromosomes — meaning each cell contains **two** of each chromosome, one from the mum and one from the dad.

3) **Gametes** have a **haploid (n)** number of chromosomes — there's only one copy of each chromosome.

4) At **fertilisation**, a **haploid sperm** fuses with a **haploid egg**, making a cell with the normal diploid number of chromosomes. Half these chromosomes are from the father (the sperm) and half are from the mother (the egg).

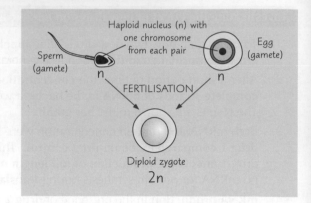

5) During sexual reproduction, any sperm can fertilise any egg — **fertilisation** is **random**. Random fertilisation produces zygotes with **different combinations** of **chromosomes** to both parents. This **mixing** of **genetic material** in sexual reproduction **increases genetic diversity** within a **species** (there's more on genetic diversity on page 92).

Gametes are Formed by Meiosis

Meiosis is a type of cell division. It takes place in the **reproductive organs**. Cells that divide by meiosis are **diploid** to start with, but the cells that are formed from meiosis are **haploid** — the chromosome number **halves**. Without meiosis, you'd get **double** the number of chromosomes when the gametes fused. Not good.

1) Before meiosis starts, the DNA unravels and **replicates** so there are **two** copies of **each** chromosome, called **chromatids**.

2) The DNA condenses to form double-armed chromosomes, each made from **two sister chromatids**. The sister chromatids are joined in the middle by a **centromere**.

3) **Meiosis I** (first division) — the chromosomes arrange themselves into **homologous pairs**.

4) These homologous **pairs** are then **separated**, **halving** the chromosome number.

5) **Meiosis II** (second division) — the pairs of sister chromatids that make up each chromosome are **separated** (the **centromere** is divided).

6) **Four haploid cells** (gametes) that are **genetically different** from each other are produced.

A Note About Homologous Pairs: Humans have 46 chromosomes in total — 23 pairs. One chromosome in each pair came from mum and one from dad, e.g. there are two number 1's (one from mum and one from dad), two number 2's etc. The chromosomes that make up each pair are the same size and have the same genes, although they could have different versions of those genes (called alleles). These pairs of chromosomes are called homologous pairs.

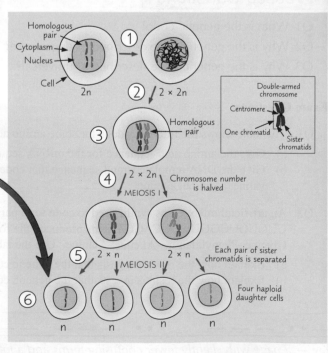

In the exams, you might need to spot **when meiosis happens** in an organism with a **life cycle you haven't seen before**, e.g. an insect or plant. Just remember that in any organism, **meiosis** is needed for **sexual reproduction** because it produces daughter cells (gametes) with **half** the number of **chromosomes** of the parent cell.

You might also be told **how many** chromosomes are in a parent cell, then asked to **complete diagrams** showing how many chromosomes will be in the daughter cells after the **first** and **second divisions** of meiosis. Remember that the **chromosome number** is **halved** during the **first division**.

Meiosis and Genetic Variation

Chromatids *Cross Over* in *Meiosis I*

During meiosis I, **homologous pairs** of chromosomes come together and pair up. The chromatids twist around each other and bits of **chromatids** swap over. The chromatids still contain the **same genes** but now have a different combination of **alleles**.

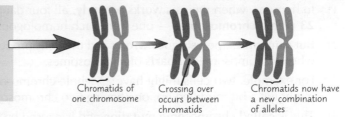

Chromatids of one chromosome → Crossing over occurs between chromatids → Chromatids now have a new combination of alleles

Meiosis Produces Cells that are *Genetically Different*

There are two main events during meiosis that lead to **genetic variation**:

1) Crossing over of chromatids

The **crossing over** of chromatids in meiosis I means that each of the **four daughter cells** formed from meiosis contains chromatids with **different alleles**:

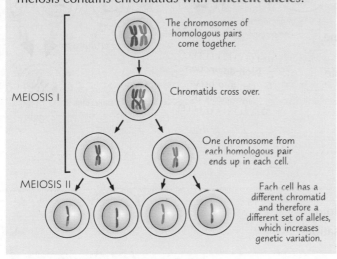

The chromosomes of homologous pairs come together.

MEIOSIS I — Chromatids cross over.

One chromosome from each homologous pair ends up in each cell.

MEIOSIS II — Each cell has a different chromatid and therefore a different set of alleles, which increases genetic variation.

2) Independent segregation of chromosomes

1) Each **homologous pair** of chromosomes in your cells is made up of **one chromosome** from your mum (**maternal**) and **one chromosome** from your dad (**paternal**).

2) When the homologous pairs are **separated** in **meiosis I**, it's completely **random** which chromosome from each pair ends up in which daughter cell.

3) So the **four daughter cells** produced by meiosis have completely **different combinations** of those **maternal** and **paternal chromosomes**.

4) This is called **independent segregation** (separation) of the chromosomes.

5) This 'shuffling' of chromosomes leads to **genetic variation** in any **potential** offspring.

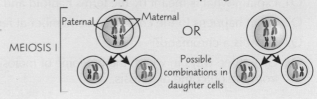

Paternal / Maternal — OR

MEIOSIS I — Possible combinations in daughter cells

Meiosis Has a *Different Outcome* to *Mitosis*

You may remember **mitosis** from page 32. **Mitosis** and **meiosis** have **different outcomes**:

	Outcomes:		
Mitosis	Produces cells with the **same number** of chromosomes as the parent cell.	Daughter cells are **genetically identical** to each other and to the parent cell.	Produces **two** daughter cells.
Meiosis	Produces cells with **half** the number of chromosomes as the parent cell.	Daughter cells are **genetically different** from one another and the parent cell.	Produces **four** daughter cells.

You need to be able to **explain** the different outcomes of mitosis and meiosis. They're different because **mitosis** only involves **one division** (which separates the sister chromatids) whereas **meiosis** has **two divisions** (which separate the homologous pairs and then the sister chromatids). There's **no pairing** or **separating** of **homologous chromosomes** in **mitosis**, and so **no crossing over** or **independent segregation of chromosomes**. This produces **genetically identical** daughter cells — unlike **meiosis**.

TOPIC 4B — DIVERSITY, CLASSIFICATION AND VARIATION

Meiosis and Genetic Variation

Chromosome Mutations are Caused by Errors in Cell Division

1) In humans, when meiosis **works properly**, all four daughter cells will end up with **23 whole chromosomes** — one from each homologous pair (1 to 23).

2) But sometimes meiosis **goes wrong** and the cells produced contain **variations** in the numbers of whole chromosomes or **parts** of chromosomes.

3) For example, two cells might have 23 whole chromosomes, one each of 1 to 23, but the other two might get a bit muddled up, one having two chromosome 6's and the other no chromosome 6.

4) This is called **chromosome mutation** and is caused by **errors** during meiosis.

5) Chromosome mutations lead to **inherited conditions** because the errors are present in the **gametes** (the hereditary cells).

One type of chromosome mutation is called **non-disjunction** — it's a **failure** of the **chromosomes** to **separate** properly. In humans, non-disjunction of **chromosome 21** during **meiosis** can lead to **Down's Syndrome**.

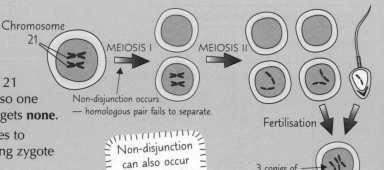

1) **Down's syndrome** is caused by a person having an **extra copy** of **chromosome 21** (or sometimes an extra copy of part of chromosome 21).

2) Non-disjunction means that chromosome 21 **fails** to **separate properly** during **meiosis**, so one cell gets an **extra copy** of 21 and another gets **none**.

3) When the gamete with the **extra copy** fuses to another gamete at **fertilisation**, the resulting zygote will have **three** copies of chromosome 21.

Non-disjunction occurs — homologous pair fails to separate.

Non-disjunction can also occur in meiosis II.

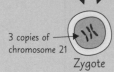

Fertilisation

3 copies of chromosome 21

Zygote

Practice Questions

Q1 Explain what is meant by the terms haploid and diploid.

Q2 What happens to the chromosome number at fertilisation?

Q3 What is a chromatid?

Q4 Give three ways in which the outcome of meiosis differs from the outcome of mitosis.

Exam Questions

Q1 *Drosophila* (fruit flies) only have four chromosomes. The diagram on the right summarises meiosis in *Drosophila*.

   a) Complete the diagram to show the chromosomes in the four daughter cells. [1 mark]

   b) Crossing over does not occur very frequently in male *Drosophila*. Explain what crossing over is and how it leads to genetic variation. [4 marks]

   c) Explain how independent segregation leads to genetic variation. [2 marks]

Q2 Turner syndrome is a genetic condition affecting females. It is caused by non-disjunction of the sex chromosomes. Females usually have two X chromosomes. Some females with Turner syndrome have only one X chromosome.

Suggest and explain how chromosome non-disjunction could cause Turner syndrome. [3 marks]

Reproduction isn't as exciting as some people would have you believe...

These pages are quite tricky, so use the diagrams to help you understand — they might look evil, but they really do help. The key thing to understand is that meiosis produces four genetically different haploid (n) daughter cells. And that the genetic variation in the daughter cells occurs because of two processes — crossing over and independent segregation.

Mutations

Aside from chromosome mutations, other types of genetic mutations can also occur — some useful, some not so.

Mutations are Changes to the Base Sequence of DNA

Gene **mutations** involve a **change** in the **DNA base sequence** of chromosomes.

Errors can also be caused by insertion, duplication, addition and translocation of bases.

1) The **types** of errors that can occur include:

> **Substitution** — one base is substituted with another, e.g. ATGCCT becomes ATTCCT (G is swapped for T).
>
> **Deletion** — one base is deleted, e.g. ATGCCT becomes ATCCT (G is deleted).

2) The **order** of **DNA bases** in a gene determines the **order of amino acids** in a particular **protein** (see p. 82). If a mutation occurs in a gene, the **sequence** of **amino acids** it codes for (and the protein formed) could be **altered**:

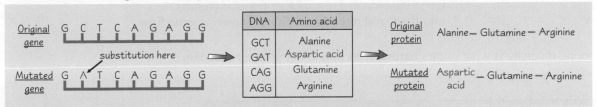

Not All Mutations Affect the Order of Amino Acids

The **degenerate nature** of the genetic code (see page 86) means that some amino acids are coded for by **more than one DNA triplet** (e.g. tyrosine can be coded for by TAT or TAC in DNA). This means that **not all** substitution mutations will result in a change to the amino acid sequence of the protein — some substitutions will still **code** for the **same amino acid**. For example:

DNA	Amino acid
TAT	Tyrosine
TAC	Tyrosine
AGT	Serine
CTT	Leucine
GTC	Valine

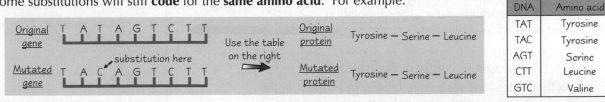

Substitution mutations **won't always** lead to changes in the amino acid sequence, but **deletions will** — the deletion of a base will change the **number** of bases present, which will cause a **shift** in all the base triplets after it.

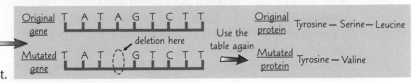

Mutagenic Agents Increase the Rate of Mutation

Mutations occur **spontaneously**, e.g. when DNA is **misread** during **replication**. But some things can cause an **increase** in the **rate** of **mutations** — these are called **mutagenic agents**. **Ultraviolet radiation**, **ionising radiation**, some **chemicals** and some **viruses** are examples of mutagenic agents.

Practice Questions

Q1 What are mutagenic agents?

Exam Question

Q1 A mutation occurred during DNA replication. The diagram on the right shows part of the original gene and the mutated gene.

a) What type of mutation has occurred? [1 mark]

b) Using the table provided, explain the effects that this mutation would have on the amino acid sequence. [2 marks]

DNA	Amino acid
AGT	Serine
TAT	Tyrosine
CTT	Leucine
AGG	Arginine

What do you get if you cross James Bond with the Hulk™?*

Mutations affect the sequence of amino acids produced — learn what happens for substitutions and deletions.

*A mutagenic agent

Genetic Diversity and Natural Selection

Genetic diversity describes the number of alleles in a species or population, and natural selection acts to increase the proportion of advantageous alleles. It's all about the most well-adapted organisms getting on with some reproduction.

Lots of Different Alleles Means a High Genetic Diversity

1) Remember, there can be **different versions** of a single **gene** — these are called **alleles** (see page 83).
2) **Genetic diversity** is the number of **different alleles** of genes in a species or population.
3) Genetic diversity **within** a **population** is increased by:

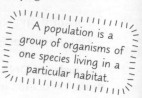
A population is a group of organisms of one species living in a particular habitat.

   - **Mutations** in the DNA — forming **new alleles**.
   - **Different alleles** being **introduced** into a population when individuals from another population **migrate into them** and reproduce. This is known as **gene flow**.

4) Genetic diversity is what allows **natural selection** to occur (see next page).

Genetic Bottlenecks Reduce Genetic Diversity

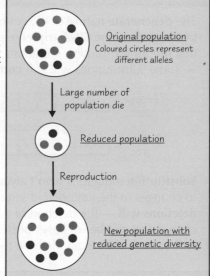

Original population
Coloured circles represent different alleles

Large number of population die

Reduced population

Reproduction

New population with reduced genetic diversity

1) A **genetic bottleneck** is an event that causes a big **reduction** in a population, e.g. when a large number of organisms within a population **die** before reproducing.
2) This reduces the number of **different alleles** in the **gene pool** and so reduces **genetic diversity**.
3) The survivors **reproduce** and a larger population is created from a few individuals.

The gene pool is the complete range of alleles in a population.

Example — Northern Elephant Seals
Northern elephant seals were hunted by humans in the late 1800s. Their **original population** was reduced to around **50 seals** who have since produced a population of around 170 000. This new population has **very little** genetic diversity compared to the southern elephant seals who never suffered such a **reduction** in numbers.

The Founder Effect is a Type of Genetic Bottleneck

1) The **founder effect** describes what happens when just a **few** organisms from a population start a **new colony** and there are only a **small number** of **different alleles** in the **initial gene pool**.
2) The **frequency** of each allele in the **new colony** might be **very different** to the frequency of those alleles in the original population — for example, an allele that was **rare** in the original population might be **more common** in the new colony. This may lead to a **higher incidence** of **genetic disease**.
3) The founder effect can occur as a result of **migration** leading to geographical **separation** or if a new colony is separated from the original population for **another reason**, such as **religion**.

Example — The Amish
The **Amish population** of North America are all descended from a **small** number of Swiss who **migrated** there. The population shows **little genetic diversity**. They have remained **isolated** from the surrounding population due to their **religious beliefs**, so **few new alleles** have been introduced. The population has an unusually high incidence of certain **genetic disorders**.

Genetic Diversity and Natural Selection

Natural Selection Increases Advantageous Alleles in a Population

Randomly-occurring **mutations** sometimes result in a **new allele** being formed. This can be **harmful**, which usually means that the **mutated allele** quickly **dies** out. However, **some mutations** can produce **alleles** that are **beneficial** to an organism (e.g. a protein is produced that works better than the original), helping the organism to **survive** in certain environments. When the allele codes for a characteristic that **increases** the **chances** of an organism **surviving**, its **frequency** within the population can **increase**. This process is known as **natural selection**. Here's how it works:

1) Not all individuals are as likely to **reproduce** as each other. There's **differential reproductive success** in a population — individuals that have an allele that **increases** their **chance of survival** are **more likely** to **survive**, **reproduce** and **pass on** their genes (including the **beneficial** allele), than individuals with different alleles.

2) This means that a **greater proportion** of the next generation **inherits** the **beneficial allele**.

3) They, in turn, are **more likely** to **survive**, **reproduce** and **pass on** their genes.

4) So the **frequency** of the beneficial allele **increases** from generation to generation.

5) Over **generations** this leads to **evolution** as the **advantageous alleles** become **more common** in the population.

Adaptation and **selection** are both key factors in **evolution** — the **gradual change** in **species** over **time**. Evolution has led to the **huge diversity** of **living organisms** on Earth.

Natural Selection Leads to Populations Becoming Better Adapted

Adaptations help organisms to **survive** in their **environment**. They can be **behavioural**, **physiological** or **anatomical**. Here are some examples:

Bob and Sue were well adapted to hiding in candyfloss shops.

1 Behavioural adaptations

Ways an organism **acts** that increase its chance of survival and reproduction. For example, **possums** sometimes 'play dead' if they're being threatened by a **predator** to **escape attack**.

2 Physiological adaptations

Processes inside an organism's body that increase its chance of survival. For example, **brown bears hibernate** over **winter**. They **lower their rate of metabolism** (all the chemical reactions taking place in their body). This **conserves energy**, so they don't need to look for **food** in the months when it's scarce.

3 Anatomical adaptations

Structural features of an organism's body that increase its chance of survival. For example, **whales** have a **thick layer** of **blubber** (fat) which helps them keep **warm** in the cold sea.

Practice Questions

Q1 What is genetic diversity?

Q2 Explain how a genetic bottleneck reduces genetic diversity.

Q3 Give an example of a behavioural adaptation.

Exam Question

Q1 Tawny owls show variation in colour. There are light grey owls and darker brown owls. Before the 1970s there were more grey owls than brown owls in Finland. Since then, climate change has been causing a decrease in the amount of snowfall in Finland. During this period, the darker brown owls have become more common.

a) Suggest why the brown owls are better adapted to living in an area with less snowfall than the grey owls. [2 marks]

b) Explain how the brown owls have become more common. [3 marks]

I'm perfectly adapted — for staying in bed...

Just remember that any mutation that increases the chances of an organism surviving (e.g. thicker blubber for keeping warm) or reproducing will increase in the population due to the process of natural selection.

Investigating Selection

Now you get to apply what you know about natural selection to bacteria and babies (amongst other things).
Natural selection affects different populations in different ways, as you'll soon discover...

Different Types of Natural Selection Lead to Different Frequency Patterns

You might remember from the previous page that **natural selection** alters **allele frequency** in a population.
Stabilising selection and **directional selection** are **types** of **natural selection** that affect **allele frequency**
in different ways. You need to learn these examples:

Antibiotic Resistance Shows Directional Selection

Directional selection is where individuals with alleles for characteristics of an **extreme type** are more likely to
survive and **reproduce**. This could be in response to an **environmental change**. **Bacteria** evolving **antibiotic
resistance** is an example of **directional selection**. Here's how it works:

1) Some individuals in a population have alleles
   that give them **resistance** to an **antibiotic**.

2) The population is **exposed** to the antibiotic,
   killing bacteria **without** the resistant allele.

3) The **resistant bacteria survive** and **reproduce**
   without competition, passing on the **allele** that
   gives antibiotic resistance to their offspring.

4) After some time, **most** organisms in the population
   will carry the **antibiotic resistance allele**.

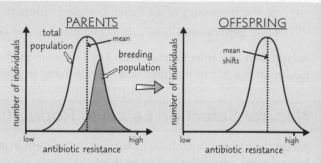

Human Birth Weight Shows Stabilising Selection

Stabilising selection is where individuals with alleles for characteristics towards the **middle** of the range are more
likely to **survive** and **reproduce**. It occurs when the environment **isn't changing**, and it **reduces the range** of
possible **characteristics**. An example of **stabilising selection** is **human birth weight**.

1) Humans have a **range** of **birth weights**.

2) Very **small babies** are **less likely** to
   survive — partly because they find it **hard**
   to **maintain** their **body temperature**.

3) Giving birth to **large babies** can be difficult,
   so large babies are **less likely** to **survive** too.

4) Conditions are **most favourable** for
   medium-sized babies — so weight of human
   babies tends to **shift towards** the **middle** of the range.

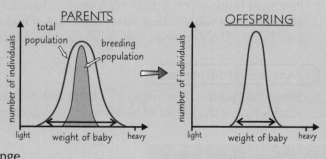

You Need to be Able to Interpret Data on the Effects of Selection

You might be asked to **interpret** information about an **unfamiliar species** in the exam. For example:

There is a population of **rabbits** with **varying fur length**. **Longer fur** helps to keep the rabbits **warmer**.
The graph shows how the **average fur length** of the rabbits **changed** over a period of six years,
which had particularly **cold winters**. The **bars** span the **difference** between
the **shortest** and **longest fur lengths** recorded.

Describe what the data shows:
Over the first two years the average fur length is about 21 mm. However, the average
length gradually increases from 21 mm to 24 mm. This shows <u>directional selection</u>.

Suggest a possible cause:
The rabbits with the <u>longer fur</u> are <u>more likely</u> to <u>survive</u> the <u>cold winters</u> than the <u>short-furred rabbits</u>. This makes them more likely to <u>reproduce</u> and, when they do, they <u>pass on</u>
the <u>allele</u> for <u>longer fur</u> to the next generation. Over time, the allele for longer fur becomes
<u>more common</u> in the population and the <u>average fur length</u> of the rabbits <u>increases</u>.

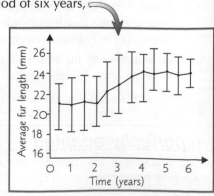

Topic 4B — Diversity, Classification and Variation

Investigating Selection

You Can **Investigate** the **Effects** of **Antibiotics** on **Bacterial Growth**

You need to know how to **investigate** the effect of **antimicrobial substances** (e.g. antibiotics, antiseptics or disinfectants) on **microbial growth**, using **aseptic techniques**.

Test the Effects of **Antibiotics** Using **Agar Plates**

1) The bacteria you will use are likely to have been grown in a **liquid broth** (a mixture of distilled water, bacterial culture and nutrients).

2) Use a **wire inoculation loop** to **transfer** the bacteria from the broth to an **agar plate** — a **Petri dish** containing **agar jelly**. Spread the bacteria over the plate using the loop.

3) Place paper discs **soaked** with different **antibiotics** spaced apart on the plate. Various **concentrations** of antibiotics should be used. Make sure you add a **negative control** disc soaked only in **sterile water**. (See page 104 for more on negative controls.)

4) **Tape** a **lid** onto the Petri dish, invert, and **incubate** the plate at about **25 °C** for **24-48 hours**. This allows the bacteria to **grow** (forming a 'lawn'). Anywhere the bacteria **can't grow** can be seen as a **clear patch** in the lawn of bacteria. This is called an **inhibition zone**.

5) The size of an **inhibition zone** tells you how well an antibiotic works. The **larger** the zone, the **more** the bacteria were inhibited from growing.

6) A **similar technique** can be used to test the effects of **antiseptics** or **disinfectants** on microbial growth.

This diagram shows an agar plate with **meticillin, tetracycline** and **streptomycin** discs **after** it has been **incubated**.

125 mg   250 mg
Meticillin — Inhibition zone
— Agar plate
Tetracycline
Streptomycin
Negative control (soaked in water)
Disc   Lawn of bacteria

- The **tetracycline** discs have **no inhibition zones**, so the bacteria are **resistant** to tetracycline up to 250 mg.
- The **streptomycin** discs have **small inhibition zones**, with the zone at 250 mg slightly larger than the one at 125 mg. So streptomycin has **some effect** on the bacteria.
- The **meticillin** discs have the **largest inhibition zones**, so meticillin has the **strongest effect** on these bacteria.

Always Use **Aseptic Techniques** to **Prevent Contamination** of Microbial Cultures

Aseptic techniques are used to **prevent contamination** of cultures by **unwanted** microorganisms. This is important because contamination can affect the **growth** of the microorganism that you're **working** with. It's also important to avoid contamination with **disease-causing microbes** that could make you **ill**. When carrying out the investigation above, you need to use the following **aseptic techniques**:

- Regularly **disinfect** work surfaces to minimise contamination.
- Work **near** a **Bunsen flame**. **Hot air rises**, so any microbes in the air should be drawn away from your culture.
- **Sterilise** the **wire inoculation loop before** and **after** each use by passing it through a **hot** Bunsen burner **flame** for 5 seconds. This will kill any microbes on the loop.
- Briefly **flame** the neck of the glass **container of broth** just after it's **opened** and just before it's **closed** — this causes air to move out of the container, preventing **unwanted** organisms from **falling in**.
- **Sterilise** all glassware before and after use, e.g. in an **autoclave** (a machine which steams equipment at high pressure).

You should also take steps to protect yourself, e.g. wash your hands thoroughly before and after handling cultures.

Practice Questions

Q1 Describe how you could investigate the effects of antibiotics on bacterial growth.

Exam Question

Q1 A group of scientists monitored how the colour of oyster shells on a beach changed over time. The graph shows the colour of the oyster shells in the scientists' initial sample and in their final sample. The oysters were mainly found on the sand, which was a mid-brown colour.

a) What type of selection is shown in the graph? Explain your answer. [3 marks]

b) Suggest how the changes shown in the graph might have taken place. [4 marks]

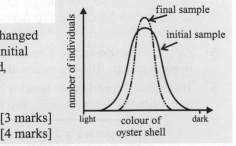

One Directional selection — the shift in the population of teenage girls...

Quite a bit to learn here — maybe try the whole cover, scribble, check thing to make sure you remember the details.

Classification of Organisms

For hundreds of years people have been putting organisms into groups to make it easier to recognise and name them. For example, my brother is a member of the species Idioto bigearian (Latin for idiots with big ears).

Phylogeny Tells Us About the Evolutionary History of Organisms

1) **Phylogeny** is the study of the **evolutionary history** of groups of **organisms**. Phylogeny tells us **who's related** to whom and how **closely related** they are.

2) All organisms have **evolved** from shared **common ancestors** (relatives). This can be shown on a **phylogenetic tree**, like this one. ⇨

3) This tree shows the **relationship** between members of the Hominidae family (great apes and humans). The **first branch point** represents a **common ancestor** of **all** the family members. This ancestor is now **extinct**. **Orangutans** were the first group to **diverge** (evolve to become a different species) from this common ancestor.

First branch point

— Orangutan
— Human
— Chimpanzee
— Bonobo
— Gorilla

4) Each of the following branch points represents **another common ancestor** from which a **different group** diverged. Gorillas diverged next, then humans, closely followed by bonobos and chimpanzees.

5) Closely related species **diverged** away from each other **most recently**. E.g. humans and **chimpanzees** are **closely** related, as they diverged very **recently**. You can see this because their branches are **close** together.

Classification is All About Grouping Together Related Organisms

Taxonomy is the science of classification. It involves **naming** organisms and **organising them** into **groups**. This makes it **easier** to **identify** and **study** them. Scientists now take into account **phylogeny** when classifying organisms, and group organisms according to their **evolutionary relationships**.

1) There are **eight** levels of groups used to classify organisms. These groups are called **taxa**. Each group is called a **taxon**.

2) The groups are arranged in a **hierarchy**, with the **largest groups** at the **top** and the smallest groups at the bottom. Organisms can only belong to **one group** at **each level** in the hierarchy — there's **no overlap**.

3) Organisms are first sorted into **three** large groups (or taxa) called **domains** — the **Eukarya**, **Bacteria** and **Archaea**.

4) **Related organisms** in a domain are then sorted into **slightly smaller groups** called **kingdoms**, e.g. all animals are in the animal kingdom. **More closely related** organisms from that kingdom are then grouped into a **phylum**, then grouped into a **class**, and **so on** down the eight levels of the hierarchy.

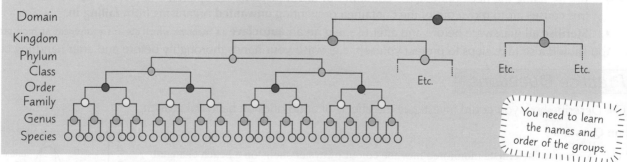

Domain
Kingdom
Phylum
Class
Order
Family
Genus
Species

Etc.
Etc.
Etc.

You need to learn the names and order of the groups.

5) As you move **down** the hierarchy, there are **more groups** at each level but **fewer organisms** in each group. The organisms in each group also become **more closely related**.

6) The hierarchy **ends** with **species** — the groups that contain only **one type** of organism (e.g. humans, dogs, *E. coli*). You need to **learn** the definition of a **species**:

> **A species is a group of similar organisms able to reproduce to give fertile offspring.**

7) Scientists constantly **update** classification systems because of **discoveries** about new species and new **evidence** about known organisms (e.g. **DNA sequence** data — see page 98).

Classification of Organisms

The **Binomial Naming System** is Used in **Classification**

1) The **nomenclature (naming system)** used for classification is called the **binomial system** — all organisms are given **one** internationally accepted scientific **name** in **Latin** that has **two parts**.

2) The **first part** of the name is the **genus** name and has a capital letter. The **second part** is the **species** name and begins with a lower case letter. E.g. using the binomial system humans are *Homo sapiens*. Names are always written in *italics* (or they're <u>underlined</u> if they're **handwritten**).

3) The binomial system helps to avoid the **confusion** of using **common names**. E.g. over 100 different plant species are called **raspberries** and one species of buttercup has over 90 different common names.

Courtship Behaviour can be Used to Help **Classify Species**

1) **Courtship behaviour** is carried out by organisms to **attract** a mate of the **right species**.

2) It can be fairly simple, e.g. **releasing chemicals**, or quite complex, e.g. a series of **displays**.

3) Courtship behaviour is **species specific** — only members of the same species will do and respond to that courtship behaviour. This allows members of the **same species** to **recognise** each other, preventing **interbreeding** and making reproduction **more successful** (as mating with the wrong species won't produce **fertile** offspring).

4) Because of this specificity, courtship behaviour can be used to **classify organisms**.

5) The more **closely related** species are, the **more similar** their courtship behaviour. Some examples of courtship behaviour include:

Geoff's jive never failed to attract a mate.

1) **Fireflies** give off **pulses of light**. The pattern of flashes is specific to each species.

2) **Crickets** make **sounds** that are similar to Morse code, the code being different for different species.

3) **Male peacocks** show off their **colourful tails**. This tail pattern is only found in peacocks.

4) **Male butterflies** use **chemicals** to attract females. Only those of the correct species respond.

Practice Questions

Q1 What is phylogeny?

Q2 What is a taxon?

Q3 List the groups of the phylogenetic hierarchy in order, starting with domain.

Q4 How does courtship behaviour help to prevent interbreeding?

Q5 How is courtship behaviour used in classification?

Exam Question

Q1 The brown trout is a species of fish and is part of the Salmonidae family. Its Latin name is *Salmo trutta*.

a) Complete the table below for the classification of the brown trout. [2 marks]

Domain		Phylum				Genus	Species
Eukarya	Animalia	Chordata	Actinopterygii	Salmoniformes			

b) The brook trout is another member of the Salmonidae family. Rarely, a brook trout and a brown trout are able to mate to produce offspring known as tiger trout. Tiger trout are unable to reproduce. Explain how you know that a brook trout and a brown trout are different species. [1 mark]

Phylum — I thought that was the snot you get with a cold...

Learning the order of the levels in the phylogenetic hierarchy is about as easy as licking your elbow... try making up a mnemonic to help (like 'Dopey King Prawns Can't Order Fried Green Sausages' for Domain, Kingdom, Phylum, Class, Order, etc). Don't be put off if you get funny Latin names in the exam — just apply what you know. Right, onwards...

DNA Technology, Classification and Diversity

Advances in DNA and molecular technology have led to advances in many other fields.
For example, scientists have been able to use the technology to help classify organisms more accurately...

Advances in Techniques Can Clarify Evolutionary Relationships

New or **improved technologies** can result in **new discoveries** being made and the **relationships** between organisms being **clarified**. This can lead to **classification systems** being **updated**. Technologies that have been useful for clarifying evolutionary relationships include:

<u>Genome sequencing</u> — Advances in genome sequencing have meant that the **entire base sequence** of an organism's **DNA** can be determined. The DNA base sequence of one organism can then be **compared** to the DNA base sequence of another organism, to see how closely related they are. **Closely related** species will have a **higher percentage** of similarity in their DNA **base order**, e.g. humans and chimps share around 94%, humans and mice share about 86%.

Genome sequencing has clarified the relationship between **skunks** and members of the **Mustelidae family** (e.g. weasels and badgers). Skunks **were** classified in the Mustelidae family until their **DNA sequence** was revealed to be **significantly different** to other members of that family. So they were reclassified into the family **Mephitidae**.

<u>Comparing amino acid sequence</u> — Proteins are made of **amino acids**. The **sequence** of amino acids in a protein is coded for by the **base sequence** in DNA (see p. 82). **Related organisms** have similar DNA sequences and so **similar amino acid sequences** in their proteins. E.g. **cytochrome C** is a short protein found in many species. The more **similar** the **amino acid sequence** of cytochrome C in two different species, the **more closely related** the species are likely to be.

<u>Immunological comparisons</u> — **Similar proteins** will also bind the same **antibodies** (see p. 44). E.g. if antibodies to a **human version** of a protein are added to isolated samples from some other **species**, any protein that's like the human version will also be **recognised** (bound) by that antibody.

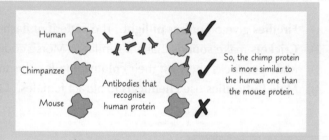

Antibodies that recognise human protein

So, the chimp protein is more similar to the human one than the mouse protein.

You Need to be Able to Interpret Data on DNA and Protein Similarities

Here are two examples of the kind of thing you might get:

	Species A	Species B	Species C	Species D
Species A	100%	86%	42%	44%
Species B	86%	100%	51%	53%
Species C	42%	51%	100%	91%
Species D	44%	53%	91%	100%

The table on the left shows the **% similarity of DNA** using DNA sequence analysis between several species of bacteria.

The data shows that species **A** and **B** are **more closely related** to each other than they are to either C or D. Species **C** and **D** are also **more closely related** to each other than they are to either A or B.

You can also use DNA base sequences to see how closely related two members of the same species are.

The diagram on the right shows the **amino acid sequences** of a certain protein from three different species.

You can see that the amino acid sequences from species **A** and **B** are **very similar**. The sequence from species **C** is **very different** to any of the other sequences. This would suggest that species **A** and **B** are **more closely related**.

Species A — Val — Ser — Phe — Tyr

Species B — Val — Ser — Phe — Phe

Species C — Phe — Glu — Val — Glu

DNA Technology, Classification and Diversity

Gene Technologies Have Changed the Way Genetic Diversity is Assessed

You might remember from page 92, that **genetic diversity** is the **number** of **different alleles** in a population.

1) Early **estimates** of genetic diversity were made by looking at the **frequency** of **measurable** or **observable characteristics** in a population, e.g. the number of different eye colours in a population and the number of people with each particular eye colour.

2) Since different **alleles** determine different **characteristics** (see page 83) a **wide variety** of **each characteristic** in a population indicates a **high number** of different **alleles** — and so a **high genetic diversity**.

3) However gene technologies have now been developed that allow us to **measure genetic diversity directly**:

There weren't many people with Sid's observable characteristics.

> For example:
>
> • **Different alleles** of the same gene will have **slightly different DNA base sequences**. Comparing the DNA base sequences of the same gene in **different organisms** in a population allows scientists to find out **how many alleles** of that gene there are in that population.
>
> • Different alleles will also produce slightly different **mRNA base sequences**, and may produce **proteins** with slightly different **amino acid sequences**, so these can also be compared.

4) These **new technologies** can all be used to give more **accurate estimates** of genetic diversity within a population or species. They also allow the genetic diversity of **different species** to be **compared** more easily.

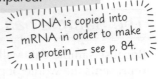

DNA is copied into mRNA in order to make a protein — see p. 84.

Practice Questions

Q1 Give one technological advance that has helped to clarify evolutionary relationships.

Q2 Suggest two techniques that could be used to assess genetic diversity within species.

Q3 Why can observable characteristics be used as a measure of genetic diversity?

Q4 How has the way in which genetic diversity is assessed changed over time?

Exam Question

Q1 The amino acid sequence of a specific protein was used to make comparisons between four species of animal. The results are shown below.

Species	Amino acid 1	Amino acid 2	Amino acid 3	Amino acid 4
Rabbit	His	Ala	Asp	Lys
Mouse	Thr	Ala	Asp	Val
Chicken	Ala	Thr	Arg	Arg
Rat	Thr	Ala	Asp	Phy

a) Which two species are the most closely related? [1 mark]

b) Which species is the most distantly related to the other three? Explain your answer. [2 marks]

These pages have a PG classification — Protein Guidance...

..on evolutionary relationships. It's the latest release. It's important that you understand that the more similar the DNA and proteins, the more closely related two species are. This is because relatives have similar DNA, which codes for similar proteins, made of similar sequences of amino acids. DNA really is the key to everything, eh?

Investigating Variation

It's a lot of work studying variation in an entire population (imagine studying all the ants in one nest) — so instead you can take a random sample and use this to give you a good idea of what's going on in the entire population.

Variation Can be Caused by Genes, the Environment, or Both

1) **Variation** is the **differences** that exists between individuals. There's variation **between** species and **within** species

2) Variation can be caused by **genetic factors**. **Different** species have **different genes**, which causes variation **between** species. Individuals of the **same** species have the **same genes**, but **different alleles** (versions of genes) — this causes variation **within** a species.

3) Variation **within** a species can also be caused by differences in the **environment**, e.g. climate, food, lifestyle.

4) Most variation **within** a species is caused by a **combination** of **genetic** and **environmental** factors. E.g. **genes** determine how tall an organism **can grow**, but **nutrient availability** affects how tall the organism **actually grows**.

To Study Variation You Have to Sample a Population

When investigating variation you usually only look at a **sample** of the population, **not** the **whole thing**. For most species it would be too **time-consuming** or **impossible** to catch all the individuals in the group. So samples are used as **models** for the **whole population**.

The Sample has to be Random

Because sample data will be used to **draw conclusions** about the **whole population**, it's important that it **accurately represents** the whole population and that any patterns observed are tested to make sure they're not due to chance.

1) To make sure the sample isn't **biased**, it should be **random**. For example, if you were looking at plant species in a field you could pick random sample sites by dividing the field into a **grid** and using a **random number generator** to select coordinates.

2) To ensure any variation observed in the sample isn't just due to **chance**, it's important to analyse the results **statistically**. This allows you to be more **confident** that the results are true and therefore will reflect what's going on in the **whole population**.

You Can Use the Mean to Look for Variation Between Samples

1) The **mean** is an **average** of the values collected in a sample. Find it using this **formula**:

$$\text{mean} = \frac{\text{total of all the values in your data}}{\text{the number of values in your data}}$$

Example:

The heights of different seedlings in a group are: 6 cm, 4 cm, 7 cm, 6 cm, 5 cm, 8 cm, 7 cm, 5 cm, 7 cm and 9 cm
To calculate the mean, add all of the heights together and divide by the number of seedlings:
Mean height = (6 + 4 + 7 + 6 + 5 + 8 + 7 + 5 + 7 + 9) ÷ 10 = 64 ÷ 10 = **6.4 cm**

2) The mean can be used to tell if there is **variation between samples**. For example:

> The **mean height** of a species of **tree** in woodland A = **26 m**, in woodland B = **32 m** and in woodland C = **35 m**. So the **mean height varies**.

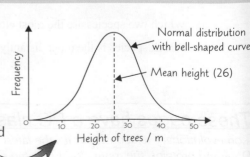

3) Most samples will include values **either side** of the **mean**, so you end up with a **bell-shaped graph** — this is called a **normal distribution**. A normal distribution is **symmetrical** about the mean.

Investigating Variation

The **Standard Deviation** Tells You About **Variation Within a Sample**

1) The **standard deviation** tells you how much the **values** in a **single sample vary**. It's a measure of the **spread** of **values** about the **mean**.

2) Sometimes you'll see the mean written as, e.g. **9 ± 3**. This means that the **mean** is **9** and the **standard deviation** is **3**, so most of the **values** are spread between **6 to 12**.

3) A **large standard deviation** means the values in the sample **vary a lot**. A **small standard deviation** tells you that most of the sample data is around the mean value, so **varies little**.

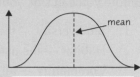

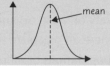

Here, all the values are similar and close to the mean, so the graph is steep and the standard deviation is small.

Here, the values vary a lot, so the graph is fatter and the standard deviation is large.

You won't be asked to calculate standard deviation in the exams, but you might be asked to interpret data that includes standard deviations.

You Can Use the **Standard Deviation** to Draw **Error Bars**

1) **Standard deviations** can be **plotted** on a graph or chart of **mean values** using **error bars**, e.g.

2) Error bars extend **one standard deviation above** and **one standard deviation below** the mean (so the total **length** of an error bar is **twice the standard deviation**).

3) The **longer** the **bar**, the **larger** the **standard deviation** and the **more spread out** the sample data is from the mean.

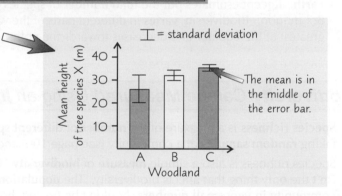

The mean is in the middle of the error bar.

Practice Questions

Q1 Why do scientists look at a sample of a population, rather than the whole population?

Q2 Why does a population sample have to be chosen at random?

Q3 What does the standard deviation of a data set tell us?

Exam Question

Q1 A student was investigating the variation in development time for two beetle species. The student recorded the development time for six beetle larvae from species A and six from species B. The results are shown in the table.

Development Time (Days)	
Species A	Species B
8	12
11	10
9	6
10	12
7	15
9	11

a) Calculate the mean development time for each species. [2 marks]

b) The standard deviation for species A is 1.3 and for species B is 2.7 (to 1 decimal place). What conclusions can you draw from this information? [2 marks]

Sex and drugs and rock and roll — it's all just standard deviation...

Bet you thought you'd finished with maths — 'fraid not. Luckily, calculating a mean is probably one of the easiest bits of maths you could be asked to do — so make sure you can. Also, make sure you understand what both the mean and the standard deviation can tell you about a bit of data. Interpreting data is an all-time favourite with the examiners.

Biodiversity

Bet you've noticed how there are loads of different living things in the world — well that's biodiversity in a nutshell.

Biodiversity is the Variety of Organisms

Before you can sink your teeth into the real meat of biodiversity, there are a few definitions you need to know:

1) **Biodiversity** — the **variety** of **living organisms** in an **area**.
2) **Habitat** — the **place** where an organism **lives**, e.g. a rocky shore or field.
3) **Community** — all the **populations** of different **species** in a **habitat**.

A species is a group of similar organisms able to reproduce to give fertile offspring (see page 96).

Areas with a **high** biodiversity are those with lots of **different species**.

Biodiversity Can be Considered at Different Levels

Biodiversity can be considered at a range of scales from the **local** to the **global**.

1) **Local biodiversity** — you could consider the **variety** of different **species** living in a **small habitat** that's **local** to you — e.g. a pond or meadow, or even your back garden. Some habitats will be more **biodiverse** than others.

2) **Global biodiversity** — you could also consider the variety of **species** on **Earth**. Recent estimates put the **total number** of species on Earth at about 8.7 million. Biodiversity **varies** in different parts of the world — it is greatest at the equator and decreases towards the poles.

Pete wasn't sure that the company's new increased biodiversity policy would be good for productivity.

Biodiversity Can be Measured Using an Index of Diversity

1) **Species richness** is a measure of the **number** of **different species** in a **community**. It can be worked out by taking **random samples** of a community (see page 100) and **counting** the number of different species.

2) Species richness is also a simple **measure** of **biodiversity**. But the number of different species in a community isn't the only thing that affects biodiversity. The **population sizes** of those species do too. Species that are in a community in very **small numbers** shouldn't be treated the same as those with bigger populations.

3) An **index of diversity** is another way of measuring biodiversity. It's calculated using an equation that takes **both** the **number of species** in a community (species richness) and the **abundance of each species** (population sizes) into account.

The number of species in a community and the abundance of each species is also known as the species diversity.

4) You can **calculate** an index of diversity (d) using this formula:

$$d = \frac{N(N-1)}{\sum n(n-1)}$$

Where...
N = **Total number** of organisms of **all species**
n = **Total number** of organisms of **one species**
$\sum$ = '**Sum of**' (i.e. added together)

The **higher** the **number**, the **more diverse** the area is. If all the individuals are of the **same species** (i.e. no biodiversity) the **index is 1**. Here's an example:

There are 3 different species of flower in this field — a red species, a white and a blue.

There are 11 organisms altogether, so N = 11.

There are 3 of the red species, 5 of the white and 3 of the blue.

So the species diversity index of this field is:

$$d = \frac{11(11-1)}{3(3-1)+5(5-1)+3(3-1)} = \frac{110}{6+20+6} = 3.44$$

When calculating the bottom half of the equation you need to work out the n(n–1) bit for each different species then add them all together.

Biodiversity

Agricultural Practices Can Reduce Biodiversity

Farmers try to **maximise** the **amount of food** that they can produce from a given area of land.
But many of the **methods** they use **reduce biodiversity**. For example:

1) **Woodland clearance** — this is done to **increase** the **area** of farmland. It directly reduces the **number** of **trees** and sometimes the **number** of **different tree species**. It also **destroys habitats**, so some species could lose their **shelter** and **food source**. This means that species will **die** or be forced to **migrate** to another suitable area, further **reducing** biodiversity.

2) **Hedgerow removal** — this is also done to **increase** the **area** of farmland by turning **lots of small fields** into **fewer large fields**. This **reduces** biodiversity for the same reasons as woodland clearance.

3) **Pesticides** — these are chemicals that **kill** organisms (**pests**) that feed on **crops**. This **reduces** diversity by **directly killing** the pests. Also, any species that feed on the pests will **lose** a food source, so their numbers could **decrease** too.

4) **Herbicides** — these are chemicals that kill **unwanted plants** (**weeds**). This **reduces** plant diversity and could **reduce** the number of organisms that feed on the weeds.

5) **Monoculture** — this is when farmers have fields containing only **one type of plant**. A **single type** of plant **reduces** biodiversity **directly** and will **support fewer organisms** (e.g. as a habitat or food source), which **further reduces** biodiversity.

Whilst **agriculture** is **important**, we don't want to **lose** too much **biodiversity**. So there has to be a **balance** between agriculture and conservation. Conservationists try to **protect** biodiversity. Some **examples** of **conservation** schemes are:

- Giving **legal protection** to **endangered species**.
- Creating **protected areas** such as SSSIs (Sites of Special Scientific Interest) and AONBs (Areas of Outstanding Natural Beauty). These **restrict** further **development**, including **agricultural** development.
- The **Environmental Stewardship Scheme** which encourages **farmers** to **conserve biodiversity**, e.g. by replanting hedgerows and leaving margins around fields for wild flowers to grow.

Practice Questions

Q1 What is biodiversity?

Q2 What is species richness?

Q3 Give three ways in which agriculture can reduce biodiversity.

Site 1 — No Field Margins		Site 2 — Enhanced Field Margins	
Bombus lucorum	15	*Bombus lucorum*	35
Bombus lapidarius	12	*Bombus lapidarius*	25
Bombus pascuorum	24	*Bombus pascuorum*	34
		Bombus ruderatus	12
		Bombus terrestris	26

Exam Question

Q1 A study was conducted to investigate the impact of introducing enhanced field margins on the diversity of bumblebees. Enhanced field margins are thick bands of land around the edges of fields that are not farmed, but instead are planted with plants that are good for wildlife. Scientists studied two wheat fields, one where the farmer sowed crops right to the edge of the field and another where the farmer created enhanced field margins. The scientists counted the number of bees of different species at each site. Their results are shown in the table above.

a) What two things does an index of diversity take into account when measuring biodiversity? [2 marks]

b) Use the data in the table and the formula below to calculate the index of diversity for each site.

$$d = \frac{N(N-1)}{\sum n(n-1)}$$

[4 marks]

c) What conclusions can be drawn from the findings of this study? [2 marks]

Species richness — goldfish and money spiders top the list...

Agricultural practices can threaten biodiversity — I never knew a field of corn could cause so much bother. Make sure you know the definition of species richness and that population size is important in biodiversity measures too. As for the formula for the index of diversity — be prepared to use it and to say what the numbers it churns out actually mean.

Planning an Experiment

As well as doing practical work in class, you can get asked about it in your exams too. Harsh I know.
You need to be able to plan the perfect experiment and suggest improvements to ones other people have planned.

Before You Start Planning, Be Clear on What You're Trying to Find Out

Like all scientists, you should start off by making a **prediction** or **hypothesis** — a **specific testable statement**, based on theory, about what will happen in the experiment. You then need to **plan** a good experiment that will provide **evidence to support the prediction** — or help **disprove it**.

A Good Experiment Gives Results that are:

1) **Precise** — precise results **don't vary** much **from the mean**. Precision is **reduced** by **random error**.

2) **Repeatable and reproducible** — repeatable means if the **same person** repeats the experiment using the same methods and equipment, they will get the same results. Reproducible means if **someone different** does the experiment, using a slightly different method or piece of equipment, the results will be the same.

3) **Valid** — valid results **answer the original question**. To get valid results you need to **control all the variables** to make sure you're only testing the thing you want to.

4) **Accurate** — accurate results are **really close** to the **true answer**.

Precise results are sometimes referred to as reliable results.

You need to be able to **design** a good experiment. Here are some things you'll need to consider:

1) **Only one variable should be changed** — Variables are **quantities** that have the **potential to change**, e.g. pH. In an experiment you usually **change one variable** and **measure its effect** on another variable.
   - The variable that you **change** is called the **independent variable**.
   - The variable that you **measure** is called the **dependent variable**.

2) **All the other variables should be controlled** — When you're investigating a variable you need to keep everything else that could affect it **constant**. This means you can be sure that **only** your **independent** variable is **affecting** the thing you're measuring (the dependent variable).

3) **Negative controls should be used** — Negative controls are used to **check** that only the independent variable is affecting the dependent variable. Negative controls **aren't expected** to have **any effect** on the experiment.

4) **The experiment should be repeated at least three times and a mean should be calculated** — this reduces the effect of **random error** on your experiment, which makes your results **more precise**. Doing repeats and getting similar results each time also shows that your data is **repeatable** and makes it more likely to be **reproducible**.

> **EXAMPLE:** Investigating the effect of **temperature** on **enzyme activity**.
> 1) Temperature is the **independent** variable.
> 2) Enzyme activity is the **dependent** variable.
> 3) pH, volume, substrate concentration and enzyme concentration should all **stay the same** (and the quantities should be recorded to allow someone else to reproduce the experiment).
> 4) The experiment should be **repeated** at least **three times** at each temperature used.
> 5) A **negative control**, containing everything used **except the enzyme**, should be measured at each temperature used. No enzyme activity should be seen with these controls.

Examiners love getting you to **comment** on **experimental design** or **suggest improvements** to **methods** — e.g. how a method could be improved to make the results more precise. So make sure you know how to **design** a **good experiment**.

Select Appropriate Apparatus, Equipment and Techniques

1) When you're **planning** an experiment you need to decide what it is you're going to **measure** and **how often** you're going to take measurements. E.g. if you're investigating the **rate of an enzyme-controlled reaction**, you could measure how fast the **product appears** or how quickly the **substrate** is **used up**. You could take measurements at, e.g. 30 second intervals or 60 second intervals.

2) Then you need to choose the most **appropriate** apparatus, equipment and techniques for the experiment. E.g.

   - The **measuring apparatus** you use has to be **sensitive** enough to measure the changes you're looking for. For example, if you need to measure **small changes** in **pH**, a **pH meter** (which can measure pH to several decimal places) would be more sensitive than indicator paper.

   - The **technique** you use has to be the most **appropriate** one for your **experiment**. E.g. if you want to investigate plant cells undergoing mitosis, it's best to prepare a **stained squash slide** so you see the chromosomes clearly under the microscope (see page 34).

Planning an Experiment

You Need to Know How to Use *Apparatus* and *Techniques Correctly*

Examiners could ask you about a **whole range** of different apparatus and techniques. Make sure you know how to use all the instruments and equipment you've come across in class and can carry out all the techniques too. Here are some **examples** of equipment you should be able to use:

- **Measuring cylinders** and **graduated pipettes** — These have a **scale** so you can measure specific **volumes**. Whichever one you use, make sure you read the volume from the **bottom** of the **meniscus** when it's at **eye level**.

The meniscus is the curved upper surface of the liquid inside the pipette.

Read volume from here — at the bottom of the meniscus.

- **Water baths** — Make sure you **allow time** for water baths to **heat up** before starting your experiment. Don't forget that your **solutions** will need **time** to get to the **same temperature** as the water before you start the experiment too. Also, remember to **check** the **temperature** of the water bath with a **thermometer** during the investigation to make sure it **doesn't change**.

- **Data logger** — Decide **what** you are **measuring** and what **type** of **data logger** you will need, e.g. temperature, pH. Connect an **external sensor** to the data logger if you need to. Decide **how often** you want the data logger to take readings depending on the **length** of the **process** that you are measuring.

Make sure you know how to do **all** the **practical investigations** described in this book. You should be able to **apply** the techniques described to **different contexts**. For example, page 40 describes how to prepare **serial dilutions** in order to find out the **water potential** of **potato cells**. You could also use serial dilutions when investigating the effect of **substrate concentration** on **enzyme activity**, to prepare solutions of varying substrate concentration.

Risk Assessments Help You to Work Safely

1) When you're planning an experiment, you need to carry out a **risk assessment**. To do this, you need to identify:
   - All the **dangers** in the experiment, e.g. any hazardous chemicals, microorganisms or naked flames.
   - **Who** is at **risk** from these dangers.
   - What can be done to **reduce** the **risk**, such as wearing goggles or gloves or working in a fume cupboard.

2) You also need to consider any **ethical issues** in your experiment. For example, if you're using **living animals** (e.g. insects) you must treat them with **respect**. This means **handling them carefully** and keeping them away from **harmful chemicals**, **extreme heat sources** and other things that might cause them **physical discomfort**.

Record Your Data in a Table

It's a good idea to draw a table to **record** the **results** of your experiment in.

1) When you draw a table, make sure you **include** enough **rows** and **columns** to **record all of the data** you need to. You might also need to include a column for **processing** your data (e.g. working out an average).

2) Make sure each **column** has a **heading** so you know what's going to be recorded where.

3) The **units** should be in the **column** heading, not the table itself.

data *heading* *units* *column*

Farm	Length of hedgerows (km)	Number of species
1	49	21
2	90	28
3	155	30

row

Watch Out for Anomalous Results

Doing repeats makes it easier to spot anomalous results.

When you look at all the **data** in your **table**, you may notice that you have a result that **doesn't seem to fit in** with the rest at all. These results are called **anomalous results**. You should **investigate** anomalous results — if you can work out what happened (e.g. you measured something totally wrong) you can **ignore** them when **processing** your results.

My best apparatus is the pommel horse...

It's not really, I just like the word pommel. Scientists are rightfully fussy about methods and equipment — I mean if you're going to bother doing an experiment, you should at least make sure it's going to give you results you can trust.

Processing and Presenting Data

Processing data means taking raw data and doing some calculations with it, to make it more useful.

Processing the Data Helps You to Interpret it

You Need to be Able to Calculate Percentages and Percentage Change...

Calculating **percentages** helps you to **compare amounts** from **samples** of **different sizes**.
To give the amount **X** as a percentage of sample **Y**, you need to **divide X by Y**, then **multiply** by **100**.

E.g. a tissue sample containing **50** cells is viewed under the microscope. **22** are undergoing mitosis.
What percentage of the cells are undergoing mitosis? Answer: $22/50 \times 100 = $ **44%**

Calculating **percentage change** helps to **quantify** how much something has changed, e.g. the percentage change in the growth rate of pea plants when a fertiliser is added. To **calculate** it you use this equation:

$$\text{Percentage change} = \frac{\text{final value} - \text{original value}}{\text{original value}} \times 100$$

A **positive** value shows an **increase** and a **negative** value shows a **decrease**.

...as Well as Ratios

1) Ratios can be used to **compare** lots of different types of quantities. E.g. an organism with a **surface area to volume ratio** of **2 : 1** would theoretically have a surface area **twice as large** as its volume.

2) Ratios are usually most useful in their **simplest** (smallest) **form**. To simplify a ratio, **divide each side** by the **same number**. It's in its simplest form when there's nothing left you can divide by.

3) To get a ratio of **X : Y** in the form **X : 1**, **divide both sides** by **Y**.
E.g. to get 28 : 34 into the ratio of X : 1, divide both sides by 34. You get 0.82 : 1.

Averages and the Range Can be Used to Summarise Your Data

1) When you've done **repeats** of an experiment you should always calculate a **mean** (a type of average). To do this **add together** all the data values and **divide** by the **total** number of values in the sample.

Test tube	Repeat (g) 1	2	3	Mean (g)	Range (g)
A	28	37	32	$(28 + 37 + 32) \div 3 = 32.3$	$37 - 28 = 9$
B	47	51	60	$(47 + 51 + 60) \div 3 = 52.7$	$60 - 47 = 13$

2) You might also need to calculate the **range** (how **spread out** the data is). To do this find the **largest** data value and **subtract** the **smallest** data value from it.

3) **Standard deviation** can be more useful than the **range** because it tells you how **values** are spread about the **mean** rather than just the **total spread** of data. A **small standard deviation** means the repeated results are all **similar** and **close** to the mean, i.e. **precise**. There's more on standard deviation on p. 101.

Like the mean, the **median** and **mode** are both types of average.
- To calculate the **median**, put all your data in **numerical order**. The median is the **middle value** in this list. If you have an **even number** of values, the median is **halfway** between the middle two values.
- To calculate the **mode**, count **how many times** each value comes up. The mode is the number that appears **most often**. A set of data might not have a mode — or it might have more than one.

Watch Out For Significant Figures

When you're processing your data you may well want to round any **really long numbers** to a certain number of **significant figures**. E.g. **0.6878976** rounds to **0.69** to 2 s.f..
When you're doing **calculations** using numbers given to a certain number of significant figures, you should always give your **answer** to the **lowest number** of significant figures that was used in the calculation.

The first significant figure of a number is the first digit that isn't a zero. The second, third and fourth significant figures follow on immediately after the first (even if they're zeros).

For example:
$$1.2 \div 1.85 = 0.648648648... = \textbf{0.65}$$
2 s.f. | 3 s.f. | Answer should be rounded to 2 s.f. | Round the last digit up to 5.

This is because the **fewer digits** a measurement has, the less **accurate** it is.
Your answer can only be as accurate as the **least accurate measurement** in the calculation.

Processing and Presenting Data

Use a Suitable Graph or Chart to Present Your Data

Graphs and charts are a great way of **presenting data** — they can make results much **easier to interpret**.

1) When you have **qualitative** data (non-numerical data, e.g. blood group) or **discrete** data (numerical data that can only take certain values in a range, e.g. shoe size) you can use **bar charts** or **pie charts**.

2) When you have **continuous** data (data that can take any value in a range, e.g. height or weight) you can use **histograms** or **line graphs.**

3) When you want to show how **two variables** are **related** (or **correlated**, see next page) you can use a **scatter graph**.

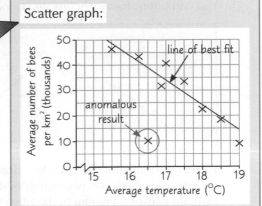

Scatter graph:

Whatever type of graph you use, you should make sure that:

- The **dependent variable** goes on the **y-axis** (the vertical axis) and the **independent** on the **x-axis** (the horizontal axis).

- You always **label** the **axes**, include the quantity and **units**, and choose a **sensible scale**.

- The graph covers **at least half** of the **graph paper**.

If you need to draw a **line** (or curve) **of best fit** on a **scatter graph**, draw the line through or as near to as many points as possible, **ignoring** any **anomalous** results.

Find the Rate By Finding the Gradient

Rate is a **measure** of how much something is **changing over time**. Calculating a rate can be useful when analysing your data, e.g. you might want to the find the **rate of a reaction**. Rates are easy to work out from a graph:

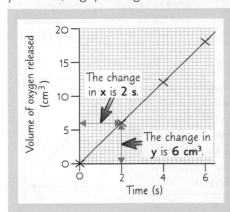

For a **linear** graph you can calculate the **rate** by finding the **gradient of the line**: $\Rightarrow$

$$\text{Gradient} = \frac{\text{Change in Y}}{\text{Change in X}}$$

So in this **example**: $\text{rate} = \dfrac{6 \text{ cm}^3}{2 \text{ s}} = 3 \text{ cm}^3 \text{ s}^{-1}$ $\leftarrow$ cm³ s⁻¹ means the same as cm³/s (centimetres³ per second)

The **equation** of a **straight line** can always be written in the form $y = mx + c$, where **m** is the **gradient** and **c** is the **y-intercept** (this is the **value of y** when the line crosses the **y-axis**). In this example, the equation of the line is $y = 3x + 0$ (or just $y = 3x$). Knowing the equation of the line allows you to estimate results not plotted on the graph. E.g. in this case, when x (the time) is **20 s**, y (the volume of oxygen released) will be $3x = 3 \times 20 = 60 \text{ cm}^3$.

For a **curved** (non-linear) graph you can find the **rate** by drawing a **tangent**:

1) Position a ruler on the graph at the **point** where you want to know the **rate**.

2) **Angle** the **ruler** so there is **equal space** between the **ruler** and the **curve** on **either** side of the point.

3) **Draw** a **line** along the ruler to make the tangent.

   Extend the line right across the graph — it'll help to make your **gradient calculation easier** as you'll have **more points** to choose from.

4) **Calculate** the **gradient** of the **tangent** to find the **rate**.

   Gradient = 55 m² ÷ 4.4 years = **12.5 m² year⁻¹**

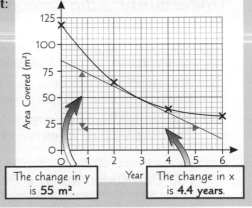

The change in y is **55 m²**. | Year | The change in x is **4.4 years**.

When calculating a rate (or anything else for that matter) you might have to **convert** between **units**, e.g. seconds and minutes. Make sure you can convert between common units of time, length and volume.

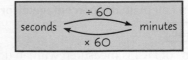

seconds ⇄ minutes (÷ 60 / × 60)

Significant figures — a result of far too many cream cakes...

Lots of maths to get your head around on these two pages, but stay calm and take your time with it all. You'll be fine.

Drawing Conclusions and Evaluating

There's no point in getting all those lovely results and just leaving it at that. You need to draw some conclusions...

You Need to be Able to **Draw Conclusions** From **Data**

1) Conclusions need to be **valid**. A conclusion can only be considered as valid if it answers the original question (see page 104).

2) You can often draw conclusions by looking at the relationship (**correlation**) between two variables:

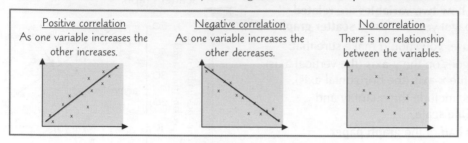

Positive correlation
As one variable increases the other increases.

Negative correlation
As one variable increases the other decreases.

No correlation
There is no relationship between the variables.

There is no correlation between the colour of your tights and the proportion of your life you spend upside down.

3) You have to be very **careful** when **drawing conclusions** from data like this because a **correlation** between two variables **doesn't** always mean that a **change** in one variable **causes** a **change** in the other (the correlation could be due to **chance** or there could be a **third variable** having an effect).

4) If there's a relationship between two variables and a change in one variable **does** cause a change in the other it's called a **causal relationship**.

5) It can be **concluded** that a **correlation** is a **causal relationship** if every other variable that could possibly affect the result is **controlled**. ⬅ In reality this is very hard to do — correlations are generally accepted to be causal relationships if lots of studies have found the same thing, and scientists have figured out exactly how one factor causes the other.

6) When you're making a conclusion you **can't** make broad **generalisations** from data — you have to be very **specific**. You can only **conclude** what the results show and **no more**.

> **Example**
>
> The graph shows the results from a study into the effect of penicillin dosage on the duration of fever in men. The only **conclusion** you can draw is that there's a **negative correlation** between penicillin dosage and duration of fever in men (as the **dosage** of **penicillin increases**, the **duration** of **fever** in **men decreases**). You **can't** conclude that this is true for any other antibiotic, any other symptom or even for female patients — the **results** could be **completely different**.

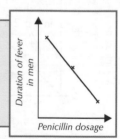

Duration of fever in men / *Penicillin dosage*

Uncertainty is the Amount of **Error** Your **Measurements** Might Have

1) The results you get from an experiment won't be completely perfect — there'll always be a **degree of uncertainty** in your measurements due to limits in the **sensitivity** of the apparatus you're using.

2) For example, an electronic mass balance might measure to the **nearest 0.01 g**, but the real mass could be up to **0.005 g smaller or larger**. It has an **uncertainty value** of ± 0.005g.

3) The ± sign tells you the **range** in which the **true value** lies (to within a certain probability). The range is called the **margin of error**.

You Can **Calculate** The **Percentage Error** of Your **Measurements**

If you know the **uncertainty value** of your measurements, you can calculate the **percentage error** using this formula: ➡

$$\text{percentage error} = \frac{\text{uncertainty}}{\text{reading}} \times 100$$

Example

50 cm^3 of HCl is measured with an uncertainty value of ± 0.05 cm^3.

$$\text{percentage error} = \frac{0.05}{50} \times 100 = \textbf{0.1\%}$$

Drawing Conclusions and Evaluating

You Can *Minimise* the *Errors* in Your *Measurements*

1) One obvious way to **reduce errors** in your measurements is to buy the most **sensitive equipment** available. In real life there's not much you can do about this one — you're stuck with whatever your school or college has got. But there are other ways to **lower the uncertainty** in experiments.

2) For example, you can plan your experiment so you **measure** a **greater amount** of something:

> If you use a **500 cm³** cylinder that goes up in **5 cm³** increments, each reading has an uncertainty of ± **2.5 cm³**.
>
> So using a 500 cm³ cylinder to measure **100 cm³** of liquid will give you a percentage error of:
>
> $$\frac{2.5}{100} \times 100 = 2.5\%$$
>
> But if you measure **200 cm³** in the same cylinder, the percentage error is:
>
> $$\frac{2.5}{200} \times 100 = 1.25\%$$
>
> Hey presto — you've just **halved** the uncertainty.

You Also Need to Be Able to *Evaluate Methods* and *Results*

1) In the exams, you might get asked to **evaluate** experimental results or methods. Here are some things to think about:

- **Repeatability**: Did you take enough repeat readings of the measurements? Would you do more repeats if you were to do the experiment again? Do you think you'd get similar data if you did the experiment again?
- **Reproducibility**: Have you compared your results with other people's results? Were your results similar? Could other scientists gain data showing the same relationships that are shown in your data?
- **Validity**: Does your data answer the question you set out to investigate? Were all the variables controlled?

2) Make sure you **evaluate** your **method**. Is there anything you could have done to make your results more **precise** or **accurate**? Were there any **limitations** in your method, e.g. should you have taken measurements more **frequently**? Were there any **sources** of **error** in your experiment? Could you have used more sensitive **apparatus** or **equipment**? Think about how you could **refine** and **improve** your experiment if you did it again.

3) Once you've thought about these points you can decide how much **confidence** you have in your **conclusion**. For example, if your results are **repeatable**, **reproducible** and **valid** and they back up your conclusion then you can have a **high degree** of **confidence** in your conclusion.

Solving Problems in a *Practical Context*

In the exams, you'll get plenty of questions set in a 'practical context'. As well as answering questions about the methods used or the conclusions drawn, you'll need to be able to **apply** your **scientific knowledge** to solve **problems** set in these contexts. For example:

> Q1 A scientist is investigating how the rate of an enzyme-controlled reaction is affected by substrate concentration. The results are shown in the graph.
>
> a) Suggest why the graph levels off at substrate concentrations higher than 0.08 M. [2 marks]

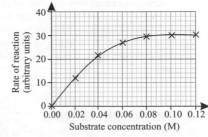

You should remember from page 12 that once all the enzymes' **active sites** are **full** (the saturation point has been reached) adding more substrate won't increase the rate of reaction any further — which is why the rate levels off.

Correlation Street — my favourite programme...

Don't ever, ever assume that correlation means cause. There, I've told you again. No excuses now. A good evaluation is a sign that you really understand what makes a good experiment, so make sure your evaluation-writing-skills are top notch.

Answers

Topic 1A — Biological Molecules

Page 5 — Carbohydrates

1   Two molecules of alpha-glucose *[1 mark]* are joined by a glycosidic bond *[1 mark]*. A molecule of water is released/a condensation reaction takes place *[1 mark]*.

2   Take a new sample of the test solution, add dilute HCl and heat it in a water bath that's been brought to the boil *[1 mark]*. Neutralise it with sodium hydrogencarbonate *[1 mark]*. Then add blue Benedict's solution and heat it in a water bath that's been brought to the boil *[1 mark]*. If the test is positive for a non-reducing sugar, a brick red precipitate will form *[1 mark]*. If the test is negative, the solution will stay blue *[1 mark]*.
The question asks to describe a test for a non-reducing sugar. Remember, the test for a reducing sugar has to be performed first. If this gives a negative result, a non-reducing sugar may still be present. That's when the test for non-reducing sugars should be performed.

3 a) Because it is made up of chains of a monosaccharide/ N-acetylglucosamine *[1 mark]*.

  b) Cellulose and chitin are both polysaccharides *[1 mark]*, made up of long and unbranched chains *[1 mark]*. The chains are linked together by weak hydrogen bonds *[1 mark]*.

  c) A molecule of water *[1 mark]* is used to break the glycosidic bond between the monosaccharides in the chain *[1 mark]*.

  d) Secretion of chitinases would protect plants against attack by insects *[1 mark]* and fungal infection *[1 mark]*, by breaking down the chitin in the exoskeleton of insects and the cell walls of fungi *[1 mark]*, which would kill the invading organisms *[1 mark]*.

Page 7 — Lipids

1   The hydrophobic tails force them to clump together in the cytoplasm as insoluble droplets *[1 mark]*. This means they can be stored in cells, as a source of energy, without affecting the cell's water potential *[1 mark]*.

2 a) Two fatty acid molecules *[1 mark]* and a phosphate group *[1 mark]* attached to one glycerol molecule *[1 mark]*.
Don't get phospholipids mixed up with triglycerides — a triglyceride has three fatty acids attached to one glycerol molecule.

  b) Saturated fatty acids don't have any double bonds between their carbon atoms *[1 mark]*. Unsaturated fatty acids have one or more double bonds between their carbon atoms *[1 mark]*.

Page 9 — Proteins

1   A peptide bond *[1 mark]* forms between the carboxyl group of one amino acid and the amino group of the other amino acid *[1 mark]*. A molecule of water is released / a condensation reaction takes place *[1 mark]*.
If you find it difficult to explain a process, such as a dipeptide forming, learn the diagrams too because they may help you to explain the process.

2   The secondary structure is coiled and folded further to form the protein's final 3D structure *[1 mark]*. More bonds, including hydrogen bonds, ionic bonds and disulphide bridges, form between different parts of the polypeptide chain *[1 mark]*.

Page 11 — Enzyme Action

1   The complementary substrate binds to the active site of the enzyme *[1 mark]* to form an enzyme-substrate complex *[1 mark]*. As the substrate binds, the active site changes shape slightly, which provides a better fit *[1 mark]*. The substrate is broken down / joined together to form the product(s) *[1 mark]*.

2   A change in the amino acid sequence of an enzyme may alter its tertiary structure *[1 mark]*. This changes the shape of the active site so that the substrate can't bind to it *[1 mark]*.

Page 13 — Factors Affecting Enzyme Activity

1 a) Competitive inhibitor molecules have a similar shape to the substrate molecules *[1 mark]*. They compete with the substrate molecules to bind to the active site of an enzyme *[1 mark]*. When an inhibitor molecule is bound to the active site it stops t substrate molecule from binding *[1 mark]*.

  b) Non-competitive inhibitor molecules bind to enzymes from their active site *[1 mark]*. This causes the active site to change shape so the substrate molecule can no longer fit *[1 mark]*.

Page 15 — Enzyme-Controlled Reactions

1   65 °C gradient = 40 cm^3 ÷ 4 s = **10 cm^{3}s^{-1}**
(accept between 8 cm^{3}s^{-1} and 13 cm^{3}s^{-1}) *[1 mark]*.

Topic 1B — More Biological Molecules

Page 17 — DNA and RNA

1

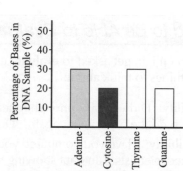

[1 mark for a bar drawn for thymine at 30%.
1 mark for a bar drawn for guanine at 20%]
Remember, thanks to complementary base pairing, there are always equal amounts of adenine and thymine in a DNA sample and equal amounts of cytosine and guanine. Double-check your answer by making sure the percentages of all four bases add up to 100%.

2 a) Nucleotides are joined between the phosphate group of one nucleotide and the (deoxyribose) sugar of the next *[1 mark]* by phosphodiester bonds *[1 mark]* in a condensation reaction *[1 mark]*.

  b) Two polynucleotide strands join through hydrogen bonding between the base pairs *[1 mark]*. Base pairing is complementar (e.g. A always pairs with T and C always pairs with G) *[1 mark]*. The two antiparallel polynucleotide strands twist to form a DNA double helix *[1 mark]*.

Page 19 — DNA Replication

1   Any five from: e.g. DNA helicase breaks the hydrogen bonds between the two DNA strands and the DNA helix unwinds *[1 mark]*. / Each strand acts as a template for a new strand *[1 mark]*. / Individual free DNA nucleotides join up along the template strand by complementary base pairing *[1 mark]*. / DNA polymerase joins the individual nucleotides together, so that the sugar-phosphate backbone forms *[1 mark]*. / Hydrogen bonds then form between the bases on each strand and the strands twis to form a double-helix *[1 mark]*. / Two identical DNA molecules are produced *[1 mark]*. / Each of the new molecules contains a single strand from the original DNA molecule and a single new strand *[1 mark]*. *[Maximum of 5 marks available.]*

Answers

ge 21 — Water

.) As the water evaporates from the surface of the elephant's body *[1 mark]*, some of the elephant's heat energy is used to break the hydrogen bonds which hold the water molecules together *[1 mark]*. This cools the surface of the elephant's body *[1 mark]*.
•) There is strong cohesion between water molecules *[1 mark]*. This results in water having a high surface tension when in contact with air, causing it to form droplets *[1 mark]*.

ge 23 — Inorganic Ions

A condensation reaction *[1 mark]* occurs between this molecule (ADP) and inorganic phosphate/P$_i$ *[1 mark]*. The reaction is catalysed by ATP synthase *[1 mark]*.
) Iron ions are a key component of haemoglobin *[1 mark]*. The iron ions in haemoglobin bind to oxygen *[1 mark]*. The haemoglobin is transported around the body in red blood cells *[1 mark]*.
•) Phosphate ions form the phosphate groups of ATP *[1 mark]*. Breaking the bonds between the phosphate groups in ATP releases energy *[1 mark]*.

pic 2A — Cell Structure and Division

ge 27 — Eukaryotic Cells and Organelles

) E.g. helps maintain pressure inside the cell/keeps the cell rigid *[1 mark]* / isolates unwanted chemicals inside the cell *[1 mark]*.
•) E.g. cell wall *[1 mark]*, chloroplasts *[1 mark]*
Ciliated epithelial cells have lots of mitochondria *[1 mark]* because they need lots of energy *[1 mark]*.
Any four (in order) from: e.g. ribosomes *[1 mark]* / rough endoplasmic reticulum *[1 mark]* / Golgi apparatus *[1 mark]* / Golgi vesicle *[1 mark]* / cell-surface membrane *[1 mark]*.
This question really tests how well you know what each organelle does. The rough endoplasmic reticulum transports proteins that have been made in the ribosomes to the Golgi apparatus. At the Golgi apparatus the proteins are packaged and sent in Golgi vesicles to be secreted at the cell-surface membrane.

ge 29 — Prokaryotic Cells and Viruses

) murein *[1 mark]*
•) Any three from: e.g. *Vibrio cholerae* replicates its circular DNA and its plasmids *[1 mark]*. / The cell gets bigger and the DNA moves to opposite poles *[1 mark]*. / New cell walls begin to form *[1 mark]*. / The cytoplasm divides to make two daughter cells *[1 mark]*. / This process is called binary fission *[1 mark]*.
Vibrio cholerae is a prokaryotic organism, so its cell wall must be made from murein and it must replicate by binary fission.
:) Having a capsule may help to protect *Vibrio cholerae* from attack by the immune system cells of the people it infects *[1 mark]*.

ge 31 — Analysis of Cell Components

mitochondrion *[1 mark]* and nucleus *[1 mark]*
The resolution of light microscopes is not good enough to show objects smaller than 0.2 μm *[1 mark]*.
It should be kept ice-cold to reduce the activity of enzymes that break down organelles *[1 mark]*. It should be kept isotonic to prevent damage to the organelles through osmosis *[1 mark]*.

Page 33 — Cell Division — Mitosis

1 a) A — Metaphase *[1 mark]*, B — Telophase *[1 mark]*, C — Anaphase *[1 mark]*.
   b) X — Chromosome/Chromatid *[1 mark]*, Y — Centromere *[1 mark]*, Z — Spindle fibre *[1 mark]*.

Page 35 — Cell Division — Investigating Mitosis

1   32 ÷ 42 = 0.76 *[2 marks for the correct answer or 1 mark for the correct calculation.]*

Topic 2B — Cell Membranes

Page 37 — Cell Membrane Structure

1   The membrane is described as fluid because the phospholipids are constantly moving *[1 mark]*. It is described as a mosaic because the proteins are scattered throughout the membrane like tiles in a mosaic *[1 mark]*.
2 a) Cut five equal sized pieces of beetroot and rinse them to remove any pigment released during cutting *[1 mark]*. Make up five test tubes with alcohol concentrations at 0, 25, 50, 75 and 100% *[1 mark]*. Place a piece of beetroot in each test tube for the same length of time *[1 mark]*. Remove the pieces of beetroot from each tube and use a colorimeter to measure how much light is absorbed by each of the remaining solutions *[1 mark]*.
   b) As the concentration of alcohol increased, the absorbance also increased *[1 mark]*. This means that more pigment was released by the beetroot as the alcohol concentration increased, so the membrane became more permeable at higher concentrations of alcohol *[1 mark]*.

Page 39 — Exchange Across Cell Membranes — Diffusion

1 a) channel protein(s) *[1 mark]*
   Channel proteins transport charged particles, such as ions.
   b) E.g. ions are water soluble *[1 mark]* and the centre of the phospholipid bilayer is hydrophobic *[1 mark]*.
   c) The rate of facilitated diffusion will slow down/level off *[1 mark]*. As diffusion progresses, the concentration gradient of the chloride ions will decrease/the concentration of chloride ions inside and outside of the cell will become the same (an equilibrium will be reached) *[1 mark]*.

Page 41 — Exchange Across Cell Membranes — Osmosis

1 a) The water potential of the sucrose solution was higher than the water potential of the potato *[1 mark]*. So water moved into the potato pieces by osmosis, increasing their mass *[1 mark]*.
   b) The water potential of the potato and the water potential of the solution was the same *[1 mark]*.
   c) −0.4 g *[1 mark]*. The difference in water potential between the solution and the potato is the same as with the 1% solution, so the mass difference should be about the same, but negative *[1 mark]*.
   The potato has a higher water potential than the solution, so it will lose water and mass.

Answers

Page 43 — Exchange Across Cell Membranes — Active Transport

1 a) Solute X. E.g. because the concentration of solute X inside the cell continues to increase over time, showing uptake against a concentration gradient *[1 mark]*. / Because the concentration of solute Y levels off, which does not happen in active transport *[1 mark]*.

Solute Y is being transported by some form of diffusion. Once the concentration of solute Y inside the cell reaches equilibrium with the concentration outside the cell, the rate levels off. This doesn't happen with active transport.

b) Energy is needed because the solute is being transported against its concentration gradient *[1 mark]*.

c) Energy is released by the hydrolysis of ATP *[1 mark]* into ADP and P_i/inorganic phosphate *[1 mark]*.

Topic 2C — Cells and the Immune System

Page 45 — The Immune System

1 Antibodies bind pathogens together / agglutinate pathogens *[1 mark]*. This allows phagocytes to engulf many pathogens at once *[1 mark]*.

2 A secondary immune response is a faster and stronger response than the primary response *[1 mark]*. This is because memory cells are produced during the primary response, which are able to recognise the foreign antigen when it is encountered again *[1 mark]*. During the second infection, memory cell B-cells can quickly divide to form plasma cells, which secrete the correct antibody to the antigen *[1 mark]*. Memory T-cells quickly divide into the right type of T-cells to kill the cell carrying the antigen *[1 mark]*.

You'll only get the full marks for this question if you explain (as well as describe) why the secondary response differs.

Page 47 — Immunity and Vaccines

1 When some individuals in a population receive the vaccine, the occurrence of the disease in the population is reduced *[1 mark]*. This means that those in the population who haven't been vaccinated are less likely to become infected *[1 mark]*. This is called herd immunity *[1 mark]*.

2 The flu virus is able to change its surface antigens/shows antigenic variation *[1 mark]*. This means that when you're infected for a second time with a different strain, the memory cells produced from the first infection will not recognise the new/different antigens *[1 mark]*. The immune system has to carry out a primary response against these new antigens *[1 mark]*. This takes time and means you become ill *[1 mark]*.

3 a) Active immunity involves the production of memory cells specific to a particular antigen. This means the immune system is able to mount a secondary immune response if the same antigen is detected again *[1 mark]*. Passive immunity only offers short-term protection because the antibodies given are broken down in the body. / Memory cells are not produced, so the body can't mount a secondary immune response *[1 mark]*.

b) It takes time for the body to produce antibodies/memory cells against the antigens in the vaccine *[1 mark]*.

Page 49 — Antibodies in Medicine

1 Monoclonal antibodies are made against antigens specific to cancer cells/tumour markers *[1 mark]*. An anti-cancer drug is attached to the antibodies *[1 mark]*. The antibodies bind to the antigens/tumour markers on cancer cells because their binding sites have a complementary shape *[1 mark]*. This delivers the anti-cancer drug to the cells *[1 mark]*.

Page 51 — Interpreting Vaccine and Antibody Data

1 a) Fewer people were being infected by Hib because they had been vaccinated against it *[1 mark]* or were benefiting from her immunity *[1 mark]*.

b) E.g. fewer people received the vaccine. / A new strain of Hib appeared, which the vaccine was less effective against *[1 mark]*.

Page 53 — HIV and Viruses

1 HIV has a core that contains the genetic material (RNA) and some proteins *[1 mark]*. It has an outer layer called the capsid, which is made of protein *[1 mark]*, surrounded by an envelope that is made from the membrane of the host cell *[1 mark]*. There are attachment proteins sticking out from the envelope *[1 mark]*.

Topic 3A — Exchange and Transport Systems

Page 55 — Size and Surface Area

1 A small mammal has a bigger surface to volume ratio than a lar mammal *[1 mark]*. This means that heat is lost more easily from small mammal *[1 mark]*. So a smaller mammal needs a relative high metabolic rate, in order to generate enough heat to mainta a constant body temperature *[1 mark]*.

Page 57 — Gas Exchange

1 Any one from: gaseous exchange surfaces have a large surface area *[1 mark]*, e.g. mesophyll cells in a plant (or any other suitable example) *[1 mark]*. / Gaseous exchange surfaces are th which provides a short diffusion pathway *[1 mark]*, e.g. the wal of tracheoles in insects (or any other suitable example) *[1 mark]* A steep diffusion gradient is constantly maintained across gaseo exchange surfaces *[1 mark]*, e.g. the counter-current system in fish gills (or any other suitable example) *[1 mark]*. *[Maximum o 2 marks available]*

2 Sunken stomata and hairs help to trap any moist air near to the stomata *[1 mark]*, reducing the concentration gradient from leaf to air, which reduces water loss *[1 mark]*.

Page 59 — Gas Exchange in Humans

1 Any two from: e.g. the lungs contain millions of tiny air sacs called alveoli, creating a large surface area for gas exchange *[1 mark]*. / The alveolar epithelium is only one cell thick, which means there is a short diffusion pathway *[1 mark]*. / The alveoli are surrounded by a dense network of capillaries, which mainta a steep concentration gradient of oxygen and carbon dioxide between the alveoli and the blood *[1 mark]*.

2 The external intercostal muscles and diaphragm contract *[1 mar* This causes the ribcage to move up and out and the diaphragm to flatten *[1 mark]*, increasing the volume of the thoracic cavity *[1 mark]*. The air pressure in the lungs decreases and air flows down the pressure gradient into the lungs *[1 mark]*.

Page 61 — The Effects of Lung Disease

1 a) Emphysema involves the loss/break down of elastin in the walls the alveoli *[1 mark]*. This means the alveoli can't recoil to expe air as well *[1 mark]*.

b) 1.7 / 3.2 × 100 = **53%** *(to 2 s.f.)* *[1 mark]*

c) Both FEV_1 and FVC are reduced, so the ratio between them stays the same as in a healthy person *[1 mark]*.

Answers

Page 63 — *Interpreting Lung Disease Data*

a) The daily death rate increased rapidly after 4th December *[1 mark]* peaking around the 7th, then decreasing afterwards *[1 mark]*. Both pollutants followed the same pattern *[1 mark]*.
You could also get the marks by saying it the other way round — the pollutants rose and peaked around the 7th then decreased, with the death rates following the same pattern.

b) There is a link/correlation between the increase in sulfur dioxide and smoke concentration and the increase in death rate *[1 mark]*.
Don't go saying that the increase in sulfur dioxide and smoke <u>caused</u> the increase in death rate — there could have been another reason for the trend, e.g. there could have been other pollutants responsible for the deaths.

Page 65 — *Dissecting Gas Exchange Systems*

E.g. the liquid preservative has entered the grasshopper's tracheae, so they are no longer filled with air (and they would appear silver in colour if filled with air) *[1 mark]*.

a) The lung tissue will float as it/the alveoli still contain(s) some air *[1 mark]*.

b) E.g. make sure the dissecting instruments are clean, sharp and free from rust *[1 mark]*. / Carry out the dissection on a cutting board *[1 mark]*. / Cut downwards and away from the body when using a scalpel *[1 mark]*. / Wash hands/disinfect work surfaces after carrying out the dissection *[1 mark]*.

Topic 3B — *More Exchange and Transport Systems*

Page 67 — *Digestion and Absorption*

a) lactase *[1 mark]*

b) The digestion products of lactose/glucose and galactose are absorbed across the epithelial cells of the ileum by active transport with sodium ions *[1 mark]* via a co-transporter protein *[1 mark]*.

Page 69 — *Haemoglobin*

a) It is composed of more than one polypeptide chain *[1 mark]*.
The reason that haemoglobin has a quaternary structure is because it has <u>more than one</u> polypeptide chain. The fact that it's made up of four polypeptides isn't important.

b) i), ii)

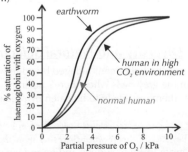

i) The curve for a human in a high carbon dioxide environment should look like a normal human dissociation curve that has shifted right (see graph above) *[1 mark]*. This is the Bohr effect *[1 mark]*. High concentrations of carbon dioxide increase the rate of oxygen unloading and the saturation of blood with oxygen is lower for a given pO_2 *[1 mark]*.

ii) The curve for the earthworm should be drawn to the left of the human one (see graph above) *[1 mark]*.
The earthworm lives in an environment with a low partial pressure of oxygen, so it needs haemoglobin with a higher affinity for oxygen than human haemoglobin.

Page 71 — *The Circulatory System*

1 E.g. they have elastic tissue in the walls *[1 mark]* so they can stretch and recoil as the heart beats, which helps maintain the high pressure *[1 mark]*. The inner lining (endothelium) is folded *[1 mark]* so that the artery can expand when the heartbeat causes a surge of blood *[1 mark]*.

2 The hydrostatic pressure in the capillary is greater than the hydrostatic pressure in the spaces around the cells *[1 mark]*, so fluid moves out of the capillary and into spaces around the cells *[1 mark]*.

Page 74 — *The Heart*

1 a) 0.2 - 0.4 seconds *[1 mark]*.
The AV valves are shut when the pressure is higher in the ventricles than in the atria.

b) 0.3 - 0.4 seconds *[1 mark]*.
When the ventricles relax the volume of the chamber increases and the pressure falls. The pressure in the left ventricle was 16.5 kPa at 0.3 seconds and it decreased to 7.0 kPa at 0.4 seconds, so it must have started to relax somewhere between these two times.

c) 16.5 − 0.5 = 16
(16 ÷ 0.5) × 100 = **3200% *[1 mark for the correct answer.]***
In this question you need to calculate the percentage increase from 0.5 kPa (blood pressure at 0.0 s) to 16.5 kPa (blood pressure at 0.3 s). To do this you find the difference between the two blood pressures (16 kPa), divide this by the starting blood pressure (0.5 kPa), and multiply the whole thing by 100.

Page 77 — *Cardiovascular Disease*

1 a) A large sample size was used *[1 mark]*.
The sample included many countries *[1 mark]*.

b) E.g. a large waist measurement could indicate that someone is overweight *[1 mark]*. Being overweight can be linked to high blood pressure *[1 mark]*. High blood pressure is a risk factor for cardiovascular disease because it increases the risk of damage to artery walls *[1 mark]*.

Page 79 — *Transport in Plants — Xylem*

1 a) The evaporation of water from plant surfaces *[1 mark]*.

b) Transpiration from the leaves at the 'top' of the xylem creates tension, which pulls more water into the leaf *[1 mark]*. Water molecules are cohesive, so when some are pulled into the leaf others follow *[1 mark]*. This means the whole column of water in the xylem, from the leaves down to the roots, moves upwards, pulling water into the stem through the roots *[1 mark]*.

Page 81 — *Transport in Plants — Phloem*

1 a) Leaves can act as a source because they are a part of a plant where solutes/products of photosynthesis are made *[1 mark]*.

b) Radioactive solutes/products of photosynthesis have been translocated to the fruits because the fruits are acting as a sink *[1 mark]*.

Answers

Topic 4A — DNA, RNA and Protein Synthesis

Page 83 — DNA, Genes and Chromosomes

1   Any five points from: e.g. in the nucleus of eukaryotic cells, DNA is stored as chromosomes *[1 mark]*. It is linear *[1 mark]*. It is wound around proteins called histones *[1 mark]*. Mitochondria and chloroplasts in eukaryotic cells also contain DNA *[1 mark]*. In mitochondria and chloroplasts, the DNA is short and circular *[1 mark]*. The DNA in mitochondria / chloroplasts is not associated with histones *[1 mark]*.

2   672 ÷ 3 = **224** amino acids
[2 marks for the correct answer, 1 mark for the correct calculation.]
Remember, only the exons actually code for amino acids. Three nucleotides code for each amino acid, so you need to divide the number of nucleotide pairs in the exons by three.

Page 85 — RNA and Protein Synthesis

1   The drug binds to DNA, preventing RNA polymerase from binding, so transcription can't take place and no mRNA can be made *[1 mark]*. This means there's no mRNA for translation and so protein synthesis is inhibited *[1 mark]*.

Page 87 — The Genetic Code and Nucleic Acids

1 a) GUG = valine
UGU = cysteine
CGC = arginine
GCA = alanine
Correct sequence = **valine, cysteine, arginine, alanine**.
[2 marks if all four amino acids are correct and in the correct order. 1 mark if three amino acids are correct and in the correct order.]

 b) valine = GUG
arginine = CGC
alanine = GCA
mRNA sequence = GUG CGC GCA
DNA sequence = **CAC** *[1 mark]* **GCG** *[1 mark]* **CGT** *[1 mark]*.

2 a) The mRNA sequence is 18 nucleotides long and the protein produced is 6 amino acids long *[1 mark]*. 18 ÷ 6 = 3, suggesting three nucleotides code for a single amino acid *[1 mark]*.

 b) E.g. The sequence produced began leucine-cysteine-glycine. This would only be produced if the code is non-overlapping, e.g. UUGUGUGGG = UUG-UGU-GGG = leucine-cysteine-glycine *[1 mark]*.
If the code was overlapping, the triplets would be, e.g. UUG-UGU-GUG-UGU, which would give a sequence starting leucine-cysteine-valine-cysteine.
Also, this part of the DNA sequence produces 6 amino acids. This is only correct if the code is non-overlapping — the sequence of amino acids would be longer if the code overlapped *[1 mark]*.

Topic 4B — Diversity, Classification and Variation

Page 90 — Meiosis and Genetic Variation

1 a)

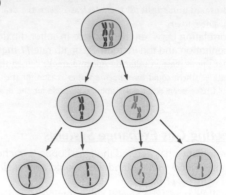

[1 mark for 2 single-stranded chromosomes (not sister chromatids) in each daughter cell.]

 b) During meiosis homologous pairs of chromosomes come together *[1 mark]*. The chromatids twist around each other and bits swap over *[1 mark]*. The chromatids now contain different combinations of alleles *[1 mark]*. This means each of the four daughter cells will contain chromatids with different combinations of alleles *[1 mark]*.

 c) Independent segregation means the homologous chromosome pairs can split up in any way *[1 mark]*. So, the daughter cells produced can contain any combination of maternal and paternal chromosomes with different alleles *[1 mark]*.

2   Chromosome non-disjunction may mean that the sex chromosomes fail to separate during meiosis *[1 mark]*. This could mean that one of the daughter cells/gametes ends up without a copy of the X chromosome, whilst another daughter cell/gamete gets two X chromosomes *[1 mark]*. If the gamete without an X chromosome is fertilised, the resulting zygote will be missing one X chromosome, resulting in Turner syndrome *[1 mark]*.

Page 91 — Mutations

1 a) substitution *[1 mark]*

 b) The second amino acid will be arginine for the mutated gene, rather than serine (as for the original gene) *[1 mark]*. The rest of the sequence of amino acids produced will not be affected *[1 mark]*.

Page 93 — Genetic Diversity and Natural Selection

1 a) E.g. the brown owls may be better camouflaged/blend in with the landscape better than the grey owls when there's no snow cover *[1 mark]*. This makes them less likely to be eaten by predators *[1 mark]*.
Snow makes everything white, so lighter coloured owls blend in better when there's snow around. They stick out more when there's no snow though.

 b) The brown owls are more likely to survive and reproduce when there's less snow cover *[1 mark]* and pass on the allele for darker brown colouring to their offspring *[1 mark]*. Over time, the allele for darker/brown colouring will become more common in the population *[1 mark]*.

Answers

ge 95 — *Investigating Selection*

) This is an example of stabilising selection *[1 mark]*. The initial sample shows a fairly wide range of shell colours from light to dark *[1 mark]*. Over time, the average colour of oyster shell has shifted towards the middle of the range, so more oysters have a mid-range coloured shell in the final sample than in the initial sample *[1 mark]*.

) Oysters at the extremes of light and dark are less likely to survive because they can be more easily seen by predators against the sand *[1 mark]*. This means that the mid-range coloured oysters have an advantage and are more likely to survive and reproduce *[1 mark]*. The advantageous alleles for mid-range coloured oysters are more likely to be passed on to the next generation *[1 mark]* leading to an increase in mid-range coloured oysters in the population *[1 mark]*.

ge 97 — *Classification of Organisms*

)

Domain	Kingdom	Phylum	Class	Order	Family	Genus	Species
Eukarya	Animalia	Chordata	Actinopterygii	Salmoniformes	Salmonidae	Salmo	trutta

[1 mark for 4 or more answers correct.
2 marks for all 7 answers correct.]

) They are unable to reproduce to give fertile offspring *[1 mark]*. Although brook trout and brown trout do sometimes mate to produce offspring, those offspring are infertile.

ge 99 — *DNA Technology, Classification* *d Diversity*

) Mouse and rat *[1 mark]*.

) Chicken *[1 mark]* because all of the amino acids in the protein sequence for the chicken are different to the amino acids for the other species *[1 mark]*.

ge 101 — *Investigating Variation*

) species A = $\frac{8 + 11 + 9 + 10 + 7 + 9}{6} = \frac{54}{6} = $ **9 days** *[1 mark]*
   mean

   species B = $\frac{12 + 10 + 6 + 12 + 15 + 11}{6} = \frac{66}{6} = $ **11 days** *[1 mark]*
   mean

) The standard deviation for species B is higher than that of species A suggesting that the values are more spread out from the mean *[1 mark]*. This indicates that there is more variety in development time for species B *[1 mark]*.

Page 103 — *Biodiversity*

1 a) The number of different species *[1 mark]* and the number of individuals/population size of each species in a community *[1 mark]*.

b) Site 1 —
N (N − 1) = 51 (51 − 1) = 2550
Σn (n − 1) = 15 (15 − 1) + 12 (12 − 1) + 24 (24 − 1) = 894
Use of N (N − 1) ÷ Σn (n − 1) to calculate diversity index of 2550 ÷ 894 = **2.85**
[2 marks for correct answer, 1 mark for incorrect answer but correct working.]
Site 2 —
N (N − 1) = 132 (132 − 1) = 17292
Σn (n − 1) = 35 (35 − 1) + 25 (25 − 1) + 34 (34 − 1) + 12 (12 − 1) + 26 (26 − 1) = 3694
Use of N (N − 1) ÷ Σn (n − 1) to calculate diversity index of 17292 ÷ 3694 = **4.68**
[2 marks for correct answer, 1 mark for incorrect answer but correct working.]
It's always best if you put your working — even if the answer isn't quite right you could get a mark for correct working.

c) The diversity of bumblebee species is greater at site 2 *[1 mark]*. This suggests there's a link between enhanced field margins and an increased diversity of bumblebee species *[1 mark]*.

Index

A

absorption of food products 67
accuracy 104
activation energy 10
active immunity 47
active sites 10, 11
active transport 42, 43
adaptations 39, 55, 93
agar plates 95
agglutination 44
AIDS 52, 53
algal cells 24
allele frequencies 93, 94
alleles 83, 89, 92-94, 99
alveolar epithelium 59
alveoli 58, 59
amino acids 8, 67, 82, 86, 91, 98
  absorption of 67
amylase 14, 66
animal cells 24
anomalous results 105
antagonistic muscles 58
antibiotic resistance 94, 95
antibodies 44-51
  in medicine 48, 49
  interpreting data on 50, 51
  structure of 44
antigen-antibody complexes 44
antigenic variation 46
antigens 44-49
antimicrobials 95
antiparallel DNA strands 17, 18
aorta 72-74
apparatus 104, 105
artefacts (microscope slides) 35
arteries 70
arterioles 70
aseptic techniques 95
ATP 22, 42
ATP hydrolase 22
ATP synthase 22
atria 72-74

B

bases 16, 17, 82, 84-87, 91
base triplets 82, 84, 86
B-cells 44, 45
Benedict's test 3
bile salts 66
binary fission 29
binomial naming system 97
biodiversity 102, 103
biological catalysts 10
biuret test 9
Bohr effect 69
bronchi 58
bronchioles 58
broth (bacterial) 95

C

calibration curve 41
cancer 33
capillaries 59, 71
capillary endothelium 59
capsids 28, 52
capsules 28
carbohydrates 2-5, 66
cardiac cycle 73, 74
  interpreting data on 74
cardiovascular disease 75-77
  interpreting data on 77
carrier proteins 38, 42
catalase 14
causal relationships 62, 63, 77, 108
cell cycle 32, 33
cell division 32, 33, 88-90
cell fractionation 31
cell membranes 25, 36, 43
  permeability of 37
  structure of 36, 37
cells 24-29
cell-surface membranes 25
cellular immune response 45
cellulose 5
cell vacuoles 24, 26
cell walls 24, 26
centromeres 32, 88
channel proteins 9, 38
chitin 24
chloroplasts 24, 25
cholesterol 36, 76
chromatids 32, 88, 89
chromosomes 32, 34, 82, 83, 88-90
  chromosome mutations 90
circulatory system 70, 71
classification 96-99
clonal selection 44, 45
codons 84-86
cohesion-tension theory 78
colorimetry 37
communities 102
competitive inhibition 13
complementary base pairing
       17, 18, 84, 85
concentration gradients 38-40, 42, 56, 57
conclusions 108
condensation reactions 2, 4, 6, 8, 20
conflicting evidence 77
conservation 103
coronary arteries 70
correlations 62, 77, 108
co-transporter proteins 42, 43, 67
counter-current systems (gas exchange) 56
courtship behaviour 97
Crick 17, 19
crossing over 89
cytokinesis 32

D

degenerate nature (of genetic code) 86, 9
deoxyribose 16
dependent variables 104, 107
diaphragm 58
diffusion 38, 39
  factors affecting the rate of 39, 56, 57
digestion 66, 67
dipeptidases 67
dipeptides 8, 67
diploid 88
directional selection 94
disaccharidases 66
disaccharides 2, 3, 66
dissections
  fish gills 64
  insects 65
  lungs 64
  plants 79
dissociation curves 68, 69
DNA
  nucleotides 16
  replication 18, 19
  storage of 82
  structure of 17
DNA helicase 18
DNA polymerase 18
domains 96
double-helix 17
Down's syndrome 90
drawing conclusions 108

E

electron microscopes
  scanning 30
  transmission 30
ELISA test 49
emulsification 66
emulsion test 7
endopeptidases 67
enzymes 9-15, 66, 67
  action of 10, 11
  factors affecting activity 12, 13
  inhibition of 13
  investigating reactions of 14, 15
  structure of 11
error bars 101
ethical issues
  with antibodies in medicine 51
  with vaccines 51
  with working with living organisms
       65, 105
eukaryotic cells 24-27, 82
evaluating 109
evolution 93
evolutionary relationships 96, 98
exchange across cell membranes 38-43
exchange organs 54
exons 83, 85
exopeptidases 67
expiration 58

Index

ilitated diffusion 38, 39, 42, 43
ning techniques 103
y acids 6, 7, 66, 67
bsorption of 67
ella 28
d mosaic model 36
nder effect 92
tose 2, 66, 67
ctional RNA 82
gal cells 24

actose 2
netes 88
exchange
fish 56
humans 59-61
insects 56
plants 57
single-celled organisms 56
urface adaptations 56
es 82, 83
netic bottlenecks 92
netic code 86
netic diversity 88, 92, 93, 99
omparisons of 99
e mutations 91
netic variation 89, 100
omes 82
ome sequencing 98
s 56
cose 2, 4, 5, 42, 43, 66, 67
bsorption of 42, 43, 67
tructure of 2
cerol 6, 66, 67
cogen 4
colipids 36
coproteins 36
cosidic bonds 2, 4
lgi apparatus 25
lgi vesicles 26
phs 107
ticules 35

itats 102
moglobin 68, 69
oloid 88
zards 105
art 70, 72-75
tructure of 72
t exchange 55
d immunity 46
tones 82
V 49, 52, 53
mogenisation 31
mologous pairs 83, 88, 89
st cells 28, 29, 52

human birth weights 94
humoral immune response 45
hydrogen ions 23
hydrolysis reactions 3, 20, 66, 67

I

ileum 43, 66
immune system 44, 45
immunity 45-47
independent segregation 89
independent variables 104, 107
index of diversity 102
induced fit model 11
initial rate of reaction 15
inspiration 58
intercostal muscles 58
interpreting data 50, 51, 62, 63,
        74, 77, 87, 98, 108
introns 83, 85
inorganic ions 23
iodine test 4
iron ions 23

K

kingdoms 96

L

lactose 2
lipases 66
lipids 6, 7, 66
loci 83
lock and key model 10
lung diseases 60, 61
    interpreting data on 62, 63
lungs 58
lymphatic system 71
lysosomes 26

M

magnification 30
margin of error 108
mass flow hypothesis 80, 81
mass transport systems 54, 70, 78
mean (average) 100, 101, 106
median (average) 106
meiosis 88-90
memory cells 45-47
Meselson and Stahl 19
messenger RNA (mRNA) 84-87
micelles 66, 67
microscopes 30, 34, 35
mitochondria 25, 27
mitosis 32-35, 89
    investigating 34, 35
    stages of 32
mitotic index 34
mode (average) 106

monoclonal antibodies 44, 48, 51
monomers 2, 3
monosaccharides 2, 3, 66
murein 28
mutagenic agents 91
mutations 90-93

N

natural selection 93, 94
negative controls 104
non-competitive inhibition 13
non-disjunction 90
non-reducing sugars 3
nuclei 25
nucleic acids 16, 86, 87
    interpreting data on 86, 87
nucleotides 16, 17
    derivatives of 22

O

optical microscopes 30, 34
    use of 34
organelles 24, 28, 31
organs 27
organ systems 27
osmosis 40, 41

P

partial pressures 68
passive immunity 47
pathogens 44-46
percentage change 106
percentage error 108
phagocytes 44, 45
phloem 80, 81
phosphate ions 23
phosphodiester bonds 17
phospholipid bilayer 36
phospholipids 6, 7, 36
phylogeny 96
planning experiments 104, 105
plant cells 24
plasma cells 44, 45
plasmids 28, 29
plasmodesmata 24
polar molecules 20
pollution and lung disease 63
polymers 2, 3, 16, 17
polynucleotides 17
polypeptides 8, 9
polysaccharides 4, 5
potometers 79
precision 104, 109
pre-mRNA 85
presenting data 107
pressure gradients 58
primary immune response 45
primary structure of proteins 8, 82
processing data 106

Index

prokaryotic cells 24, 28, 29, 82
proteases 67
proteins 8, 9, 82
  structure of 8
protein synthesis 84, 85
proteomes 82
pulmonary artery 72-74
pulmonary vein 72-74

Q

quaternary structure of proteins 8, 68

R

radioactive tracers 81
random samples 100
range 106
rate of reaction 107
ratios 106
reducing sugars 3
repeatability 104, 109
reproducibility 104, 109
resolution 30
ribcage 58
ribose 16
ribosomes 16, 26-28, 85
ringing experiments 81
risk factors 62, 63, 76
RNA 16, 17, 82, 84, 85
RNA polymerase 84
rough endoplasmic reticulum (RER) 26

S

saturated fatty acids 6
secondary immune response 45
secondary structure of proteins 8
semi-conservative replication 18, 19
SEMs 30
serial dilutions 40
sexual reproduction 88
significant figures 106
smoking and lung disease 62
smooth endoplasmic reticulum (SER) 26
sodium ions 23, 42, 43, 67
specialised cells 27
species 96, 97, 102
species richness 102
spirometers 60
splicing 85
squashing cells 34
stabilising selection 94
staining cells 30, 34
standard deviation 101, 106
starch 4
stomata 57, 78
structural proteins 9
substrates 10-12
sucrose 2
surface area to volume ratios 54, 55

T

tables 105
tangents 15, 107
taxa 96
taxonomy 96
T-cells 44, 45, 52
TEMs 30
tertiary structure of proteins 8, 11, 44
thoracic cavity 58
tissue fluid 71
tissues 27
trachea (humans) 58
tracheae (insects) 56
transcription 84
transfer RNA (tRNA) 84-87
translation 85
translocation 80, 81
  experiments 81
transpiration 78, 79
transport proteins 9
triglycerides 6, 7

U

ultracentrifugation 31
uncertainty 108, 109
units (converting between) 107
unsaturated fatty acids 6

V

vaccines 46, 47, 50, 51
  interpreting data on 50, 51
validity 104, 108, 109
valves
  in the heart 72-74
  in veins 70
variables 104, 109
variation 100, 101
veins 70
vena cava 72-74
ventilation 58, 60, 61
ventricles 72-74
viruses 28, 29, 52, 53
  replication of 29, 52

W

water
  loss (control of) 57
  properties of 20, 21
  transport in plants 78
water potential 40, 41, 71
  investigation of 41
Watson 17, 19

X

xerophytes 57
xylem 78, 79